DATE DUE

MAR 2 3 2016	
OCT 3 0 2017	

BRODART, CO.   Cat. No. 23-221

Premarital Sex in America

PREMARITAL SEX IN AMERICA

How Young Americans Meet, Mate, and Think about Marrying

MARK REGNERUS

JEREMY UECKER

UNIVERSITY PRESS

2011

OXFORD

UNIVERSITY PRESS

Oxford University Press, Inc., publishes works that further
Oxford University's objective of excellence
in research, scholarship, and education.

Oxford   New York
Auckland   Cape Town   Dar es Salaam   Hong Kong   Karachi
Kuala Lumpur   Madrid   Melbourne   Mexico City   Nairobi
New Delhi   Shanghai   Taipei   Toronto

With offices in
Argentina   Austria   Brazil   Chile   Czech Republic   France   Greece
Guatemala   Hungary   Italy   Japan   Poland   Portugal   Singapore
South Korea   Switzerland   Thailand   Turkey   Ukraine   Vietnam

Published by Oxford University Press, Inc.
198 Madison Avenue, New York, NY 10016

www.oup.com

Oxford is a registered trademark of Oxford University Press

Library of Congress Cataloging-in-Publication Data
Regnerus, Mark.
Premarital sex in America : how young Americans meet, mate,
and think about marrying / Mark Regnerus and Jeremy Uecker.
p.   cm.
Includes bibliographical references and index.
ISBN 978-0-19-974328-5
1. Premarital sex—United States.
2. Young adults—Sexual behavior—United States.
3. Man-woman relationships—United States.
I. Uecker, Jeremy. II. Title.
HQ27.R44 2011
306.73'308420973—dc22
2010014447

5 7 9 8 6 4

Printed in the United States of America
on acid-free paper

Contents

Acknowledgments

Thanks especially to Terry Cole, Deeann Regnerus, Nicolette Manglos, Guli Fager, Eric Stumberg, Brad Wilcox, and Alex Weinreb for numerous conversations on the subject matter. Betsy Stokes continued her excellent editing practices. Our editor at Oxford, Cynthia Read, is still a pleasure to work with.

Thanks also to a variety of people for their assistance, support, ideas, invitations, or data access: Glenn Stanton, Norval Glenn, Jenny Trinitapoli, Kevin Dougherty, jimi adams, Joe Potter, Mark Warr, Tom Pullum, Susie Meghdadpour, Janell Regnerus, David Regnerus, Mark Hayward, Nicole Ryan, Noble Kuriakose, Christian Smith, Jenell Paris, Jim Furrow, Dave Atkins, Kevin Reimer, Don Baucom, Rebeca Marin, Cisco Chaves, Brad Breems, Amy Burdette, Ryan Weimar, Amanda Robb, Bob Hummer, David Kallison, Kelly Lee, Elizabeth Marquardt, Conrad Hackett, Chuck Stokes, Ana Paula Verona, Brett and Heather Arabie, Amy Weinreb, Keri Stumberg, Kathleen Vohs, Michael McCullough, Amy Adamczyk, Terra McDaniel, Kersten Priest, Margarita Mooney, Jennifer Johnson-Hanks, Bob Woodberry, Chandra Muller, Kelly Raley, Rob Crosnoe, Marc Musick, Jennifer Marshall, Margaret Talbot, Sarah Watson, Mary Lingwall, Chris Bachrach, Mike Langford, Nicole Angotti, Paula England, Jack Thomas, and our sociology course students, who always help us understand this stuff.

We wish to acknowledge the hard work that the Add Health research team at UNC-Chapel Hill continues to do. The same goes for the NSYR research team, especially Chris Smith and Lisa Pearce. Thanks to the Lilly Endowment for continuing to fund the NSYR, and to those NSYR investigators who conducted in-person interviews for Waves II and III. We remain obliged to the Population Research Center of the University of Texas for their exceptional administrative and technical assistance.

Finally, Mark owes his family—Deeann, Samuel, Elizabeth, and Ruth—a continuing, deepening debt. Without their tolerance of his writing habit, books like these just never could materialize. Jeremy is immensely grateful for the constant support and encouragement from his wife, Elisabeth, and the fresh motivation and perspective supplied by his daughter, Annie.

Premarital Sex in America

ONE

Introduction

A S THE TITLE betrays, this is a book about premarital sex. In other words, this book is about the vast majority of Americans. In December 2006, researchers from the Guttmacher Institute released a report about the historic and contemporary prevalence of premarital sex, and they received an avalanche of media attention for it.[1] Their news: about 95 percent of the American public had their first experience of sexual intercourse before they got married. The report also suggested that this is nothing new—even most Americans born in the 1940s reported having sex before marriage.[2] But having sex before you're married doesn't mean you had sex by age 18, or even age 25 (although opportunities for premarital sex are certainly increasing). This book is about the heterosexual decisions and relationships of unmarried Americans *between the ages of 18 and 23*, and our best data estimate suggests about 84 percent of them have already had sex.

Ironically, we won't actually use the term *premarital sex* very often. Not because the sexual relationships we will describe here aren't actually premarital—they are—but because the term itself has changed meanings. Historically, it implied a sexual relationship between a *couple* who eventually got married. Most sexual relationships among contemporary young adults, however, no longer result in marriage. And an increasing share of American adults aren't marrying at all. Yes, premarital sex has lost much of its association with marriage, at least marriage to a particular partner.[3] It now tends to refer to any act of sexual intercourse that occurs prior to a *person's* getting married. Whether it's a person's first sexual partner, an old boyfriend, a one-night stand, or someone's eventual spouse, the "who" has become less important than the "when" in the use of the term.

But to insist on scholarly consistency is pointless: the term means what most people now think it means, which is *any and all sex before marriage*. And that is what this book is about. Since American women and men are now marrying for the first time at the (all-time-high) average age of 26 and 28, respectively, more and more premarital sex is occurring than ever before.

Taylor Hamilton can attest to that. She is 20 years old, a rising junior at a university in Pennsylvania, and she shares a rented townhouse with several girlfriends. She has a girl-next-door look to her and is thoughtful and serious, yet humorous, peppering our interview with both pensiveness and laughter. Although she is a self-professed agnostic, two of her housemates are what she describes as "hardcore Christian." She likes them anyway, a testimony to modern norms of navigating diversity. Indeed, Taylor seems gifted at the art of balance. She negotiates her studies, her diverse friendships, and her romance in a way that many young women struggle to. Taylor is sexually active with her boyfriend of three years, Michael. She's actually never had sex with anyone else; nor has he. She contends that there's a big difference between hooking up—a trend we cover at length in chapter 4—and the sexual relationship she experiences with her boyfriend. She likes the security of it, while remaining grateful that it's not as binding as marriage: "It's been one of the things that, like, isn't changing in my life. I love (that)."

More than any previous generation, Taylor and nearly all of her peers resist pushing their beliefs on anybody. Should people wait until they're married to have sex? "Sure, if it's right for them." "Whatever you want to do is fine." "It's up to them." "No pressure." "Nobody else can answer that question for them." But this live-and-let-live mantra doesn't mean sexual standards have vanished. Indeed, Taylor's disdain for the college hook-up culture is palpable. When asked what's required for people to have sex, she speaks emphatically:

> They better at least be able to talk about it. That's what I told one of my friends. She was like, "Yeah, but I feel so weird asking him to use a condom." I was like, "Well, then you're not ready," because if you can't talk about stuff like that and what would happen if I got pregnant, or you know, all that stuff, if you can't talk about it openly then . . . just, just wait. . . . If you begin to talk about it, you have to be mature enough to, like, actually think about what the real consequences are and what you would do in that situation and take the appropriate precautions, you know. And if you're not on birth control because you're scared to

ask your mom or you're scared to go to the doctor and get a pelvic (exam), you're not ready. You're just not.

This standard, however, is not typical. The ability of young Americans to communicate effectively with their sexual partners remains stunted, as we will detail in chapter 3.

Taylor learned what she knows about sex from personal experience, her penchant for online research, and extensive hearsay among her friends. She didn't learn much from her mother. While the two of them get along fairly well, they "don't talk about sex, that's for sure." Hers is a common response among young adults in America. It's as if in spite of the heightened sexualization of media and film, American parents just can't bring themselves to have an ongoing dialogue about sexuality with their teenage or young-adult children. Parents much prefer a "don't ask, don't tell" policy: We hope our kids won't ask us about what we did, so we won't have to tell them. And in return, we won't ask them about what they're doing.

Taylor's mother knows she's on the pill, but that's the extent of her mother's interest in conversation: "When she found out, she was like, 'Are you sure? Are you sure you're ready?' We never discussed it any further." Echoing upper-middle-class white parents' anxiety about their children's educational future and career, her mother's interest appears limited to "a safety concern," according to Taylor. "She was like, 'Are you sure nobody's forcing you? Or, 'You know all the facts?' All that kind of thing." In fact, American parents' oversight of their teenage and young-adult children tends to be wide but shallow, resulting in children who long for—but seldom experience—real intimacy with their parents. Instead of pursuing a deeper relationship, many parents settle for just knowing that their kids are "safe."

Even though Taylor has been with her boyfriend for three years now, she hasn't had a pregnancy scare during that time. Many young women have, as we detail in chapter 2. Although they are each other's first sexual partner and she's on the pill, they sporadically use a condom as further insurance, a minority practice we've noted in others' accounts as well. More commonly, condoms are shed in favor of the pill among couples in seemingly secure relationships.

The idea of premarital sex was never a moral issue for Taylor. Her parents lived together before marrying and have never counseled her against that strategy. In keeping with her class culture, Taylor's mother warns her against being financially tied to a man. Accordingly, Taylor is very career-oriented: she intends to pursue a doctoral degree in physical therapy. Marriage is not for sex; it's for settling down and having kids, as we'll discuss at length in chapter 6. That's why she wants to marry someday:

> I'm hoping I'll get my career together and get married and have kids and I'll be able to do both, which I kind of know is not really all that possible. Um, I think I'll probably, hopefully I can do, like, get my career going then take off and have kids and stay at home with them for awhile and do like, part-time maybe. Or then go back when they're older. Um, I want to be at home for the most part when they're little. . . . I don't want to just go to school and then go straight into having babies, you know, do nothing with all my education.

Plenty of today's upper-middle-class young women are like Taylor. They want a career and a stable marriage and a family, and they recognize that achieving all three may be a challenge. But they certainly anticipate reaching all three goals. At some point, they suspect, they might even park their career (for a time) in favor of childrearing. This is a new script for a segment of young Americans who don't consider themselves very religious or conservative about sex but in fact often display fairly traditional sexual behavior patterns.

Indeed, the "script" is a theme we return to throughout the book. A script can be thought of like the script that an actor follows in enacting a play. Regular people do the same thing in normal life, although we're seldom conscious of it. We follow unwritten scripts that tell us what to think, how we ought to act in certain situations, what we should say and when.[4] Such scripts define and organize our social experience, and are developed through social interaction with other people, by observing them and by learning from them. We then use these scripts not only to guide our own behavior but to assess and judge the behavior of other people. Indeed, a key motivator of human behavior is to enact the common scripts around us. We may or may not even like our scripts, but we tend to stick to them. We might think "outside the box," but we don't often act outside it. Sexual scripts in particular specify not only appropriate sexual goals—what we ought to want—they also provide particular direction for responding to sexual cues, for figuring out what to do and what not to do and when, who leads, and what's inappropriate to ask for.[5] There is, nevertheless, wide variation in the sexual and family scripts that Americans enact, and our political and religious home cultures have much to do with that. We'll revisit this "red sex, blue sex" division at length in chapter 7.

WHAT IS EMERGING ADULTHOOD?

Recently we heard, in the span of just a few hours, claims both that "13 is the new 18" and "21 is the new 16." Confused? That's understandable. But this is the conundrum of emerging adults, the group of Americans about which this book is written.[6] Many American children are being tacitly pressed forward—by peers, parents, and the marketplace—into adolescence and toward adulthood earlier than ever. But then they're halted before they actually self-identify as adults. They remain in a "holding pattern" for several years, until marriage, career responsibilities, childbearing, and/or simple maturation force them to recognize their adult status and identity.

Historically, the transition from adolescence to full adulthood included five elements: economic independence from one's parents, residing outside of their home, conclusion of schooling (and commencement of work), marriage, and children. Marriage and parenthood were the traditional anchors of these five, since the majority of the population didn't pursue higher education, many women didn't join the labor force, and sometimes independence from parents never quite materialized in the way we imagine it today. Our contemporary world, however, looks very different. Adulthood "emerges" much more slowly for most of us, and for many it no longer includes all five of these criteria. In 1960, 77 percent of women and 65 percent of men had met all five criteria by age 30. Among today's 30-year-olds, only 46 percent of women and 31 percent of men could say so. And whereas 70 percent of 25-year-old women in 1960 had engaged in all five traditional adult-status actions, only one in four had done so in the year 2000.[7] *New York Times* columnist David Brooks captures the essence of this phenomenon and hints at this group's sexual and relational patterns:

> Now young people face a social frontier of their own. They hit puberty around 13 and many don't get married until they're past 30. That's two decades of coupling, uncoupling, hooking up, relationships and shopping around. This period isn't a transition anymore. It's a sprawling life stage, and nobody knows the rules. Once, young people came a-calling as part of courtship. Then they had dating and going steady. But the rules of courtship have dissolved. They've been replaced by ambiguity and uncertainty. Cell phones, Facebook and text messages give people access to hundreds of "friends." That only increases the fluidity, drama and anxiety.[8]

Brooks believes that emerging adulthood is no longer about transitioning from adolescence to adulthood. Instead, it's a "sprawling life stage" of its own.

Emerging adulthood has fluid boundaries; when exactly it starts and concludes isn't fixed. Most 19-year-olds would fit in, but some wouldn't. Many 27-year-olds could be included, but plenty could not. In essence, emerging adulthood is characterized by freedom and an openness to new ideas, a time to try on responsibilities for size without having to commit to them. Most traditional college students are emerging adults—they have adult-style freedoms but lack some or all of the typical adult responsibilities: work, marriage, and children. They can put off those responsibilities for years, never committing, changing jobs and relationships. Some exhibit little interest in stability. That's why it's difficult to put age brackets around emerging adulthood; it resists being tied down, because its inhabitants resist settling down. That is the very definition of emerging adults, the subjects of our study.

But for the sake of clarity and because we have limited interview data from youth older than 23, when we talk about emerging adults in this book, we are referring to Americans between 18 and 23 years of age. Our primary interest is in the population of *unmarried* young people recently out of high school, up through the conclusion of what is typically considered the college years. The sexual behavior of *married* young adults looks different from that of unmarried people—in large part because of the consistent "supply" of sex and the relative security of the relationship.

THE SEXUAL SIGNIFICANCE OF TURNING 18

There is a wide and popular disparity between the perceived morality of the sexual relationships formed by teenagers and those of emerging adults. When queried in the 2002 National Study of Family Growth (NSFG), only 15 percent of adult men and women believed that it was okay for two consenting *16-year-olds* to have sex. What a difference two years makes, however. When the same question was put to the same people—but this time the topic was consenting *18-year-olds*—fully 55 percent said that was okay. Perhaps ironically, when we narrow the sample down to the oldest group of people who were asked the question—people between 40 and 44 years old—the contrast is the most striking: only 6 percent of them think consensual sex between

16-year-olds is all right, while 46 percent of them say the same if the participants are a mere two years older. At face value, there is something about turning 18 that makes adults far more accepting of the sexual decisions of young people. Being 18 is a powerful yet largely symbolic marker of adulthood that means a change in status and privileges, if not always responsibility. The power of this marker suggests a strong association in Americans' minds between legal adulthood and the age of moral responsibility.

Turning 18 also historically connotes a move out of the parents' house, at least seasonally, into a state of being "on your own," capable of making your own decisions. Sociologist Amy Schalet notes in her comparative study of American and Dutch parents that the former tend to have serious misgivings about the sexual behavior of their children so long as they are "under their roof."[9] But in reality how many 18-year-olds are truly on their own, entirely out of the house and self-supporting? Fewer today than ever before: among 20-year-old women like Taylor, only 6 percent have completed all five transitions that have historically marked heterosexual adulthood: leaving home, finishing schooling, becoming financially independent, getting married, and having a child.[10] In 1960, this was true of five times as many young women.

The bottom line is that 18-year-olds today simply don't identify with adulthood. When we ask our introductory sociology class—comprised largely of college freshmen and sophomores—how many of them think of themselves as adults, seldom do more than 10 percent of them raise their hands. These are America's emerging adults: accelerating in sexual desire and interest and at the cusp of their peak fertility and virility, yet slowing down to meet growing educational expectations, pursue expanding career pathways, and savor the joys of friends and self-actualization.

THE SCOPE OF HETEROSEXUALITY IN EMERGING ADULTHOOD

It's important to note up front that this is largely a book about heterosexual behavior. Save for this trio of paragraphs and a number of references in later chapters, we won't directly evaluate GLBTQ relationships in this book. Some will label our focus as heteronormative—that is, privileging heterosexual expressions to the neglect of alternative sexualities—but the primary reason for avoiding an extended treatment of different sexual forms and identities is that it would have to be a much longer book in order to pay adequate attention to other patterns, to say nothing of the dynamics by which they form and the courses they take. We recognize that sexuality can be fluid and certainly spans a spectrum, and that our decision to limit our analyses to common forms of heterosexual practice is thus somewhat arbitrary.

Plenty of heterosexual emerging adults, including some in our survey and interview samples, no doubt feel sexual desire and exhibit behavior that wouldn't be considered exclusively heterosexual. How many? Table 1.1 displays the frequencies of same-sex attraction, behavior, and self-identification as homosexual or bisexual among men and women aged 18–23, drawn from the 2002 NSFG, a nationally representative dataset. It's obvious from this that there are indeed *degrees* of same-sex sexual involvement, and that actual same-sex behavior is far more common than self-identification as homosexual. Nearly triple the number of women as men report same-sex attractions (18.1 percent vs. 6.9 percent) and engaged in same-sex sexual behavior (14 percent vs. 5.2 percent). But only about half as many women as men self-identify as homosexual (1 percent vs. 2.1 percent). Exactly twice as many women as men identify themselves as bisexual (4.6 percent vs. 2.3 percent). Each of these categories displays a clear uptick since adolescence, except for women's reports of bisexual and homosexual self-identifications— the former declines and the latter remains stable, at one percent.

While this table raises plenty of good questions that we don't explore further here, it also serves to remind us that while women's sexuality tends to be more fluid than men's, a heterosexual orientation remains the norm among emerging adults. And it is for that reason as

TABLE 1.1 Same-Sex Behavior, Attraction, and Identity, in Percent, Never-Married 18- to 23-Year-Olds

	Is at least somewhat attracted to members of same sex	Has had sexual contact with a same-sex partner	Identifies as homosexual	Identifies as bisexual
Men	6.9	5.2	2.1	2.3
Women	18.1	14.0	1.0	4.6

Source: NSFG

well that we have elected to focus here on heterosexual relationship conduct, and will leave to other fine analysts and other books the topics of same-sex attraction, orientation, and behavior.[11]

THIS BOOK'S PARAMETERS AND DIRECTION

So this book explicates the sexual ideas, habits, and relationships of heterosexual emerging adults. In particular, we're after answers to several important questions about emerging adults:

What are their sex lives and relationships like?
What do they wish for? And what do they actually do?
Are there "new scripts" in American heterosexuality?
How prevalent are nontraditional forms of sex, and what do people think of them?
What is the college sex scene like? Are the stereotypic depictions accurate?
What about young Americans who are not in college?
What role does porn play in sex today?
Do emerging adults like their sexual relationships? How long do their relationships last?
Where does marriage fit into young adults' plans?
How do culture and religion color their sexual scripts?

We answer each question using both nationally representative survey data as well as in-person interviews. To use only national survey statistics to answer our questions would be farsighted: it would give us the big picture, but could encourage all manner of misinterpretations of the data. Survey researchers often seem perfectly comfortable speculating about the people behind the variables without listening to their stories. While personal anecdotes may not matter much to social scientists, they often mean *everything* to our interviewees. Stories of what happened to them and people they know carry exceptional weight in their own understanding of sex and relationships.

To stick with *only* their stories, however, would encourage us to extrapolate from the accounts of the few to the experiences of the many. Since nearsightedness and farsightedness are both problems that need correction, we hope to have avoided the shortcomings of each by utilizing both survey and in-person interview research methods.

As a result of our insistence on national representativeness, lots of readers will find their own stories within these pages. Most should, in fact. Some, however, will not see themselves here at all and might think that somehow we must've gotten it wrong. We just ask that you remember that this is a social study, and that not every individual fits the trends that characterize the American public when glimpsed as a whole.

The majority of our survey findings come from the third wave of the National Longitudinal Study of Adolescent Health (Add Health), the largest, most extensive data set available about American young people. Add Health suits our purposes for a number of reasons. First, its interviewers asked a detailed set of questions not only about the respondents' sexual activity patterns, but about each romantic and/or sexual relationship reported by a respondent. Second, Add Health is a longitudinal "panel study" that allows us to track changes in respondents' own attitudes and behaviors over time. Respondents were questioned twice (waves 1 and 2) while they were in high school and then again (wave 3) when they were 18–28 years old. Each wave of Add Health includes a large number of respondents, and 15,197 completed the wave-3 survey (which took place between July 2001 and May 2002). When we restricted our analyses only to those respondents who are no longer in high school and who are no older than 23, we were left with a working wave-3 sample size of 11,729.[12]

In addition to Add Health, we examined data from three other surveys: the National Survey of Family Growth (NSFG), the College Women's Survey (CWS), and the College Social Life Survey (CSLS).

The NSFG is a nationally representative survey of Americans aged 15–44 that concentrates on fertility, health, and parenting. As such, the NSFG asked detailed questions about sexual behavior and includes a considerable number of emerging adults. Our working NSFG sample size of 2,580 young adults comes from the 2002 series of interviews.[13] The CWS is a national study of college women conducted in the Winter of 2001 and directed by family scholars Norval Glenn (University of Texas at Austin) and Elizabeth Marquardt (Institute for American Values). Glenn and Marquardt's telephone survey of 1,000 college women focused on their attitudes, values, and behaviors with respect to sex, dating, and marriage.[14] The online CSLS, directed by Stanford sociologist Paula England, has so far collected data from over 10,000 undergraduate students across numerous universities, spanning 2005–2008. While it is not representative of young adults—or even of college students—it is a valuable source of information and the most recent of the data sources.[15] Because these three surveys are smaller than Add Health and cross-sectional in nature, we use them only when they address issues not adequately covered by Add Health.

The combination of these four survey-based studies gave us plenty of numbers to crunch. But rather than flood the text with complicated statistics of interest only to a specialized audience, we've relegated the more complicated statistical models (such as regression) to Appendix A.

Of course, the most meaningful perspectives on any topic can often best be discovered through deep conversations with real people. Thus we supplement our statistics with in-person interviews with emerging adults from the National Study of Youth and Religion (NSYR). Its second wave included approximately 70 interviews with respondents ages 18–21 between June and December 2005, and its third wave included 230 interviews with respondents ages 20–23 between May and September 2008.[16] The selection process for these interviews took into account a range of demographic and religious characteristics including region, residence (urban/suburban/rural), age, sex, race, household income, religion, and school type. The purpose of the interviews was to gather extended follow-up information about respondents' family, religious, and social lives—including a lengthy conversation on sexuality and sexual behavior—and to compare responses to those offered at earlier waves.[17]

We also draw upon approximately 40 interviews that we conducted ourselves with undergraduates at the University of Texas (2007–2009). These could not replace the more nationally representative interviews from the NSYR, but they do help shed more light on the detailed processes of pursuing or refraining from sexual involvement among college students, as well as their conduct within sexual relationships. Interviewees' names and occasionally their geographical state of residence (to a similar city or state within the region) have been changed, to protect their identity and ensure their confidentiality. (Additional information on the interview data collection process is included in appendix B.)

NAVIGATING THIS BOOK

In the following chapters, then, you'll learn our best understanding of what's happening among heterosexual young adults and why. Chapter 2 focuses on the sexual practices, partnerships, and patterns of *individuals*, including documenting virginity rates, the number of lifetime and recent sexual partners reported, experience with different types of sex, sexually transmitted infections, and contraceptive habits. Its purpose is to document what's going on broadly.

Most of the sex that Americans have, however, is within the context of some sort of relationship. But due to common data limitations, the vast majority of what we know about sexual behavior is from individuals and about the individual. Very little is popularly known about sexual relationship dynamics. Chapter 3 serves to remedy that. There we cover the prevalence of premarital sexual relationships, the speed with which unmarried couples begin having sex, the average duration of these sexual relationships, partner age differentials, the experience of nonromantic sexual relationships, and the extent to which partners engage in sexual activity that they dislike but tolerate for the sake of the relationship. Basically, we explore how and why sex happens when it does. We draw extensively upon the theory of sexual economics, a seldom-considered series of social structures and market dynamics that powerfully shapes the ability of individuals to get what they want—whether they want more sex or less, and whether or not they want it in the context of a relationship. The theory's explanatory power is remarkable, reaching into Americans' minds, bedrooms, and marriages.

Chapter 4 considers the sexual culture and sex lives of American students enrolled in four-year traditional colleges and universities. There are some powerful stereotypes out there about the sex lives of college students. But are they true? What is the college sex scene really like? Are "hookups" now the norm among collegians? How has social networking and texting affected the sexual landscape on campus? We compare students' sexual behaviors with those of young adults that aren't in college, since many Americans do *not* go straight into a traditional four-year college when they graduate from high school. Yet collegians tend to receive a great deal of media attention about sex. How different is the sexual behavior of these two groups?

Chapter 5 delves into how emerging adults emotionally experience their sexual relationships and activity patterns. Men's and women's experience of sex and relationships is typically quite distinct. They often want different things from their relationships, and they often get different things. Some types of sexual relationship tend to lead to contentment, while others tend to elicit distress. We explore the differences and why they appear.

Chapter 6 explores the idea of marriage in the minds of emerging adults. The vast majority of them still wish to get married some day. And yet the institution itself seems altogether disconnected from not only where they are in their lives but also where many of them wish to go next. Marriage becomes a future event that will simply happen somehow.

Distinctions among emerging adults remain pronounced, though, including political and class differences in sexual activity patterns, fertility preferences, ideas about homosexuality, cohabitation, and abortion, and the pursuit of early marriage. Religion is only one aspect of these cultural distinctions about sex, and it is seldom the most influential one. In chapter 7 we trace how culture conflict in America unites different types of sexual actors over common interests, grievances, and perspectives about how sex is meant to fit into life.

Chapter 8 ends the book by highlighting the twin ideas that reappear throughout the manuscript—sexual scripting and sexual economics—before concluding by discussing ten distinct myths about emerging-adult sexual behavior.

TWO

The Partnerships and Practices of Emerging Adults

CAMI, LIKE TAYLOR from chapter 1, is an attractive 20-year-old woman from the Northeast. She too is a rising junior in college. Both are bright, articulate, pleasant, and are respected by the adults in their lives. Unlike Taylor, however, Cami is a virgin. When we spoke with her back in high school, she was a devout Catholic and one of our very few interviewees who articulated an extensive religious ethic about sex. Two years later, she is not as active in the faith as she was in high school—a typical scenario in the college years. She's even aware of her waning religiosity: "I wish I was [more religious] sometimes. I feel like I need to, like, make that one of my priorities. . . ." She confesses she never really did read the Bible all that much, but she had been faithful at Mass. She labels herself "the typical remorseful Catholic," though her happy demeanor hardly exudes guilt.

Cami has pledged to remain a virgin until marriage, though she admits to having done "everything but [intercourse] and oral sex." She's generally conservative about the topic of sexuality and is very pro-child, raving about how her cousins are "all starting to have babies. It's great. . . . It's so fun having so many cousins. I love it." She doesn't, however, object to the use of contraception and in fact is on the pill herself: "I actually have to use birth control because, ironically enough, my period's like, really irregular, so I wasn't getting it after I got it initially. So I had to go on it to get it." She recognizes some irony but doesn't feel like being on the pill threatens her personal pledge in the least.

She's had two short-term romances since we last spoke with her and has been on the receiving end of rejection in each: "Sometimes I feel like I have issues, like I'm not very good at it or something, because they never really last very long, and there's not very many. I don't really know." For Cami, romantic relationships are "like training for learning how to have a relationship that could lead to marriage."

Her two short-lived relationships might not have offered Cami much "training," but they did expose concerns about her body image. Despite the fact that all but the most discriminating men would say Cami is beautiful, she struggles to agree. Her older sister has suffered from bulimia, which was a wake-up call for her. It helps that home is a haven for her, and that she and her mother communicate well and speak frankly into each other's lives. Despite the body-image struggle, Cami hasn't considered using sex to feel better about herself. Sex is not the key to making a relationship work, she insists, despite what she sees as the modus operandi of many girls, who "seem to think that's what you have to do to have intimacy with a guy. And not that I have a dispute with intimacy with guys, but I wouldn't want it to be like that. I feel like you should, I don't know, I just feel like it's pretty shitty right now," referring to the overtly sexual manner in which she sees young men and women relating. She knows she's in the minority, and she doesn't like that. But neither does she vocally contest the norm:

> I feel like it's kind of unfortunate that so many people are having sex. I feel like it's pretty casual, you know? Like I have some friends too that I've grown up with that've told me things, and some of my friends have had many sexual partners. . . . It just shows a lack of self respect, [but] it's like they don't see it that way and I don't tell them that because I feel like it would be pretty judgmental.

Table 2.1 shows just how much in the minority Cami is among her peers. Like 27 percent of young women in America, Cami is not presently in a romantic relationship of any sort. Of course that she is a virgin is even more uncommon. Note, however, how accurate she is in her perception about women's relationships with men—she knows that sex and dating are widely considered an inseparable pair. Indeed, this is the current situation for two-thirds of all unmarried emerging-adult women. Only 4 percent of all 18–23-year-old women are currently in a romantic relationship but *not* sexually involved with the person whom they are seeing. In other words, among all emerging adult women in any form of romantic relationship, only about 6 percent are not having sex of some sort.[1] (The figure for men is slightly

TABLE 2.1 Current Relationship Status, in Percent, Never-Married 18- to 23-Year-Olds

	Men	Women
Current Relationship Status		
Not in a relationship	40.0	27.4
Dating and having sex	52.5	66.4
Dating but not having sex	4.6	4.0
Just having sex	2.8	2.2

Source: Add Health

higher, only because fewer of them report being in a romantic relationship, a very common survey artifact.) Kathleen Bogle, author of *Hooking Up: Sex, Dating, and Relationships on Campus*, concludes the same—dating within this demographic involves sex.[2] Cami is clearly trying to live against the grain, and she knows it'll only get harder to live up to the promise that she made to herself. Right now she fits in fine with the share of young women who aren't in a relationship at all. But she's hopeful about the future, despite the clear lack of social support around her: "I've never felt that driven to do it, but I feel like the older I get, the more solidified this is and the more I feel like if someone really respects me they'll respect my beliefs too. So I think it'll be possible." Certainty is out, it seems.

Cami perceives that not all the change in sexual attitudes has come about simply because younger generations think and act differently than older ones. And she's right. Many of today's oldest Americans—who have long ago ceased their active socialization of their own children—think differently about sex than did the oldest Americans 30 years ago. According to data from the General Social Survey (GSS), 57 percent of the oldest group of respondents (ages 65–89) to the survey in the early-to-mid-1970s said premarital sex was "always wrong." That figure has dropped to 39 percent among the same age group in 2002. It's now a minority opinion even among the oldest Americans. All of these numbers suggest a sea change—considerable, linear, yet slow—in the realm of American heterosexuality.[3]

For Cami, however, waiting on sex is a formula for relationship success: "For me personally, I think if you wait, it would probably be a really good way to know that you were in love and the guy thought you were valuable enough to wait for." She is an idealist, no doubt, and yet many would admire her ideals—including plenty of her sexually active peers.

MODERN VIRGINITY AND SEXUAL ALTERNATIVES

So not all Americans between 18 and 23 have had sexual intercourse. But a large majority already has, and plenty that haven't have expressed themselves sexually in other ways, such as giving or receiving oral sex, or manual stimulation. Interviewees often use the term "hand job" when referring to manual stimulation of a man and "fingering" or "feeling up" when referring to manual stimulation of a woman. A study of over 200 midwestern young adults classified virgins in two ways: total abstainers and those who came close but didn't have actual inter-course.[4] Half of the "came close" group participated in a variety of other sexual activities like those noted above. Total abstainers did not participate in any. They were, however, generally characterized by a lack of sexual opportunities.

Others masturbate. According to data from the online College Social Life Survey (CSLS), 30 percent of college men reported that they'd masturbated in the past 24 hours, while an additional 26 percent didn't want to answer the question. By contrast, only 8 percent of women said they'd masturbated in the past 24 hours, while 21 percent didn't answer the question. While masturbation is often a replacement behavior for men—meaning men who don't have sex regularly are *more* likely to report elevated rates of masturbation—the opposite is true of women: women who don't have sex regularly are also *less* likely to report recent masturbation. In other words, men who are virgins are much more likely to masturbate than are women who are virgins.

Reasons why young adults avoid sexual intercourse are numerous and not often different from the ones they offered as teenagers: they haven't found the right person or relationship yet; God (or their family) expects them to wait until marriage; they are apprehensive about sex; or they don't feel the desire to pursue sex just yet.

So before we launch into a detailed examination of sexual behavior rates and relationship dynamics—which take up the majority of this book—we want to clarify that plenty of young adults are still virgins, and these shouldn't be thought of as abnormal or sexually stunted. They are, nevertheless, not the norm.

Sociologists often talk about "on-time" and "off-time" behaviors over the life course, about what is considered "age appropriate" in a society or community, such as when a person is ready to get married. Or how young is too young to have a child? When is it too late to have a child? There may be biological and developmental answers to these questions, but they're often swamped in importance by the power of the *social* answers to them. The same is true of first sex, which is why the film *The 40-Year-Old Virgin* portrays a collective effort to rid the main character of a trait that he's socially supposed to have lost about two decades earlier. In fact, on-time and off-time ideas pervade our thinking. For example, middle-class Americans now reject the thought of a 20-year-old marrying or having a child, yet they presume the same 20-year-old is interested in sex. Never mind the tight historical and biological links between sex, marriage, and fertility: a good life in the minds of many Americans now involves delayed marriage and child-bearing but accelerated sex.

While we don't have the data to make strong claims here about shifts in virginity rates over time, other scholars of human sexuality have done exactly that. Among some of the oldest Americans ever interviewed about premarital sex, a strong gender gap was evident. Among people born before 1900, 37 percent of men but only 3 percent of women reported having had premarital intercourse by age 18.[5] That gender gap was probably not as profound as it appears. It's quite likely that women felt far more pressure to give a socially desirable answer to the question than did men. Things have certainly changed, though: the popularity of sex by age 18 has since grown in a steady, linear fashion. In every successive 10-year birth cohort in that study, premarital virginity rates at age 18 have declined among both men and women. In *Forbidden Fruit*, nearly two-thirds of all 18-year-olds reported having already had vaginal sex, up from 57 percent of 17-year-olds, 33 percent of 15-year-olds, and just under 10 percent of 13-year-olds.[6]

Much media attention continues to accompany periodic reports about the sexual behavior of high schoolers. Scholars of adolescent sexuality and health peer into each year's new CDC estimates and claim success or failure for this or that program.[7] But the big picture remains clear, regardless of year-to-year fluctuations: young Americans are, on average, losing their virginity earlier than their parents did and certainly earlier than their grandparents. Particular teenagers may thwart this pattern, but the trend has not significantly changed course. If our estimate that around two-thirds of 18-year-olds are sexually experienced is on target, one thing is sure: those who defy the odds and retain their "V card" well into their 20s are an increasingly unique group. What are they like?

To begin, they're about twice as rare as they were *before* they turned 18. Estimates from the Add Health study suggest about 16 percent of all young adults—those between 18 and 23—have not had vaginal intercourse. If we include respondents up to age 27, the figure is cut in half once more, down to 8 percent. And remember, this figure is only about vaginal sex. What do these virgins have in common? Table A2.1 (in appendix A, pp. 252–53) displays statistical-model estimates of different characteristics used to predict who remains a virgin in early adulthood and who does not. Those most likely to remain a virgin tend to exhibit the following traits:

- They're in college, especially four-year degree programs, or else are college graduates.
- They're more religious, especially in terms of how central it is to their identity.
- They're not prone to getting drunk.
- They don't consider themselves popular.

A few characteristics of emerging-adult virgins are gender-specific:

- Asian men are more likely than white men to be virgins.
- Regular churchgoing is more a hallmark of virginity in men than it is in women.
- Politically conservative women, by party or self-identity, are more likely to be virgins.

A few other traits display a weaker association with virginity, including a better father-daughter or mother-son relationship during adolescence and a proclivity toward avoiding risks in general.[8] While lack of physical attractiveness is popularly associated with virginity—due obviously to lower perceived "market value"—this doesn't apply to women. In a study of the 2002 National Survey of Family Growth (NSFG), higher body mass index (BMI) displays no statistical association with being a virgin, age at first sex, or frequency of sex.[9] Dozens of our interview transcripts both with teenagers and young adults—together with survey analyses of data from the NSFG—reveal little obvious connection between physical attractiveness and sexual experience.

Other studies note virgins are more likely to hold a "marital orientation" and are less tolerant of deviant behavior in general. One study even found that virgins were more likely to be firstborns.[10] Together with these other studies, our interviews and survey data findings suggest that emerging-adult virgins can be classified into one or more of these categories: the *very religious*, the *risk averse*, those with *high expectations*, and those with *limited attractiveness*.

For some emerging adults, these categories overlap. That is certainly the case with Cami, who is fairly religious, not much given to partying, somewhat studious, and positive and hopeful about sex within marriage. But she wouldn't characterize herself as pursuing chastity per se. She's simply a confident, attractive young woman who is focused on school and wants sex to wait. Her virginity is not accidental, and she has not regretted waiting.

Religiosity

The first group of emerging-adult virgins, the very religious, is probably the largest. Religiosity is often the primary reason for maintaining virginity into the 20s, according to developmental psychologist Jeffrey Arnett.[11] And in the 2002 NSFG, 44 percent of respondents who had not yet had sex cited religion and morality as their primary reason for abstaining. It was by far the most common answer. Sunny, an 18-year-old evangelical and abstinence pledger from Oregon, remains as conservative about men as she was when we spoke to her two years ago. She's not in a hurry to pursue a relationship; the one romantic relationship she has had since then lasted only a month and was a "stupid" thing, she thinks. Even though they did nothing more than hold hands, she feels like it was improper, that she let others down and wasn't keeping her commitments. For Sunny, dating is about marriage, and if marriage isn't a future possibility, then dating is not just a waste of time, it's actually wrong. She laments what she sees as the extreme self-centeredness of sexual relationships today: "It's just now, and me, and nothing else." She feels no compulsion to lower her high standards and is confident about marriage in her future. The right man will be revealed: "I think it'll be okay. I know there are people out there that have character."

If we could see 10 years into her future, however, would Sunny be singing the same tune? In his book on emerging adulthood Jeffrey Arnett describes "Nancy," a 28-year-old virgin for whom the road has not been an easy one: "It's hard, it's really hard now," she laments.[12] Indeed, with age it becomes more difficult to altogether avoid sex (unless a person is antisocial, truly afraid of relationships, or has little to offer in the sexual marketplace). A group of friends who share Nancy's reticence about nonmarital sex support each other, and this is the essence of the *plausibility structure*, a central idea in sociology that is defined as a network of people who collectively profess and affirm a particular set of norms (guidelines for behavior) and values (beliefs about what's important). It doesn't much matter what the values or norms are or how odd they may seem to outsiders; social support (encouragement) and social control (pressure to conform) lend them legitimacy and make sure they persist. All ideas—no matter how new or old or popular or unpopular—require social support and control in order to stay relevant and persuasive. Churchgoing and religiosity often provide social support and social control for those who remain virgins into young adulthood. On the other hand, however, since organized religion is a key source of Americans' social interaction and a central place to meet people, it actually increases sexual opportunity. So virginity in the pews becomes quite rare, given enough time.

Risk Aversion and High Expectations

The risk-averse and those with high expectations are often—but not always—the same people. For some of the former, social awkwardness and the quality of being shy limits their opportunity for social interactions that could turn sexual. For others, the risks of pregnancy or an STI seem to overwhelm all advice about how to mitigate those risks. To the risk-averse, only avoidance is 100 percent effective. While they may appear to outsiders as sexually naïve, such naïveté is often understandable and may even be strategic. Brad, a 20-year-old Texan, hasn't had oral or vaginal sex and uses his ignorance of how to have sex—that is, the script he'd be expected to follow if were he in a sexual situation—to delay the experience: "I'm not gonna lie . . . I wouldn't have the foggiest idea what to do," he confesses. It's not that he's opposed to sexual activity; indeed, he's had opportunities. He's just actively trying not to figure out how to make it happen, because he doesn't want to at present. Impending exams, work schedules, or the lack of a condom offer convenient excuses to say no. While some may find Brad's ignorance humorous or his disinterest odd, neither is terribly uncommon. What virgin, after all, is entirely clear about what a sexual relationship entails? And for plenty of virgins—including people like Brad—the naïveté can be intentional. They use the unknown territory of a sexual relationship as a convenient way to remain as they are. Sex can wait.

Jerry is not risk-averse, but he does exhibit high expectations, which are almost endemic to Asian American college students. He's thoughtful and strategic about his future. Nineteen years old, the Maryland native was beginning his college career, but classes had not yet started, so he was not yet a part of campus culture. Neither religious nor particularly conservative about sex, Jerry nevertheless had not had sex and didn't speak of any other types of sexual behavior recounted by many "technical virgins" (those who haven't had intercourse but have experienced other types of paired sexual experience, like oral sex). Asian culture, with its conservative priorities about hard work and achievement, plays a cautionary role for him that religion otherwise might. During adolescence, Asian teenagers are the least likely to hear from their parents about sexual matters, and they are the last—on average—to have experienced intercourse.[13] They're more likely to give heed to parental advice, and to limit experiences that could divert them from meeting the social expectations placed upon them. As a result, sex waits.

Limited Attraction

Finally, there is the question of attractiveness. Some people wouldn't mind having sex but haven't yet managed to do so because of others' limited interest in them.[14] But lack of objective physical attractiveness seldom actually equals no sex. *Subjective* attractiveness—what respondents think about their own appearance—matters more. According to Add Health, only 13 percent of virgin women consider themselves "very attractive," compared with 28 percent of nonvirgin women. The same goes for men: only 20 percent of virgins think they're very attractive, down from 30 percent of nonvirgins. Virgins are also apt to report being less self-confident than nonvirgins—but not less happy, as we'll discover in chapter 5.

Regardless of perceived or real attractiveness or confidence, this common phenomenon—which we call *accidental temperance*—is far more characteristic of men than women. Why? Because women always have value on the sexual market. This is just a fact. Women's virginity, in other words, is generally by choice. Men's may or may not be. In chapter 3, we will expand upon the inescapable "market dynamics" of sex.

Whatever the reasons for it or the wishes to keep or get rid of it, virginity continues to receive bad press in public discourse and in most emerging-adult subcultures, especially in the wake of the debate over abstinence-based sex education. Virginity and the endorsement of it is seen by many as naïve, doomed to fail, or even oppressive. But the fact is that very many Americans reflect negatively on the circumstances in which—or the timing of when—they lost their virginity. Most emerging adults—70 percent in Jeffrey Arnett's study—think they were too young to have lost their virginity when they did. If this were a book on first sexual experiences, we could fill it with awkward accounts.[15] The primary reason for their regret is less about morality than psychology: they were too young to appreciate the emotional significance of what they had done. Many describe themselves as being "young and stupid."

Planned rather than more spontaneous first sexual experiences are far more characteristic of older teenagers and young adults than of younger teens, prompting fewer accounts laden with regret. By then it was normal or average—or even slightly past the average age—and they knew it, so they were more prepared.

In sum, then, emerging-adult virginity is unusual but hardly unheard of. It characterizes about 16 percent of the population of Americans between 18 and 23 years old. Being a virgin at one's wedding, however, is considerably rarer than this.

SERIAL MONOGAMY

Among all the ideas and norms about sexual relationships among emerging adults today, one emerges from the pack to dominate all the others. It's *serial monogamy*, the primary sexual script among emerging adults today. And it's into this pattern that most Americans put their energy. We have fewer confidants and close friends than in previous decades, despite the opportunities afforded by online social networking.[16] Emerging adulthood mirrors this nation of isolates who regularly—but often only temporarily—move into and out of intimate relationships.[17] Emerging adults are not doing *without* relationships, as journalist and *Unhooked* author Laura Sessions Stepp worries.[18] They just look different. They're more tenuous. Emerging adults seem more aware of other options. In a 2007 Texas survey of adults, respondents in romantic relationships of all sorts were asked to report their level of agreement with this statement: "I often think that there may be someone better for me out there." Thirty percent of those under age 25 agreed, while only 12 percent of those aged 25–44 did.[19]

Even while emerging adults consider other options for sexual partners, they still powerfully criticize deviations from the norm of monogamy, even if the monogamous relationships are fairly brief. You're only allowed one sexual partner at a time, and to overlap is to cheat, and cheating remains a serious norm violation that gives the victimized party not just the uncontested right but often a perceived moral obligation to end the relationship. Even though Gabriela, a 23-year-old from Texas, has had numerous sexual partners, she is quick to police the norm of exclusivity: "You're supposed to be in a monogamous relationship with another person and you're not supposed to be with anybody else." That's the deal. It's also how most Americans of any age think about sexual relationships, including marriage. While accounts of "open" relationships or swingers are be-ginning to proliferate, the idea of nonmonogamy still doesn't fly among the vast majority of Americans, even otherwise-tolerant emerging adults. In an entertaining piece published in *New York* mag-azine, Philip Weiss waxes mournfully about his desire to have sex with other women and yet maintain his marriage unscathed.[20] Weiss con-cludes that sexual exclusivity has managed to, and will continue to, withstand all revolutionary impulses thrown at it. It's testimony to the power of culture to combat primordial predilections for sexual variety.

So the number of sex partners people have over a lifetime—or how long those relationships last—is increasingly considered less important to emerging adults than is their monogamous conduct while in those relationships. The same goes for "friends with benefits," a topic to which we return in chapter 3. They too tend to be exclusive, if short-lived relationships.

HOW MANY PARTNERS?

One way to assure sexual variety in a serially-monogamous-yet-marriage-esteeming culture such as ours is to pursue it early, then eventually capitulate and "settle down" to the stable sex life that Weiss bemoans. And that is what seems to be happening. In step with historical change in young-adult virginity rates, the number of sexual partners that young Americans claim to have had has also risen. Among people born in the 1920s, 70 percent of men and 12 percent of women reported more than one partner before marriage.[21] (As with historical accounts of virginity, so with premarital partnerships: differences in how socially desirable it has been to admit multiple sexual partners likely enhance the gender gap.) Table 2.2 displays the number of lifetime and recent sex partners among contemporary emerging adults. We already know that 16 percent of young men and women report no sexual partners yet. About the same number report having had only one partner, leaving just over two-thirds reporting more than one lifetime sexual partner. About 25 percent say they've had 5–10 partners. At the top end, 15 percent of emerging adult men and 10 percent of women tell us they've already had sex with more than 10 people.[22]

The numbers are of course smaller when we consider only sexual partnerships *in the past year*. In that light, 63 percent of men and 72 percent of women report no more than one partner. At each level above one partner, however, there are more men than women

TABLE 2.2 Number of Sex Partners, Lifetime and Past Year, Never-Married
18- to 23-Year-Olds

Number of Partners	Men		Women	
	Lifetime	Past year	Lifetime	Past year
0	16.1	24.0	16.0	22.6
1	16.9	39.1	16.0	49.7
2	12.3	16.5	11.9	14.6
3	9.1	8.5	11.1	6.2
4	7.1	3.6	8.5	2.4
5–10	23.7	7.1	26.3	4.0
11+	14.8	1.3	10.3	0.4

Source: Add Health

reporting. The most frenetic of sex lives—averaging a new partner about once every month of the past year—are truly exceptional, comprising only about one percent of the population and three times as many men as women. Kari, an 18-year-old Texan, had sex with four men in three months after she broke up with her boyfriend. She regrets it, saying, "I wish none of it ever happened," but it did. And it points out two hallmarks of men and women's sexual behavior that we will explore further in chapter 3. First, men are game for more sexual partnerships than women are, on average. Kari had no problem attracting sexually willing men. But a man's partner count generally cannot rise *as rapidly* as a women's can—since, all other things being equal, her sexual marketability is consistently greater than his.

When compared with the benchmark University of Chicago sex study, the "recent sex partner" figures do not appear to have changed much since the early 1990s. Sociologists reported then that—among 18- to 29-year-old never-married men—41 percent had had one sex partner in the past year, 31 percent reported 2–4 partners, and 14 percent reported five or more. Among never-married women of the same age, 57 percent had had one partner, 24 percent had reported 2–4, and 6 percent reported five or more.[23] Tables A2.2 and A2.3 (in appendix A, pp. 254–55) display statistical-model estimates predicting respondents' number of lifetime and recent sexual partners, respectively, as a function of a variety of individual traits and behaviors. The results from both tables suggest certain conclusions about who's most likely to have more sexual partners today:

- Popular men (according to their own self-description) have more partners.
- People who first have sex before age 16 have more partners.
- People who have gotten an abortion (or whose partner did) have more partners.
- People who like to take risks have more partners.
- People who get drunk more frequently have more partners.
- African American men, when compared with white men, have more partners.
- College students and college graduates have fewer partners.
- More politically conservative women have fewer partners.

Most of these conclusions are not surprising, since more permissive sexual behavior has long been associated with, for instance, drunkenness, a proclivity for risk-taking, and popularity. More surprising is what's *not* significant here: why is religiosity largely unrelated to recent sexual partnering? Although religiousness suggests sexual conservatism, it too—like sex—involves social interaction and participation and provides a natural setting for meeting members of the opposite sex. And why, according to the model results, do evangelical women report more recent partners than do mainline Protestants? In *Forbidden Fruit*, we noted the relational nature of evangelicalism: marriage matters. Relationships matter. Such an intensively relational culture lends itself to romance and thus to sexual relationships. For mainliners like Presbyterians and Episcopalians, on the other hand, those things matter *later*—after other important things like finishing college and jump-starting a career are in place.

But it's considerably more difficult to predict recent sexual partnering than lifetime patterns, since there is much more fluctuation in what a person is known to do over one year than over five or ten years. Many interviewees, like Kari, reported uncommon sexual activity patterns (such as multiple partners in rapid succession) for brief periods of time that didn't seem characteristic of their long-term relationship pattern. For that reason, even factors that tend to predict virginity—religious service attendance, planfulness, and father-daughter relationship quality—don't notably predict recent partner counts for nonvirgins.

Far more influential on number of sex partners are behavior patterns like frequent drunkenness and early sexual experience. We're not claiming here that the direction of influence always flows one way. It is plausible that men who have more partners may presume for that reason that they are more popular (and in at least one obvious way, they are); women who have more partners may feel out of step with "conservative" morality and increasingly distance themselves from that identity; people who have more partners may self-medicate depressive symptoms by drinking more; and a decision to have an abortion can result from an unplanned pregnancy with "the wrong person." So we can't prove which causes which or if they build on each other. We do know that out there in the real world, these phenomena are co-occurring with considerable regularity. When you see one, you're more apt to see the other.[24]

Remembering Previous Partners

Men report more sexual partners than women do. Period. Everywhere. A *New York Times* article in 2007 noted how in study after study of sexual partnerships, in virtually every corner of the earth, the conclusion was always the same.[25] Mathematicians balk at such a claim, arguing that it is statistically impossible for heterosexual men to have more partners *on average* than heterosexual women since each new partner for a man is also a new partner for a woman. So why such persistently divergent self-reports? There are several plausible answers, and it's likely that more than one of them is true:

1. There are a small number of women, such as sex workers, who seldom show up in research samples and—if counted—would raise the average score of women to be equal to that of men.
2. Men are more likely than women to count nonvaginal sexual experiences (like oral sex) as contributing to their overall number of partners.
3. There exists a social desirability bias and a double standard, wherein men tend to claim more partners—and women tend to claim fewer—than they've actually had.
4. When asked to recall, women enumerate partners, which leads to underestimation; men, on the other hand, use rough approximation, leading to overestimation.

This last explanation, offered by psychologist Norman Brown, fits the evidence well when study participants are given plenty of time to think about their answers.[26] In reality, surveys seldom offer respondents the time to actually stop and enumerate in their minds their past partnerships. In our interviews, most women knew the number immediately. If they didn't, they stopped to count. (We allotted everyone ample time to do so.) But Devon, a lanky 19-year-old from Seattle, exemplifies the male tendency toward rough approximation. When asked how many people he'd ever had sex with, Devon responded, "only like 10 people, maybe 10 to 15." Another reported "20 to 30" total partners, which included at least a couple of prostitutes during trips abroad. Indeed, men often appear to lose track—or not care enough to recall correctly—after 6 or 7 partners.

A study comparing in-person interviews with self-completed sex questionnaires notes persistent divergence in women's counts when comparing the two methods of data collection. When asked by an interviewer, only 3 percent of women admitted having four or more sexual partners in the past 12 months. But when they could discreetly write the answer down themselves, 9 percent said so. This social desirability gap increased with the age of the women, indicating less embarrassment among the youngest cohort.[27] In sum, all four of these reasons for the "apparent" gender gap in self-reported partnerships enjoys some degree of validity and likely accounts for part of the gap.

How Many Is Too Many?

In a question submitted to Carolyn Hax, the *Washington Post* advice columnist who has become the Ann Landers of progressive younger adults, a woman asked:

> What is the acceptable number of sexual partners a woman should have by the time she is 35? My boyfriend has been badgering me, and I lied and said 10, thinking that is low, and he went ballistic, questioning my virtue, etc. The funny thing is, he has been with at least 50 women!

No matter the answer, the question reveals Americans' enduring interest—even among seemingly secure, self-confident, educated careerists—in figuring out the norms and scripts of our own and each other's sexual lives. It's as if reading about what others think and do somehow gives us permission to do what we've already done, to consider doing what others are doing, or to simply figure out how we're supposed to feel about our own past and present. We want someone to tell us we're *normal*, that we're neither prudish nor promiscuous.

A humorous street definition of promiscuity (derived from an Alfred Kinsey quote about nymphomaniacs) is "more partners than you've had," meaning both that any count is relative and that it's always *other people* that are promiscuous. There is certainly something to this idea, since very few young Americans identify themselves as promiscuous. (It's like self-identifying as a racist: We all know there are plenty of them out there, but no one wants to thinks he is one.) This is one type of social desirability bias known as self-deception, in which people are not intentionally dishonest but hold opinions about themselves that most others—were they to know the facts—would disagree with.

In some circles of young women, however, there does exist a working definition of "too many." It begins around 10, the start of double digits. One young woman interviewed in another study suggested that if you've had more than 10 partners, you should lie about it if asked.[28] This "too many" view is part social support and part social control. Women especially police each other here, both over what is too much to give away to a man and what is too little. Gabriela, a Hispanic woman from Texas and a recent college graduate, would never dream of letting her male friends know that she's had nine partners (one of whom gave her Chlamydia). But Philip, a 22-year-old from Kansas and a self-identified "late bloomer," wished his number were higher; he'd only had oral sex—and that with only one person. When asked why he was uncomfortable with that number, he fumbled around a little but then identified social norms by name:

> Um, I guess, because, with a lot of my friends, I mean, [it's] for pleasure and because I think a lot of my friends, it's higher as well, even though I know with some of my friends it's not. Um, but, I guess, just to be more, I'd like to have more relationships with people and I'd like to be more socially normal, I guess.

Numbers alone, however, provide little sense of the context of such partnerships—how long they lasted, why they formed, or if they were romantic or only sexual. Most emerging adults knew people who, like Kari, "went off the deep end" or "went crazy" for a spell. In fact, such stories were almost exclusively about women, precisely because such behavior is not socially expected of them. Promiscuity, by definition, concerns unexpectedly high numbers of sexual partners, and since Americans still expect women to have fewer partners than men, it stands to reason that women are far more likely to be considered promiscuous than men who act the same way.

Hannah, whose story will be featured at length in chapter 7, was a 19-year-old from Alabama who was hoping to delay her first sexual experience at least until she was engaged. But she lacked the plausibility structures—including social control, support, and role models— to help her do that. The first time we spoke with her as a 17-year-old, Hannah said she had performed oral sex on someone once, which she professed regretting. Yet two years later when asked whether she'd been sexually active over the past couple of years, she names the word but immediately rationalizes:

> I wouldn't call it promiscuous. I tried to keep it as serious as I could. There were a couple times where I made my mistakes. I've probably had maybe 8 or 9 partners, but then again there's some girls I know around here that have had 8 or 9 partners before they get out of high school, because it's just gotten that out of hand. So I don't see myself as, you know, extremely active or promiscuous, just that I've had my experiences to show me just what my beliefs really should be.

Like the popular rule of thumb noted above, Hannah didn't think she was promiscuous, despite having eight or nine partners in less than two years. "I really don't look fondly at girls that have been with 3, 4, 5 different guys in a month kind of thing," Hannah asserts. Those are rare indeed.

While complicated statistical models are helpful and necessary in distinguishing the factors that shape the patterns of sexual behavior we see, these estimations can also unwittingly cloud our understanding of real people. None of us experience our lives in pieces—our gender, our age, the religious part of us, the part that's in college, the part that drinks too much on occasion, etc. When social scientists state disembodied facts about the influence of any particular trait or behavior (like race, gender, or religiosity), the picture of reality can get confusing. We might overestimate the effects of something just because it's "statistically significant." To help counter this approach, we report below the percentages of young adults (who fit simple sets of different personal descriptions) that told Add Health interviewers that they've had more than five sexual partners in their lifetime:[29]

- Asian American women who are planful and enrolled in college: 16 percent
- White men who are popular, like risks, drink regularly, and attend church irregularly: 43 percent
- White women who had high father-daughter relationship quality as teens: 19 percent
- African American men, in college, with married parents: 48 percent
- White women who drink regularly and have had an abortion: 73 percent
- African American men, not in college, who like risks and had sex before age 16: 58 percent

- White women who are churchgoing, politically conservative, attend college, and have married parents: 11 percent
- Hispanic men, not in college, who are Catholic: 31 percent
- White women who are politically liberal, attend college or graduated, and attend church infrequently: 29 percent
- Hispanic women who are in college or graduated, have married parents, are Catholic, and attend Mass some: 0.6 percent
- Asian American men who are planful, in college or graduated, and didn't have sex before age 16: 5 percent
- White men who are evangelical, politically conservative, in college or graduated, and churchgoing: 9 percent
- African American women who are in college or graduated and attend church at least occasionally: 27 percent

MORE IN THE SEXUAL REPERTOIRE

There's more variety to emerging-adult sexual experience than just vaginal sex. As we noted, not a few virgins told us in our conversations with them that they had not yet had intercourse but had "done other things." By that, some of them meant oral sex and told us so, while others referred to forms of sexual touching and mutual masturbation. At this age, the idea of "technical virginity" becomes much less important than it was in high school. On campus—and certainly outside the orbit of higher education—the chatter about who's gone exactly how far with whom tends to diminish. This is because virginity itself becomes increasingly rare, and new social circles tend not to treat sex as newsworthy as it was in high school. And the speed with which people "round the bases" within new relationships tends to accelerate as they age. All of this makes the debate about whether one is or is not a "real virgin" (not having had vaginal intercourse) largely moot or uninteresting.

It nevertheless remains a concern among the pool of emerging adults who are dating but not having sex, especially if the abstinence is for religious reasons. In *Forbidden Fruit* we discovered that technical virginity was a social class issue—not a religious one—primarily found among teenagers who were paranoid about the hazards of pregnancy before college. But that's no longer true just a few years later. In college, technical virginity emerges as a religious phenomenon: vaginal sex becomes "the line" past which many Christians believe they ought not to venture before marriage. While Sunny, the 18-year-old evangelical we met earlier, seems bent on avoiding any hint of sexual contact, many other Christian virgins don't join her in that.

Laura, an evangelical 19-year-old college student, wrestles with the subject of sexual activity with her equally devout Baptist boyfriend Geoff. Two months into their relationship, they found themselves on his bed having a far more difficult time studying than pulling each other's clothes off. They had oral sex nearly daily for three months and never spoke about it, since to mention it in normal conversation would force them to admit to each other that what they were doing was, in her words, "wrong because of church and because of what the Bible says" about sex: "We knew it was wrong. We knew we shouldn't do it, but we never brought it up, because as humans we like it. And so if you don't talk about it, then we don't have to acknowledge that it's wrong." Remarkably, we heard the very same anticonversational logic from several other Christian young adults who were in romantic relationships. When Geoff finally spoke up, new boundaries got established and an older (30-something) married couple agreed to become "accountability partners" for them. When we asked Laura why they didn't just consider getting married—an act which within their religious system would legitimate any sex they wanted to have—Laura responded with a litany of reasons why marriage just wouldn't work yet, why Geoff wouldn't be willing, and why their parents wouldn't support it. Clearly, however, their new system isn't working, either: when we checked in with Laura several months later, she and Geoff were back to their old habits, neither talking about it nor admitting it to their accountability partners.

Oral Sex as Part of the Sexual Script

Oral sex and other types of sexual activity are common within the sexual repertoire of emerging adults. This is nothing new; already in 1994 the University of Chicago sex study had begun to conclude that oral sex was squarely in the script of adults' sexual activity. Sociologist Edward Laumann and his colleagues noted then that "if there has been any basic change in the script for sex between women and men, it is the increase in the incidence and frequency of fellatio and cunnilingus," the formal terms for oral sex that women perform on men and vice versa.[30] The historical prevalence of oral sex is uncertain and subject to speculation and the evaluation of art and historical documents, letters, and diaries. Some researchers believe its present popularity—especially among women as *recipients* of oral sex—is a relatively recent phenomenon. They attribute the increase in practice to the increasing exposure to women's orgasms in pornographic video.[31] Yet it cannot simply be a product of the expansion of online pornography, since Internet use in the early 1990s was a fraction of what it is today. Others attribute it to the heightened comfort of women in telling their partners what they do and do not want in sexual activity. Regardless of the origin of its popularity, it cannot be entirely new, since overall rates of both giving and receiving oral sex were in the 70–85 percent range among even the oldest cohorts in the Chicago study.

Just as with numbering sexual partners, there can be measurement error here as well: in many studies, women and men each claim to receive oral sex more often than they give it. Both cannot be correct. Often the measure is subject to interviewees' evaluation of their own behavior.[32] But asking directly about "fellatio" and "cunnilingus" is awkward; they are strange words not used by many. Instead, people (including researchers) often say "oral sex" as a way of referring to either of these, but of course this term fails to distinguish between the two types.[33] Despite the potential for confusion, women and men in the NSFG do not offer widely divergent estimates of giving and receiving oral sex, so we combined both responses in Table 2.3, which displays the self-reported "ever done it" prevalence of oral sex and anal sex in never-married adults aged 18–23. Unlike with sexual partner estimates, these numbers largely line up across men and women. The majority of young adults who've ever experienced oral sex have already done so by age 18. All ages report a relatively tight range of between 70 and 85 percent.

Most emerging adults aren't inclined to label oral sex as "sex." "Technically I don't really count that as sex," stated Brian, a 20-year-old from Illinois. Jessica, a 19-year-old from Minnesota, doesn't either: "Most people my age only think of sex as intercourse," she claimed. Sean, a 22-year-old from Alabama, agrees: "To me sex is when you can, you know, reproduce. And you can't do that if you are doing anything oral, you know." Others simply put regular intercourse in a separate category. That's true of Philip, the 22-year-old from Kansas who'd had oral sex but never intercourse. When we asked him whether oral sex was sex, he relayed the ongoing debate in his mind:

I was actually thinking about that on the way over here, but I was leaning towards "no." [*Okay. Why not?*] Because, like, sex is defined as intercourse, and that's kind of how we learned it in school and, like, I think anything else is almost, like, just like skin-to-skin touching. But obviously, to a, you know, a higher degree.

TABLE 2.3 Noncoital Sexual Activity of Never-Married 18- to 23-Year-Olds, in Percent

	Men		Women	
	Oral	Anal	Oral	Anal
Overall	78.3	23.8	78.9	25.1
Age				
18	69.8	18.0	71.7	21.2
19	74.4	14.6	75.1	19.0
20	77.6	25.4	77.3	27.8
21	88.3	31.0	79.7	23.4
22	82.0	21.4	84.7	28.4
23	76.8	36.6	85.8	33.2
Race/Ethnicity				
White	82.8	23.6	85.1	28.5
Black	75.4	23.9	76.0	19.9
Hispanic	68.4	25.2	66.8	12.8
Other	64.0	20.9	49.8	21.2

Source: NSFG

Yet most emerging adults perceive oral sex differently than teen-agers do because—especially within their relationships—oral sex becomes part of foreplay. Megan, a 21-year-old Texan, remarks, "You don't usually have oral sex without, like, real sex." In romantic relationships—which young adults experience at higher rates than do teenagers—the two acts are no longer conceived of as distinct actions from which to choose but as parts of the same overarching act (of sex). Patrick, a 21-year-old from Oklahoma, delineates this well: "When I was in high school and stuff, like before girls had birth control and things like that, it [oral sex] was a more common alternative . . . and so in that sense, it was like what you did instead of sex."

But to some young adults who are pursuing sexual abstinence, sex and oral sex can still be very much equated. Rosario, a 19-year-old evangelical from Arizona, lumps all sexual activities together: "What I believe is when you get married [you should] go all out, have fun. But until then . . . I don't think that you should get really involved. And when I say really involved, like, no sexual intimacy whatsoever." And yet much of how young adults perceive sexual matters comes from what they've experienced themselves. Cali, an 18-year-old member of a Nazarene church in Montana, actively deliberates about the morality of being a Christian who participates in some forms of sexual activity. Like Laura, she has not had vaginal sex but has had oral sex with her boyfriend of two years, whom she hopes one day to marry. Cali senses moral ambiguity yet suspects she'll continue to live with the tension:

> I guess I'm definitely a child of my day and age. Because there's no way oral sex is like clean-cut okay. Like there's nothing specifically about it in the Bible but if you talked to any pastor, they'd probably not be all that keen on saying it was all right. [*So how do you feel about that?*] Um, I don't know. . . . It's true that there's a slippery slope, and so they really try to caution you away from it, but, I mean, I don't know. It's one of those things. It's not, I'm sure I'm just justifying, but it's something that I'm really, I don't know, I can't say for us. I know I'm speaking a horrible illogical argument. 'Cause for us it's okay, but for them [other people] it's stupid.

Cali and Laura—in step with many religious young Americans—reflect a common perspective among conservatives about sex. They're *selectively permissive*: the moral rule remains right and good and in effect, yet it does not apply to them at present, for reasons too nuanced and difficult for them to adequately describe. It's not that they're hypocritical. Rather, they feel the powerful pull of competing moral claims upon them: the script about what boyfriends and girlfriends in love want or are supposed to do for and to each other, and the script about what unmarried Christian behavior should look like. They want to satisfy both but find themselves rationalizing.

These moral debaters, however, are the exceptions: for most emerging adults oral sex is differentiated from vaginal sex and is either experienced along with it or as a less intense substitute for it, especially early in—or outside—relationships. By emerging adulthood, vaginal intercourse has become the preferred method of sex for most. Other sexual activities function as a supplement to or an on-ramp for vaginal intercourse.

Sociologist Scott Christopher's study of premarital sexual practice claimed that the standard chronological pattern for whites and Hispanics—but not for African Americans—is as follows: progression of sexual activity from kissing to touching breasts, then genitals, then oral sex, then intercourse (and eventually, if ever, anal sex).[34] For African Americans, who tend to be earliest to intercourse among adolescents, kissing progresses more uniformly to intercourse, with no recognizable pattern for other sexual activities. They are, as one set of scholars named it, "very conventional" in their sexual repertoire.[35] Jalen, an 18-year-old African American from Boston, exemplifies this pattern. When asked how his thinking about physical involvements and sex has changed over the past couple of years, Jalen responded by noting the recent addition to his repertoire of (performing) oral sex:

> I used to think . . . like I never wanted to do oral before. Like I was like, "I ain't never doing that," at least not until I get married and then I don't know. For some, I guess always hearing about it and like I was never really disgusted with the idea in the first place. So like, just hearing about it more and more, and then I had my girl, and I'm like, yeah. I fell in love with her, and like, she ain't my wife, but she is my wifey. So, I was like, "I'll try it." So, that was really it. I mean I tried it, and it wasn't like, it didn't make me vomit. It wasn't disgusting, and I actually enjoyed it, because I seen how much pleasure she was getting from it. So, that's pretty much the only thing that changed.

Anal Sex: Too Edgy or New Addition?

While any growth in the prevalence of oral sex is debatable and likely modest, we cannot say this about heterosexual anal sex. Anal sex is a relatively new addition to the sexual script of some emerging adults—and has been attempted by about one in four. Among no age group in the NSFG or NHSLS does the prevalence of anal sexual experience ever reach 45 percent, and the oldest cohorts do *not* display the highest prevalence rates, suggesting that its prevalence has increased much more recently than that of oral sex. Only 16 percent of 18- to 24-year-olds in the NHSLS survey in the early 1990s said they had ever experienced anal sex, a number that is higher than the figure reported by 50- to 54-year-olds, who'd had decades longer to have tried it.[36] Table 2.3 reveals that twice as many 23-year-old men (compared with 18-year-olds) reported having ever had anal sex. The rate of increase was slightly smaller for women but revealed a comparable overall pattern.

Published studies of anal sex prevalence among college students reveal very divergent numbers. One study conducted at a southeastern public university revealed that 9 percent had ever had anal sex, while another—this one among students in an upper-division women's health course at California State University-Chico—reported 32 percent, up from an earlier estimate of around 15 percent of freshmen. Still another study found 23 percent of one midwestern university's nonvirgins claiming they'd had anal sex, suggesting that particular sexual marketplaces develop their own norms about what's included in the local sexual repertoire, and what's not.[37]

By age 23, then, somewhere around 30 percent of Americans claim to have experienced anal sex. What are these young adults like? In regression models of oral and anal sex (in Table A2.4, sorted by gender; see appendix A, p. 258), there are simply fewer clear, consistent patterns when compared with predicting patterns of vaginal intercourse.[38] What *is* consistent across most models predicting either oral or anal sex is:

- Race: Most white emerging adults display significantly higher prevalence of each when compared with Hispanics, and African American men report less anal sex than do white men.
- Religiosity: Churchgoing is associated with less of each type of sex, and it is the strongest (negative) predictor of both types of sexual behavior for men.

Although it has been practiced among a stable and small minority for a long time, anal sex owes its recent growth in popularity to two emergent phenomena: ubiquitous access to pornography, and the increasing normalization of the idea of—though not necessarily the endorsement of—gay male sex within the popular imagination. Again, we're not claiming that anal sex is somehow new, since its practice has been possible since the advent of humankind. But among heterosexuals (especially whites), attempting anal sex is becoming more common, to the degree that a significant minority has at least tried it. Among how many it is a standard form of sex is difficult to estimate, though our hunch suggests it is a very small figure. As two students of sexuality astutely note, "Polite conversation and Victorian values lead most people to leave this sexual practice among the 'unspoken' aspects of social life."[39] But what was once unspeakable is not anymore, even among those who vehemently dislike it.

Elizabeth, a 20-year-old working in New York, is among the majority of young Americans who has not had anal sex and among whom the idea is not particularly inviting. While permissive about some aspects of sex, she finds the idea of heterosexual anal sex repulsive and feels no compulsion to hide it or to avoid sharing her opinion on the matter: "I think anal sex you should totally avoid. I think it's really not a good idea, just because it's really bad for you, for your insides, you know?" Megan hadn't tried it, either:

I don't want it. Just seems painful. [*Do you know anybody who has?*] Yeah. [*What do they say about it?*] It's painful [laughs]. That's pretty much all I got from her. Most of the people who have, have only tried it once and don't want to ever do it again. [*And why do they try it?*] They're drunk and their boyfriends really wanted to try it. [*And why did they really want to try it?*] Why did their boyfriends? I don't know. It's some weird sexual thing guys have. [*Do you think that's common?*] Yeah.

Elizabeth and Megan are like many young American women: they have not experienced anal sex, don't especially wish to, and note that plenty who have didn't like it. We will learn just how many dislike it yet tolerate it (and why) in chapter 3.[40]

Despite the "weird sexual thing" Megan perceives that "guys have," most of the sexually active men with whom we spoke either weren't all that interested in anal sex or were interested only for the thrill of trying something unknown. No male interviewee with whom we spoke identified it as a permanent fixture in his repertoire. Patrick, 21, from Oklahoma, hadn't ever tried it, but knew friends who had:

As far as anal, I know, like, I've never done that, and I don't really have a, um, it's not really my thing. But um, three of my friends, like, it's kind of come up. Like when they were drunk they said something like maybe they've tried it or something. But I don't think it's like a regular thing at all, just something that, um . . . [*Like experimental or something?*] Yeah. It's, it definitely wouldn't be usual, but um, oral and intercourse, I think those are pretty standard.

Sean, 22, from Alabama, had attempted it once with a girlfriend, but was not enamored of the idea:

We kinda tried it once, but it hurt her too much, so. [*Is that something you would wanna do?*] Um, I don't know. Yeah, I guess. Yes and no. Nothing that I, like, want really bad, but I wouldn't turn it down with her, you know.

Based on previous studies and our own analyses and interviews, we can confidently make these claims about anal sex:

- It's a relatively new addition to the American heterosexual repertoire.
- It's been attempted by a large minority but not a majority.
- It's been adopted by a very small minority.
- Preference for it appears associated with the pursuit of novel stimulation and psychological arousal.
- It's more commonly experienced within a stable relationship, not a short-term one.
- Women almost never ask for it, and few women report enjoying it.

The trends about sexual partners and types of sex that we've out-lined above are hardly limited to emerging adults in America. Great Britain has witnessed significant increases in lifetime heterosexual partner counts, as well as reports of anal and oral sex, in a mere one decade, from 1990 to 2000. The same is true in Sweden and Denmark: partner numbers and the practice of anal sex increased, the age at first sex declined by 4–5 years, and the gap in time between menarche and first sex halved from seven to three years—all this when comparing persons born before 1920 with those born after 1960. Again, in Swe-den: three or more lifetime partners are more likely to be found among persons aged 16–24 than among adults older than that. The prevalence of multiple sex partners and casual sex has increased significantly over time as attitudes toward casual sex have become increasingly more per-missive: Since 1989, the percent of Swedes saying sex should be limited to stable relationships has declined from 53 to 37 percent among men, and from 65 to 43 percent among women. Even casual sex without a condom has grown in popularity.[41]

There is little systematic evidence of a pronounced increase in sex parties or partner swapping among emerging adults, although anec-dotal examples can always be found. Tara, a 20-year-old state univer-sity student from Louisiana, is an outlier who helps us locate the norm. Having lost her virginity in eighth grade (in a threesome), she estimates she's had between 30 and 45 sexual partners, some of whom were in orgy-like and threesome settings. Her account, however, was a very uncommon one. Thus while there may be some truth to group sex rumors that give rise to media reports and consequent parental fears, adults almost always overestimate the percentage of young people involved. Far, far more common among both teenagers and adults is standard relational sex and hookup sex involving only two persons.

In sum, then, oral sex is a common part of the sexual repertoire of many heterosexual emerging adults. Whereas once it had functioned primarily as an alternative sexual practice to intercourse, it now tends to be considered foreplay. Anal sex is not in the repertoire of most, at least not yet. Its place is not yet clearly defined and may never be. Given that most Americans, especially women, strongly prefer vaginal or oral sex to anal sex, its practice could well wane in popularity or remain a "tried that once and that was enough" sort of activity. Before then, however, anal sex may grow in popularity sim-ply for the novelty attached to it and online porn's disproportionate coverage of it.

A MORE DIFFICULT CONVERSATION: SEXUALLY TRANSMITTED INFECTIONS

The Centers for Disease Control and Prevention grabbed the headlines for awhile in March 2008 when they announced that one in every four teen girls in the United States—over three million—have at least one sexually transmitted infection (STI).[42] Some populations are at even greater risk: just under half of African American teen girls were reported to have had an STI. While indicative of current trends, the alarming CDC estimate is higher than most other existing prevalence estimates. Yet even if their estimates are too high, there can be no doubt that STIs are a growing problem among emerging adults. Medically managing STIs is not cheap, either; $8 billion per year is spent diagnosing, curing, or treating Americans' STIs.[43]

Table 2.4 displays the percent of never-married respondents who've been told by a doctor in the past year that they have an STD (sexually transmitted disease). The Add Health survey refers to STD while we use the acronym STI here. We use the STI acronym simply because several of the most common sexually transmitted conditions are in fact curable infections and do not engender disease or life-altering conditions if properly diagnosed and treated; other STIs can't be cured, but are typically manageable. (But when referring to the Add Health survey question, we use their terminology).

The snapshot estimate in Table 2.4 suggests that one in four African American young adult women have been told recently that they have an STD, and extrapolating from that number over time offers credence to the CDC's estimate. The real rate of such infections over the course of several years may well be higher. Other race and ethnic group estimates

TABLE 2.4 Percent of Never-Married Respondents Ages 18–23 Who Have Been Told by a Doctor That They Had an STD in the Last Year

	Men	Women
White	3.2	10.5
Black	10.0	24.7
Hispanic	2.9	12.9
Asian	1.7	6.2
Overall	4.3	13.0

Source: Add Health

are considerably lower, however. Overall, 13 percent of young women and 4 percent of men report that they'd learned of an STD in the past calendar year. The gender discrepancy is due in part to women's greater susceptibility to some STIs (to say nothing of the disproportionate physical risks to them of undetected STIs) as well as their greater likelihood of pursuing testing. This gender difference is evident in Figure 2.1, which displays the likelihood of getting tested for an STI in the past year, sorted by gender and number of lifetime sexual partners. Interestingly, among both men and women, testing habits actually tail off among those who've had more numerous partners.

While many young adults fear STIs, actual reported experience with one was relatively uncommon in our interview pools. Those who did report an STI also tended to describe more colorful sexual histories, although such a history is hardly a requirement. Tara, the 20-year-old we introduced in the previous section, has HPV (human papillomavirus) but has never acquired anything else, despite the fact that sex with "the majority of those guys" involved neither a condom nor any other form of birth control. HPV is not one virus, but a family of around 100 different viruses, some of which are more ominous than others. While HPV can be controlled, it can't be cured. Its most pernicious types, however, can be prevented by the vaccine Gardasil. It works best, however, if administered before sexual activity commences, which has given rise to the political heat about Gardasil among many parents who don't wish to think of their daughters yet as potentially sexually active.

Tara's HPV went undetected for a time, in keeping with the pattern in Figure 2.1, where only about 50 percent of young women who've had more than 10 lifetime partners actually got an STD test in

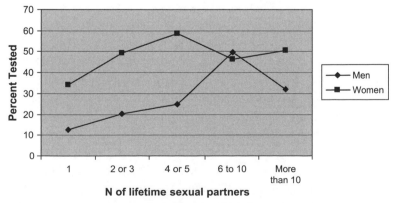

FIGURE 2.1 STD Testing in Past Year by Number of Lifetime Sexual Partners. *Source*: Add Health.

the past year. Her HPV developed into precancerous cells which were removed by cryotherapy, a method that kills such cells by freezing them. (Indeed, her annual pap smears continue to reveal abnormal cells and prompt repeated cryotherapy treatments.) Tara, never one to be entirely honest with her partners, was "scared to death about telling" David, her boyfriend at the time. So she didn't tell him. Jalen, the 18-year-old from Boston, has had seven sexual partners in his lifetime, most of whom he explicitly identifies as friends-with-benefits. He's currently in an exclusive romantic relationship. He intends to start college in the fall and has developed ideas for career pursuits, so in those ways he seems planful. But sexually, he is rather reckless. He and his girlfriend have sex regularly but don't often use a condom or any other contraception. He calls it playing "Russian roulette," and he claims it's addictive. And he has experienced that disproportionate African American representation when it comes to STIs. He has had Chlamydia before, and most of his friends have had gonorrhea, a curable STI that similarly continues to infect African Americans in disproportionate numbers. Although confident that the two of them are infection-free, Jalen nevertheless worries about pregnancy, for obvious reasons. Like many young Americans, he doesn't like to think about abortion but wouldn't rule it out. He just likes unprotected sex more.

Talk of HIV/AIDS among heterosexual young adults is uncommon except among African Americans like Jalen, precisely because that is the subpopulation most evidently at risk of HIV infection. Indeed, over 60 percent of all new HIV infections among Americans under age 25 are estimated to involve African Americans.[44] Calvin, a 21-year-old from New York who stopped counting after 15 sexual partners, describes his experience with gonorrhea and the testing process:

> Well, it was the same girl that I was telling you about that I was with for a year, and my first girl that I was with without using a condom. And she used to always tell me, like, "Ah, I'm so clean. I'm the cleanest chick you'll ever meet. Blah, blah, blah. . . ." And I'm like, "All right. Cool." So she's like, she suggested it [an STI test]. She's like, "Oh, we should go to the clinic and get checked out." "All right." So I go down to the clinic, and after they do the test, you got called back a week later. They told me to come down there. I'm like, "Aw, shit. I gotta come down there? Why do I gotta come down there for?" So I go down there, and they start giving me the pamphlet, like, I think it was gonorrhea. They were like, "Yeah, this is what it is. This is how you get it, and here, take these pills. You gotta take these for ten days." I'm like, "Fuck." And

then now, I'm thinking about everything. Like, was that pre-cum really pre-cum? Or was that the discharge they was talking about? And that funny feeling in my bladder—was that the stuff in me the whole time?" And I'm questioning everything. And at the same time, I'm like [thinking] it's good that she took me down there, but it's like, did she do something? I just got all these different questions in my mind now. And even now, it's an experience to me. Those fucking pills made me throw up. I had to, like, time [taking them] when I was going to eat. And then it happened again. It happened again while I was with her.

The chance of being infected (or in Calvin's case, reinfected) with an STI varies by lots of things, including which STI you're talking about. Yet many emerging adults treat them all as a monolithic mass in their minds, where every STI carries an equal risk of acquisition. The truth couldn't be more different. Some STIs, like Chlamydia and gonorrhea, can be gotten rid of and are typically passed from person to person by infected bodily fluid such as blood, semen, and vaginal or pre-ejaculate fluid (what Calvin referred to as "pre-cum"). Syphilis and gonorrhea are also considerably rarer than they used to be. Others, like HPV and genital herpes (HSV–2), can only be monitored and controlled and are transmitted through incidental contact with an infected skin lesion. Herpes remains remarkably common in adults—one in four women and one in eight men—though it has witnessed a slight decline in prevalence over the past decade. HPV infections, on the other hand, are increasing, and since few men ever exhibit HPV-related symptoms, this in particular is a difficult infection pattern to curb. (Indeed, many men either don't know or don't care if they're infected with HPV.) Herpes can also be transmitted from a person's genitals to a partner's mouth—or vice versa—during oral sex. Dental dams can mitigate this in oral sex performed on women—and condoms for oral sex performed on men—but the use of each remains rare. Although the empirical association between oral sex and STIs is obvious, the cognitive association is simply not yet strong enough to merit such risk-reductive approaches. People may carry a condom with them, but seldom a dental dam. No interviewee ever mentioned the term to us, though plenty discussed oral sex. The association of oral sex and STIs simply hasn't sunk in yet.

Condoms cannot eliminate the risk of passing along an STI, but correct condom use is very effective. The problem is that most people don't use condoms correctly, and erroneously equate *typical* and *correct* (or perfect) condom use in their minds.[45] Correct use is, of course, flawless: the condom goes on correctly (on the first try) and early, before contact with any seminal or vaginal fluid. This, however, is quite uncommon in real sexual situations. Indeed, slipping on a condom is often a late part of the sexual script for many, just prior to vaginal insertion and well after pre-ejaculate fluid begins to flow. To do so earlier is thought to interrupt sexual spontaneity. The bottom line remains clear: condoms tend to work as advertised if used correctly, but correct use isn't all that typical in reality. One group *is* more likely to pursue correct condom use: those seeking higher education. They are more consistent in their contraception use, and so it's no surprise that they're also less likely to acquire an STI. In the Add Health study, there's a linear and statistically significant correlation between educational status and testing positive for gonorrhea, trichomoniasis, and Chlamydia. Those who only finished high school find themselves with more STIs than those who are in—or who've graduated from—college.

While there is no doubt that the population of young Americans with STIs is growing—and hence an STI experience is becoming more normal—the subject remains a very sensitive one for many. Acquiring an STI prompts uncomfortable questions about the source of the infection—especially for those in stable relationships—as well as agonizing decisions about potentially embarrassing revelations to present and future sexual partners, to say nothing of the physical discomfort and health risks. Testing for STIs also reveals gendered norms about appropriate sexual desire and expression: women especially agonize over STIs, not just because of potential relationship or fertility consequences but because of the "moral devaluation" that accompanies ideas about STIs and sexual "uncleanness" among young women.[46] For some, discovering they have an STI—or worse, someone else discovering it—prompts association as a "bad girl" or "fallen woman," regardless of their sexual activity patterns or number of previous partners. If it's an STI that cannot be cured—like HPV or herpes—the mental and emotional "transgression" is typically even more difficult to overcome. Considering how frequent such diagnoses are—and how few emerging adults talk about them when asked in person—it's probable that social stigma about STIs has not yet diminished in step with their rising prevalence.

CONTRACEPTIVE USE

Elizabeth, the 20-year-old New Yorker we introduced earlier, works as a nanny. She was briefly in college but was not currently enrolled when she was interviewed. She experienced a pregnancy scare the very first time she had sex, which was during a brief summer fling earlier that year. Indeed, pregnancy scares are *remarkably common* among emerging adults. Although we're aware of no nationally representative dataset that has asked a direct question about their frequency, the theme recurred with a great deal of regularity in our interviews. A study of 32 women's visits to a health center for emergency contraceptive services describes well the unpredictability of a woman's reactions to a pregnancy scare, ranging from panicky to nervous to upset to nothing at all.[47] Holly, a 19-year-old from Oregon, described two such scares. Her reactions varied according to who the father would have been:

> I've had two [pregnancy scares] in my life, and it was horrible. The time that it was with Josh, it wasn't that bad, just because I knew he was there for me. He was gonna be there no matter what happened, no matter what I decided. So I mean, I was horrified, but it was okay 'cause I had a support system. And the next time it was with Trevor, but it was after we'd broken up. But we were still kind of hooking up, just 'cause we were idiots. And I don't know, I was almost two weeks late and I was completely and totally having a meltdown, because he wasn't somebody that I could go to, and I knew that.

Very many emerging-adults we spoke with told us that they "usually" use a condom but that sometimes they didn't. Sometimes interviewees were too drunk to remember a condom. Other times they didn't have one handy, and were horny. Many have traveled to a pharmacy to purchase a pregnancy test at least once, and some more than once.

Sexually active women in stable relationships typically report using some form of longer-term hormonal contraceptive but often not until well after they become sexually active. Elizabeth's pregnancy scare did not, however, occur because she failed to use contraception but because she believed—perhaps realistically, perhaps not—that the condom her partner used had broken. Indeed, this was the most common script offered by a majority of women seeking emergency contraception.[48] The resulting panic—in which she told her mother about what had happened and took a pregnancy test—was all for nothing; she wasn't pregnant.

In the Add Health data, only 51 percent of unmarried sexually active respondents said they use contraception "all of the time." Twenty-one percent said "most of the time." Seven and nine percent said "half of the time" and "some of the time," respectively. And 12 percent said "none of the time." Tim, a 19-year-old Texan, explains how these choices are often made:

We forgot like once or twice. But 95 percent of the time . . . [*Forgot? I mean, what do you mean forgot? Didn't have it?*] Forgot as in like . . . yeah, she just really wanted to have sex. [*So, it wasn't forgotten. It was on purpose.*] Well, I mean, she could have remembered to bring it with her . . . [*For some people that would mean "Oh, we can't do this."*] I was careful. I never actually ejaculated into her. . . . [*When you didn't have a condom . . .*] Right.

Despite its reputation as a poor method of contraception, Tim's occasional use of withdrawal is hardly uncommon. Data analyses of the NSFG reveal that the percentage of adult women who've ever used withdrawal as a means of contraception *increased* from 41 percent in 1995 to 56 percent in 2002.[49] Perhaps surprisingly, withdrawal can be relatively effective in preventing pregnancy, far better than doing nothing at all. Indeed, when undertaken correctly, withdrawal is nearly as effective as typical (not correct) condom use in preventing pregnancy (but not STIs). Realistic estimates of typical use indicate that about 18 percent of couples using withdrawal as their primary means of contraception will become pregnant in a year, only slightly more than those practicing typical condom use (15 percent, vs. 2 percent for correct use).[50]

Table 2.5 displays contraceptive choice at most recent sex among emerging adults, using data from the 2002 NSFG study. Surprisingly, 13 percent of men and 16 percent of women said that withdrawal was what they used the last time they had sex. While it's far below condom and pill use, it's still the third-most common method of contraception in any given act of intercourse and rather popular among college students.[51] Far fewer respondents use the rhythm method, in part because few emerging adults really understand fertility cycles. Many of

TABLE 2.5 Types of Contraceptive Use (of Self or Partner) at Last Sex, Contracepting Never-Married 18- to 23-Year-Olds

	Women	Men
Condom	52.4	66.8
Pill	45.9	49.0
Withdrawal	15.5	13.2
Depo-Provera, injectables	8.6	5.1
Rhythm or safe period by calendar	1.9	0.8

Source: NSFG.

Note: Columns sum to more than 100% because many respondents report using more than one method.

our undergraduate students, for instance, are sexually active, but when we ask about fertility in class few can tell us the most fertile days in the course of a woman's period. Even many women don't know. A condom or pill renders the question moot.

Condoms remain the preferred option among emerging adults, especially while still in their teens and in the early stages of any sexual relationship. Eventually, however, romantic relationships that involve sex and commitment often discontinue condom use and turn exclusively to the birth control pill. Taking away the only thing that separates two people—a piece of latex—is understood by many in the age of STIs as a sign of commitment and intimacy. Few men prefer condoms to the feel of unprotected sex, though they remain the go-to option for their ability to prevent most STIs. Transitions to the pill, however, have been increasingly hamstrung by recent tussles over insurance coverage of birth control pills, especially in college clinics. A month of the pill now typically sets back users anywhere from $20 to $80, depending on the type.[52] While condoms vary widely in price and style, they remain more affordable, versatile (since they can also prevent STIs), and conducive to erratic patterns of sexual intercourse.

Christine, a 20-year-old college student from Louisiana, was in the process of making the transition from condoms to the pill, and offered another common explanation for inconsistent contraceptive practices. It took Christine a while to figure out what time of day she could best tolerate her birth control pill, which she claimed upset her stomach. (So far as we know, this is an uncommon side effect.) The morning didn't work, so she tried later in the day, which worked better but made it more difficult to remember. So she occasionally forgets. As a result, when she and her boyfriend have sex, they typically augment the pill with a condom: "It's like double protection, pretty much, because sometimes I forget." Such a multimethod strategy is common among young Americans, since the pill does nothing to mitigate STIs.

Table 2.6 reinforces how sporadic actual contraceptive use really is among emerging adults. The overall contraceptive use rate at most recent sex—about 72.5 percent—is not substantially higher than the rate derived from the same question asked when they were teenagers, which was 68 percent. Very many unmarried young Americans continue to flirt with (presumably) unintended pregnancies. Hannah, the 19-year-old from Alabama we heard from earlier, exemplifies the "not every time" mentality common among many who aren't enrolled in (and haven't graduated from) traditional, four-year colleges. Like Christine, she disliked the side effects of the pill: "The hormones—they made me a less

TABLE 2.6 Percent of Never-Married 18- to 23-Year-Olds Who Used
Contraception Last Time They Had Sex, by Gender and
Educational Attainment

	Men	Women
Did not go to college	65.2	60.7
Went to college but received no degree	71.4	69.2
Enrolled in two-year college	79.6	77.4
Enrolled in four-year college	75.2	81.8
Earned associate's degree	85.8	76.9
Earned bachelor's degree or higher	85.7	88.6
Overall	71.6	73.0

Source: Add Health

happier person." In response, Hannah and her boyfriend "made a responsible decision. We sat down and talked about it, that if I wasn't going to be on contraceptives—like pills or patches or anything—that we were going to try and use the condom as much as possible." They didn't every time, however:

> Um, we try to yes, every time. There are some times when it's kind of a spur-of-the-moment . . . nobody's around kind of thing. And we just don't happen to have it with us. But we always make sure that we think, 'Do we really want to do it? Do we want to take this chance?' And we both agree, 'All right, that's what we're going to do.' We're going to accept the consequences, no matter what.

Hannah's method lends itself to pregnancy scares—and to the real thing. Had they ever had such a scare? Of course. It was like a scene straight out of the film *Juno*.

> (We) had one scare. . . . my period was a couple weeks late and we went, we got an EPT and we went to the Handy Way and he's pacing around the Handy Way and I'm, you know, it was very comical and it turned out to be nothing. And it's been about four or five months and I don't have a belly, so I guess the pregnancy test was good. Since then I guess, we've probably cut down a lot [on sex]. You know, it used to be any time that we had a chance, and now it's just every once in awhile. We've really cut down, and it kind of was a little bit of a reality check.

Thao, on the other hand, is in college. A 19-year-old from California, he has witnessed multiple pregnancy scares with his girlfriend, all the result of their intentional failure to use contraception. The repetition of the scares embarrasses him, and yet the heat of the moment and their preference for condom-free sex consumes them, he claims. Afterward, "we rationalize that it will be probably okay." So far, it has been. But the odds are against them: if they have sex regularly for a year, their probability of pregnancy is over 80 percent. Others, like Consuela, are far more apprehensive. A 20-year-old woman from a border city in which teen pregnancy is a major social problem, Consuela has always been future-minded, including in her sex life. Only once has she not used contraception during sex—when she was drunk at a party. She freaked out, by her own account, and took six pregnancy tests in order to be completely sure that she wasn't expecting. Others rely on the morning-after pill as a go-to birth control method when in a pinch.

College graduates—the group most prepared to handle a pregnancy financially—nevertheless exhibit the highest contraceptive rates, at 86–89 percent. Those who never went to any sort of college and can typically least afford a pregnancy (financially) display the lowest rates: 65 percent among men and only 61 percent of women. This phenomenon reflects what social scientists call the demographic-economic paradox: those persons most able to financially support children are least likely to be having them. While in America this paradox is not yet contributing to depopulation among the upper-middle class, it is in European countries like Spain and Italy, where fertility rates have dropped significantly.

CONCLUSION

The purpose of this chapter is to lay the groundwork about emerging adults' sexual behavior before we consider the character and aspects of their sexual relationships. Using both survey and in-person interview data, we detailed what is known about the sexual habits of emerging adults: who is a virgin and why, how many sexual partners people report having, and how the sexual repertoire of behaviors has expanded. When combined with previous studies, our results indicate some subtle changes over time—such as diminishing virginity rates—and more overt change, such as the rise in rates of experimentation with anal sex. Contraceptive use remains uneven, especially among young Americans who are not pursuing higher education. Even those who say they use it often report instances of unprotected sex. While overall STI rates appear to be climbing, actual self-reports of them among interviewees remain sporadic. Pregnancy scares remain more common, which makes sense given the overwhelming tendency toward typical rather than correct contraceptive use.

THREE

Inside Sexual Relationships

Equality may perhaps be a right, but no power on earth can ever turn it into a fact.

—*Honoré de Balzac*

MOST OF THE sexual statistics we're used to seeing and thinking about are of the individual. Every story and statistic noted in chapter 1 and 2 was about the individual. This is not surprising, since it's the easiest unit of analysis to collect data about.[1] We speak of individuals as being sexually active. Friends ask each other about how their sex life is, making the subject of inquiry—a sex life—the possession of a person, not the domain of a relationship. Many of us have come to think of sex as an individual action that happens to involve another person. This is no small change. But within the paradigm of serial monogamy, only one thing remains stable: the individual. Since we may or may not choose to embed ourselves in enduring relationship structures, fewer of us draw identity from them anymore.

But sexual relationships are worth knowing about, because they exist. They're real, even if they're short-lived, and all relationships exhibit characteristics that vary among them. Some last longer than others; some involve age disparities; some exhibit clear power differentials; some involve less romance; some are comprised of partners with very different levels of sexual interest. In this chapter, we explore what the sexual relationships of emerging adults are like, what share of them are romantic as distinct from nonromantic ones that are only about sex, how quickly they form, how long they last, what the "scripts" are for how to enter and maintain them, how sex is negotiated, how common it is that partners dislike particular sexual activities, and who among them continues to tolerate these disliked activities, who doesn't, and why. Before all that, however, we begin with a theory about how to understand the formation of sexual relationships.

THE ECONOMICS AND TIMING OF SEXUAL RELATIONSHIPS

There is a basic economics that typically precedes emerging-adult relationships and constitutes the social setting in which they develop. In their review article "Sexual Economics," social psychologists Roy Baumeister and Kathleen Vohs remind scholars of the important economic and market principles that characterize and shape the genesis of sexual relationships between unmarried adults.[2] Just as the sale of a house is not simply a transaction between two parties but is connected to the local economy and housing market, they remind us that sexual activity within a community is interconnected as part of a sexual market. Sexual markets are like economic markets: we all inhabit them, and they affect everyone.[3]

Thus sex is not entirely a private matter between two people, Baumeister and Vohs assert. Instead, it becomes part of an economic and social system in which couples participate. Think about it: men and women are always looking around and listening to friends and peers, observing each other's strategies and evaluative criteria, trying to figure out if their own experience is "normal." Many wonder if they're with someone who's "good enough," speculate about whether they're pursuing someone who's "out of their league," or wonder what they should expect sexually from their partner based on what they know or presume to know about what other couples are doing. Baumeister and Vohs's theory is impressive and convincing; some of its key aspects— reinforced by literally dozens of studies—are worth repeating here.

Although sociologists have spilled plenty of ink characterizing men and women as similar creatures and gender differences as the result of "social construction" (in other words, a human creation), there remain real differences between men and women in the domain of sexuality. On average—and that is always a critically important caveat to keep in mind—men and women desire sex for different reasons, show differing levels of interest in sex, and experience sex differently. Men initiate sex more often than women do. They tend to be more sexually permissive than women. They refuse sex less often, and rate their sex drive as stronger than women's. They exhibit different patterns of masturbation, fantasizing, emphases (on pleasure, romance, commitment, permissiveness, and sexual conquest), and even differences in how malleable their sexuality is.[4] Author Steven Rhoads humorously observes, "The libidos of perfectly ordinary men, when fully understood by women, seem deformed or disreputable to them. Many women strongly resist an accurate presentation of male sexuality."[5] To be sure, we have interviewed numerous young women who assert at least as much interest in sex as men, if not more. But they are far less common than the stereotype they thwart. Sexual economics doesn't deny in the least that women like sex, just that the vast majority of them seem to like it less than men do and prefer to have it in a committed relationship.

Of course this prompts the question: why then do unmarried young women have sex? While there are literally hundreds of reasons that people have sex—and a pair of our colleagues here at the University of Texas recently documented 237 of them—the pursuit of pleasure is of course often part of the equation.[6] But it's not the sole or primary motivation among most. Sexual economics theory would argue that sex is about acquiring valued "resources" at least as much as it is about seeking pleasure. When most people think of women trading sex for resources, they think of prostitution, and money as the terms of exchange. But this theory encourages us to think far more broadly about the resources that the average woman values and attempts to acquire in return for sex—things like love, attention, status, self-esteem, affection, commitment, and feelings of emotional union. Within many emerging adults' relationships, orgasms are not often traded equally. Stacy, a 20-year-old from Missouri, said she never experienced an orgasm with her current partner (who's not a boyfriend). But intercourse with him "makes me feel sexy, like almost confident."

While Channing, a 22-year-old from Texas, mentions the pleasure that sex provides, she also notes "the connection to other people, and just feeling that someone likes you and wants you, and feeling attractive and all that." These sorts of resources are far more commonly involved in sexual interaction than are money or material goods. Although traditionally, men have implicitly (or explicitly, if necessary) offered women resources in exchange for sex, it's a rare woman that would give men resources in exchange for sex. As Baumeister and Vohs observe, women don't pay for sex. It's as simple as that. There are male prostitutes, to be sure, but their clients are almost always other men.

When we asked one interviewee about whether she discusses her sexual relationships with her friends, she described a conversation that shed light on the sexual economy. She had asked a girlfriend about whether the sex had been "worth her time":

> Was it good? [laughs]. Basically because, I mean, some girls will start dating someone new, and the first time they have sex with this person, it's kind of like, the main question is, "Was it at least good for you?" [*So do girls talk about that a lot?*] Yes. [*And, I assume the answer isn't always yes.*] Right. [*So, then what?*] What do you mean? [*Then what do . . . girls talking about this decide? Is it just saying, "Oh well, that's the way it goes?"*] Depends on how much you like him. [*Okay.*] I mean, the more you like him, obviously the less sex matters. [*Why?*] Because, I mean, he's making up for it in other areas. [*What areas?*] Personality. [*What does that mean?*] He's fun to be around, he's funny, smart, he has more going for him than just the . . . good looker guy who's good in bed.

Other women draw a more direct line between sex and access to financial resources. While attractiveness and a good personality remain paramount concerns for many young women, Abby—a 22-year-old from Colorado—notes with surprise her own penchant to remain with a boyfriend she didn't really love or desire:

> I kind of was surprised at how I sort of dated this guy for a little while. Not for very long but, umm, and he was very wealthy [laughs]. And I was really surprised at how difficult it was to not, to like, break up with him. Because I didn't wanna go out with him anymore, but it was like, "Oh, but he's always showering me with gifts" [laughs]. There was that thought, like, maybe I should stick with it for a little while.

A recent study of 475 University of Michigan undergraduates documents that men are more likely to report making attempts to trade resources for sex while women are more likely to report attempted trades of sex for resources, just as sexual economics theory would predict.[7] Fully 27 percent of men who were not in a committed relationship reported offering someone favors or gifts in exchange for sex. On the other hand, nearly 10 percent of women reported attempting to trade sex in order to acquire something. Such trades aren't often conscious or spoken but rather reflect a subtle quid pro quo mentality. Consuela, the 20-year-old we met in chapter 2, describes one such relationship that hadn't yet quite attained boyfriend status but was sexual:

He's the nicest guy ever. He does anything and everything. And he does whatever makes me happy. It's just, not his physical features. But even—we've had sex before—even at that I'm not super-interested in it. And when he calls, I'm not like all really excited. Just kind of there. I don't know what that is, but I feel kind of obligated [to have sex with him] because he's bought me stuff, he brought me up here again from home, he helps me, he knows my mom.

Even among the very religious and sexually conservative in America, the economy of sex prevails, especially among young women who wish to wait until marriage to have sex.[8] While sex (and virginity) is thought of as a great "gift" to give, observing this value of it implies there's an economy to it. When asked why she wasn't into hooking up, Casey, a 20-year-old virgin from Arizona, waxed economic:

Why would I want to like, I see it as I'm giving them a gift by letting them spend time with me, and you know, be somewhat physical with me. You know, that's a gift—you giving yourself. And why would I wanna give that for free, you know?

Baumeister and Vohs therefore claim that the sexual activity of women has exchange value, whereas men's sexual activity does not. So even though in one sense, a man and a woman who are having sexual intercourse are both doing similar things, socially they are doing quite different things: he is primarily satiating sexual desire, while she may be doing that as well but also tends to acquire desired resources in return for the sex. Patrick, a 21-year-old from Oklahoma, knew this well. When asked whether sex with his girlfriend made him feel closer to her, he was frank: "I don't get the reassurance that I think that they [women] get with that." Megan, whom we met in chapter 2, was bluntly economic when we asked her whether—when interested in starting a relationship with a man—being willing to have sex would be an attractive quality in a woman:

I don't think so. [*Because?*] Because you're not giving [the man] much to look toward. [*Okay.*] I mean, not that you should use sex as like a bargaining play. [*Do people do that?*] Sure, all the time . . . [*Bargaining for what?*] What they want out of the relationship. [*Which is?*] Like a lot of people are like, "No sex for you until this happens." [*Until what happens?*] Whatever they want happens.

Megan didn't get specific about what women want, because different women want different things. But to her, the exchange of sex for resources was a no-brainer. It's the way it is. Some men have more resources to offer, and some women can command a higher price. Indeed, Baumeister and Vohs list 13 different individual factors and six market factors that affect the terms of sexual exchange. Physical attractiveness is only one of the individual factors. Sean, a 22-year-old from Alabama who'd had three partners so far and was sexually active with his current girlfriend, noted the price that a beautiful woman can command if she so wishes: "I mean if I really like her a lot, then I wouldn't have any problem waiting." On the other hand, drastically lowering the price of valuable goods is ironically unattractive: "If a girl just like threw herself at me then I would . . . question who she's been with or how promiscuous she is. That's the only thing that would turn me off."

The Timing and Price of Sex

So when does sex actually commence in a relationship in which sex is consensual and men desire it more than women? The theory provides a clear—though certainly contested—answer: sex begins in relationships when women decide that it does. In a fascinating study, researchers oversaw a unique experiment in which attractive young male and female researchers separately approached other-sex strangers on a college campus, expressed their attraction to them, and then made one of three randomly selected requests: would you go out with me tonight, would you come over to my apartment tonight, or would you go to bed with me tonight? Fully 75 percent of men—but not a single woman—agreed to the last of these, the invitation to casual sex.[9] In the study of human behavior, social scientists rarely happen along such stark statistical contrasts as this one between men and women. On a random Sunday evening in December 2009, we logged on to Austin's Craigslist "personals" site and tallied men's invitations for women to have casual sex with them and compared them with women's invitations to men for the same. A total of 166 invitations had been posted by men that day to women (and an additional 73 by men to other men); a mere three invitations to men for casual sex were posted by women. While such a count is hardly a scientific study, the contrasting numbers reinforce this sexual economics thesis: Women can have sex when they wish to; men can only hope for it.

In another compelling study, researchers asked 242 college students about when they expected sexual intercourse to first occur in relationships and when it actually did. Not surprisingly, men expected sex after fewer dates than women did.[10] The authors, however, calculated differences between expectations and reality separately by gender. So whose expectations jived with reality? The women's: the correlation between when women thought sex should start and when they actually began having sex in their own relationships was 0.88, indicating a high and very significant degree of association between the two ideas. (A figure of 1.0 would have been a perfect correlation.) For men, the correlation was 0.19 and statistically insignificant, meaning that when they want sex to start and when it actually does are two very different things. Another study of university students revealed that while gender differences in sexual fantasizing are beginning to narrow, there remains a greater correlation between sexual fantasy and real sexual experiences for women than for men.[11] The bottom line is this: *women are the sexual gatekeepers within their relationships*. We realize this may be perceived as a provocative claim, and many women may not sense this personal power in their own situation, but it's a claim that the theory—and our data analyses and a variety of other studies—agree upon. Not a few women, ignorant or disbelieving of basic sexual economics, imagine that power is found in *generating* male desire. On the contrary, most any woman with a pulse can generate some male desire.

One dilemma with making this claim about sexual gatekeeping is that it implies that women's choices are the one thing that is malleable, that "boys will be boys." At least in one sense, that is the case: men's sexual behavior is more stable and their sex drives more consistently elevated, making it both more difficult to predict variation in their behavior or to programmatically alter it with reliable success.[12] Although the "cost" of sex is negotiated between partners *and* reflects the narratives about sex within the community at large, in the end a woman must agree to the transaction (in a consensual relationship).[13] Patrick can attest to this. He began sleeping with his first girlfriend on her terms: "We talked about it before that, but she made it clear that it wasn't going to happen until she was ready. And so, um, I just kind of waited until she was ready and then she told me she was." When discussing the frequency with which she has sex in her cohabiting relationship with David, Tara—the 20-year-old from Louisiana we met in chapter 2—describes this ongoing sense of control:

> David is so pushy about sex. In the morning he's so like, "Roll over" [and have sex]. And I'm just like, "Ughh." Like, I like to have sex, but I don't think you should have to have it." [*Do you pretty much do it whenever he wants?*] I pretty much do it whenever *I* want.

Allison, an 18-year-old from Illinois, asserted her control over the two sexual relationships she's been in: "I don't have any [sexual] regrets. I was always the one who never, I'd never do anything if I didn't feel okay about doing it. You know, I don't care if you [her partner] don't like it. Too f-ing bad." Kaci, a 19-year-old evangelical Christian from Texas, describes virtually the same in her relationship with her boyfriend, who's studying to be a youth minister. While they stop just short of intercourse, "he's always in the mood to kiss, to do something, but then, it's like, all a matter of when *I* feel like kissing, you know, making out or whatever. That's when things happen."

This claim about sexual gatekeeping, however, flies in the face of what millions of young women feel. Many don't sense that they have control of the sexual aspect of their relationship, and we've heard plenty of passivity from young women when it comes to discussing how and when sex "happens." The average young woman might read this claim about gatekeeping and wonder, "So why doesn't it work that way for me?" Even Tara confessed that she doesn't know how to attract men apart from sex appeal. We don't disagree with these sentiments at all. Indeed, young women often feel like they have to bargain sex for relational stability. Here's why: just because women control the flow of sex within their relationships does *not* mean they're free to do sexually as they please. That is, they don't single-handedly control the price of sex. That is negotiated between two individuals in the *social context* of the prices that other, similar couples set, which is why deciphering sexual norms is such a prominent theme among teenagers and young adults, especially women. They want to know what they're supposed to do and what they can expect.

Clearly this is the domain in which women tend to lose power, as Kathleen Bogle notes in her study of college hookups. Initiating sex with men—especially quickly—hands men the keys to the future direction of the relationship.[14] This is not to suggest that intense power plays inhabit every sexual relationship, or that every sexual act exhibits competitive undertones. Rather, this sheds light on why many young women feel like "the system" thwarts them, even while we are claiming that they retain a good measure of control. The real problem for women lies in how the negotiation of sex takes place—that is, locating the "price." Sexual negotiation of this sort occurs within the context of powerful yet malleable cultural stories about what ought to happen in relationships and when (that is, what is normal for the crowd you're in). Those narratives have changed over time and become considerably more friendly to early sexual experience and, in keeping with the theory, much more tailored to men's sexual interests than to women's. When we asked Michelle (20, from Oklahoma) about how long she'd been in her last relationship before it became sexual—by her decision—she responded by illuminating the social nature of trading information about pricing sex:

> It was like, three months. [*What do you think of that? Long? Average? Short?*] Umm . . . it's short actually, now when I think about it. But actually we had known each longer than that . . . I guess we had been together for three months, but we had been talking for another couple months before that. So five months. Which is, I mean, I guess, an average amount of time for people usually. [*How do you know this?*] Because just from like friends and stuff, they'll be with a guy for not even a month, and be sleeping with them. [*Do you talk about this, among friends?*] Yes.

However, people almost always guess "the going rate" for sex incorrectly: the expectations-and-reality study noted earlier found that nearly everyone thinks that they themselves expect sex later in a relationship than the average person does. The men expected sex for themselves after about six weeks, while they believed the average man would expect to have sex within only three weeks. Women, on the other hand, expected sex for themselves after 13 weeks, but believed the average woman would expect it in less than four weeks.[15] Just like young Americans define promiscuity as a trait that only characterizes other people, so too with their own sexual expectations—they see themselves as more conservative than the average person when in fact they might very well *be* the average person.

The actual price range for sex varies widely, as Baumeister and Vohs point out. Sex might cost little or nothing—a few drinks or some attention and compliments, or simply a promise to be discreet about the liaison. Typically it's more expensive than that, such as a perceived commitment to being in an exclusive relationship for a while. The highest price a man can pay is a lifetime promise to share all his wealth, income, and affections with a woman exclusively. Charging the delivery of a public promise of lifelong marriage in exchange for sex is uncommon today. As noted earlier, between 90 and 95 percent of Americans experience sex before marriage, so the price for sex is seldom that high.[16]

So just how high is the price of sex among most unmarried young adults in America? Not very high at all. The timing of sex within relationships provides us a good indicator of the "cost" of sex to men. That is, how long does it take before sex commences within young adults' relationships? If it's a short amount of time, we presume women are expecting much fewer resources from men. If it's considerably longer, then women are expecting more. Table 3.1 displays the length of time that young adults report having known a recent sexual partner before commencing a sexual relationship with him or her. Fully 36 percent of all young men's relationships become sexual in less than two weeks, and 70 percent in less than six months. Women's claims are slightly more conservative: 22 percent of their relationships become sexual early, within two weeks, while 61 percent of them do so before the six-month mark.

If we analyze these data by persons instead of by relationships, we can state that 20 percent of all sexually active young men have had sex with someone the first day they met her. That is certainly not typical of sexual relationships and characterizes unusual, short-term relationships such as a one-night stand. But it's true: one in five emerging-adult men have "scored" on the first day at some point in their past.[17] On the other end of the spectrum, only 13 percent of sexually active young men have waited more than a year to commence a sexual relationship.

An alternate indicator of the going rate for sex is the lifetime sexual-partner count of men who have few resources to offer. In the Add Health study, 22-year-old adult men who never enrolled in college—or who have dropped out—and are *not* presently employed full-time report having had 7.4 lifetime sexual partners, on average. Among 22-year-old high-school dropouts that figure rises to 8.6 partners.

TABLE 3.1 Time Respondent Had Known Partner at First Sex in Relationship, in Percent, among all Nonmarital Sexual Relationships (Past and Current), 18- to 23-Year-Olds

	Men	Women
Time to First Sex		
2 weeks or less	36.0	21.6
2–4 weeks	12.8	11.1
1–5 months	21.5	28.7
6–12 months	10.7	13.5
1 year or more	19.0	25.1

Source: Add Health

When contrasted with male college graduates, it's obvious that the *economic* resources or promise that men offer are of decreasing value to a potential sexual partner. Such graduates report on average 4.9 lifetime partners, well below the numbers displayed by men who at least according to one indicator of resources—the standard of economic trajectory—have much less to offer a partner.

As we reviewed the transcripts of young men whom we've tracked in the NSYR over the course of six years and three separate meetings, it became obvious that these survey numbers are no fluke. Among one quartet of 20-year-old men who either never went to college or dropped out—none of whom are in the full-time labor force—we heard lifetime partner estimates of 10, 15, 20, and 100. If historically men were willing to work for sex—that is, *earn* the attentions of a potential partner by displaying commitment, life skills, and/or a promising trajectory—the modern man certainly doesn't have to. It's a different world, wherein the physical risks of sex have been dramatically lowered and the independent, economic trajectories of women dramatically raised.

Commencing a Romantic Relationship with Sex

So while we don't have the data to directly determine what the average price of sex actually is, we can gather from this assessment of time-until-sex, together with partner estimates and previous studies, that it's currently not very high. Putting sex before romance, however, is a suboptimal strategy if one's intention is to begin a long-term, committed relationship. (Of course, such an intention certainly isn't always the case.) In her study employing hypothetical scenarios, psychologist Pamela Regan concludes that people who would have sex on a first date with someone they just met are simply not considered marriageable, in contrast with those who wait for commitment. Men who've had numerous sexual partners in the past are the quickest to perceive diminished attractiveness in a woman after first intercourse.[18] In the Add Health relationship data, 8 percent of both men and women reported having had sex first—before sensing romance—in at least one of their two most important relationships so far. That means that in key relationships, 92 percent of young adults said that nurturing romance and love came first, before sex. It is difficult to make it work the other way around. And yet many try. Indeed, it's one of the most common reasons women give for "discounted" sex—as a means to increase their chances of long-term commitment. Regan's interviews with young women reveal the ill-fated logic of sex for the hope of security:

- "I guess that I want affection and I want someone to think of me a lot. I figure that if a guy isn't really interested and I put out he will stay longer and get to know me and then realize that I'm a decent person and we'll have a relationship" (Female, age 19).
- "I felt that sleeping with this particular person and sharing an intimate moment with him would be a good way to make him attracted to me and to want to go out with me. Maybe I confused sex and love. I wanted to feel loved and I thought maybe sex would fulfill that gap. But it didn't work." (Female, age 20)
- "I hope that if I have sex with the guy right away then the relationship will last longer and he will stick around if for nothing more than the sex at least" (Female, age 19).[19]

Of course, very many sexual decisions among emerging adults are not made with long-term relational intentions. Many "just happen" in social settings well known to lubricate sexual events—like parties, clubs/bars, and other gatherings. Numerous interviewees who told us they would wait for sex until they felt really comfortable with someone, or until they knew they wanted to be in an intimate relationship with someone, nevertheless admitted to some sex occurring outside of their intended paradigm. Abby told us that she would have to be in a relationship with someone in order to have sex with him, but later in the interview recalled cheating on an ex-boyfriend twice with two different men, even after moving in with him. Thus while many young adults' own description of their ideal scenarios for sex are closely tied to stable romantic relationships, their real lives often exhibit short-term deviations from this.

THE STUBBORN DOUBLE STANDARD

Women who begin having sex in their relationships "too soon" can be vilified by their peers (though not their friends) with all manner of descriptive terms, but there is no comparable way to trash a man's reputation. There is no male version of "slut" or "whore," nor does it seem that there ever will be one. "Womanizer" and "man whore" just don't convey the same sense of disdain. There isn't a reverse "walk of shame" in which men stumble home after a night at their girlfriend's residence hall or sorority house, enduring the judgmental glances of their peers. It doesn't exist. Indeed, young men are often jealous of other men's sexual access, while women are more apt to be vindictive toward each other than toward the men who pursue them.

This is the conundrum of the sexual double standard: the sexual choices of men are tolerated far more readily than those of women. Why? Back to economics: women who allow—or worse, encourage—sex too soon in a relationship are thought to make it more difficult for other women around them who would prefer "costlier" sex, that is, greater relationship commitments before sex. Women who agree to have sex without strings drive down the possible "price" of sex for other women around them. (Remember, the sexual marketplace is a social thing in which people are constantly trying to decipher what is normative and where men prefer low-commitment sex). So there's really no such thing as entirely discreet sex, even if a couple never mentions it to another soul, because every sexual act is a data point for both men and women in establishing the proper price of sex in subsequent relationships. What matters most, of course, is not some real standard documented somewhere but rather perceptions of social norms and the stories (scripts) about how sex is supposed to happen, and when, and among whom. The double standard is robust, based on economic interests and perhaps biological sex differences, and collectively still upheld by both sexes.[20] Anyone can call it wrong and harmful, but it's not going to disappear through any effort of collective will or even normative change, because it is a fixture of the social and economic system in which sex occurs. Until sex is desired and experienced by women and men equivalently, there will be a double standard about it.

Even Gabriela, who's had more partners than most of her boyfriends have, senses the rootedness of the system. When asked about whether she thought her own sexual history will be an issue in future relationships, she anticipates that it will:

Probably a lot, because the boyfriends that I've had, they've, they don't like it. [*How do you know?*] They like, they just, they say it. You know, like, "Why did you sleep with him? I wish I would have been the first person that you slept with." I've had two boyfriends that have said that. [*What do you think of that?*] I think it's complete shit. Because they didn't. They did whatever they wanted. Why can't I? [*Do you feel like there's a double standard?*] Yea. [*Still?*] Yea. [*What do you think of it?*] I think it's, I don't like it. My mom has double standards with me and my brothers all the time, and guys do it to girls all the time. [*Do you think it's, do you think Latinos have more of a double standard than other people?*]

Um, probably. From, like, from American culture, yes. But in every culture I can think of men are always allowed to do so much more than women.

Sociologist Paula England reveals her surprise and dismay that the sexual double standard is still alive in the ongoing, online College Social Life Survey (CSLS) of over 10,000 college students.[21] She and her coauthors are struck by "how little gender revolution we see in sexual and romantic affairs." Instead, they conclude, "the standard, vague though it is, has shifted to a less restrictive line for each sex but remained dual." Indeed, the double standard has eased a bit in the last several decades in the West, due largely to the advent of accessible and reliable birth control methods, which have radically lowered the objective risks of sexual intercourse for both women and men. In other words, due to the diminished hazards of sex, women have become a bit more like men (who prefer lower-cost sex), rather than men becoming more like women (who tend to prefer higher-cost sex).[22] The latter will not occur. Men have traditionally been sexual pursuers, but historically they would have had to offer women protection, economic stability, and/or the promise of marriage and children in order to get access to sex. She may have enjoyed sex, but it was far too risky to provide it without significant concessions in return.

This risk is not very relevant anymore, since young women are delaying their pursuit of stability, marriage, and children—and unlike in previous centuries, they need not marry at all to secure them. Women can now live fruitful, secure, productive, and happy lives without a long-term commitment to a man. As an unintended consequence, the value (to women) of the resources that men exchange for sex has diminished—and become largely emotional or relational—even as the price (to men) of sex that women can legitimately "charge" has likewise diminished in men's eyes.

In response to this modern turn, the frequency with which male interviewees report that women have initiated sexual relationships with them—just for the fun of it—is increasing (though it's not the typical experience). Patrick noted how his girlfriend was the most consistent initiator of sex, in contrast to the stereotypical couple:

The first time she did. Um, actually every time. . . . I think . . . [*The first time, every time, or . . . ?*] Well, the very first time with uh, with um, each person. She has, because I guess I didn't want to have her do something she wasn't comfortable with. But, um, generally my experience has been that I don't have to persuade them. Like I mean, that came off weird [laughs]. Um, I think girls like sex. Like, I was kind of under the impression maybe that girls didn't like sex as much as guys did or something, and so when like you got them to have sex with you, it was like you were getting them to do something they didn't want, and I didn't like the idea of that.

Although Patrick's experience is not standard, it is more common today than it would have been 25 or 50 years ago. Some will look upon this as good news, signaling the emancipation of women from a sexual conservatism that sought to control their pleasure. Others bemoan the low exchange rate for sex today, suggesting it seriously hampers the ability of young adults to make and keep "expensive" relationship promises like marriage. Like them or not, more egalitarian sexual standards go hand-in-hand with more sexual permissiveness.[23] It cannot be any other way.

The losers in this discounted sexual marketplace are clearly women who would prefer a high price for sex: those who want to remain virgins until marriage (and yet who wish to get married). They are increasingly put in a bind in their pursuit of a lifelong relationship, constrained by how the sexual decisions of their peers alter market expectations about the price of sex. Many feel pressure to "take what they can get" and commence a sexual relationship with a marriage-minded man before marriage, or risk the real possibility that in holding out for a chaste man to marry they will wait a lot longer than they would like to, watching the pool of available, ideal men shrink before their eyes.

CASUAL SEX AND FRIENDS WITH BENEFITS

So the value men have to offer in the sexual marketplace (stability, family, wealth) has clearly diminished. And so has the cost of sex. What motivation exists for men to be anything, then, besides the stereotypic "take what you can get" kind of man? Not a lot, unless a man already wishes to be something different than that. No wonder 75 percent of them would have immediate sex with a complete stranger if offered: it's not just discounted, it's free. In contemporary exchange terms, this action strikes most young men as an entirely rational approach to sexual relationships. And it brings us to the subject of nonromantic sexual relationships, which include both casual sex and "friends with benefits." Most young adults don't actually use the term "friends with benefits," at least not when they describe such relationships for themselves. Some associate these with casual sex, but this is not quite accurate. Casual sex implies no relationship at all, as in a one-night stand or a chance meeting of strangers. This is not, however, an accurate description of the majority of nonromantic sexual relationships, which tend to last longer than a night and are commonly generated by people who already know each other. Abby, who has had "eight or nine" sexual partners, distinguishes between the two: "I mean I never had, like, a non-emotional sexual relationship, if that's what it is, but I've had sex with a friend before. [*You've maintained your friendship?*] Yeah, actually perfectly, it was like never any problem at all." Others, like Megan, find the friendship idea much more difficult to sustain: "There's a lot of people that have just purely sexual relationships, but it's because they know that it won't affect their friendship or relationship. [*Does it?*] Depends on the person. It would affect my friendships."

Megan echoes one conclusion from a *New York Times* article entitled "Friends with Benefits, and Stress Too." The *Times* report describes a Michigan State study that sheds new light on these relationships.[24] Paradoxically, the authors find that friends-with-benefits relationships actually impede openness rather than foster it. Talking about the relationship could spell its doom. In fact, to admit real feelings for the person with whom they share their body is something many study participants feared. Only 1 out of 10 actually blossom into a romantic relationship, due in part to another ironic finding—that the relationships themselves exhibit little passion. Since making passionate love is often about an emotional as well as a physical connection, perhaps it's not surprising that such associations spark but fail to generate a real fire.

Regardless of whether the sexual association lasts, it's far more common for women than men to pursue such a relationship with someone who's a known commodity than with a random person. In other words, truly casual sex is far less attractive to women than it is to men. (Remember, *no* woman agreed to it in the study discussed earlier.) Retaining a measure of control over the "who" is important to many women who pursue this route—thus the establishment of *friends* with benefits.[25]

If men generally prefer a lower price for sex, then many of them should be inclined to engage in sex that is more associational than relational (and romantic). So exactly how much associational sex is going on? Table 3.2 displays the percent of all past and present sexual relationships that are nonromantic, that is, between partners who do

TABLE 3.2 Percent of Nonmarital Sexual Relationships That Are
Nonromantic (Past and Current), 18- to 23-Year-Olds

	Men	Women
Overall	29.1	18.0
Race/Ethnicity		
White	28.8	17.9
Black	33.4	19.0
Hispanic	29.4	17.3
Asian	18.7	17.6

Source: Add Health

not claim to be romantically involved with each other. They aren't dating; they're just having sex. These relationships are comprised of a mix of casual sexual encounters and friends-with-benefits. In keeping with the theory of sexual economics, women claim considerably fewer nonromantic sexual relationships than men (18 percent vs. 29 percent). This may be in part because they are genuinely pursuing fewer such relationships—as the theory would expect—or it may be because they are more apt than men to identify a given sexual relationship as romantic. Unfortunately, we cannot distinguish between these two here.

These are not small numbers: on average, nearly one in four sexual relationships among 18- to 23-year-old emerging adults is about sexual desire only, not romance. Splitting the results by race/ethnicity reveals little new information about women, but it does distinguish among men: African American men report the highest percent of nonromantic sexual relationships (33 percent), just above Hispanics and whites and well removed from Asian American men, at 19 percent. Sexual economics theory makes obvious sense of this: when there's a larger pool of women than men in a community, Baumeister and Vohs note a lower average price of sex there. When one in nine African American men between the ages of 20 and 34 is incarcerated, the resulting imbalance cannot help but to affect the sexual marketplace and its dynamics.[26] Available men are rarer and hence have more bargaining power in their relationships, enhancing their access to sexual variety (which is desired by a cross-section of men, not just African Americans). Demetrius, a 21-year-old from North Carolina, is one of those, and he knows it:

My relationships right now begin and end with sex. If I'm going to take you out, then more than likely we've already had sex. And it does create a problem because a lot of females are like, "That's what you get after you've taken me out." So that's why . . . [*They expect that.*] Yeah, they expect the dates and all that before you have sex. I'm saying, just save myself four months just in case things don't work out, you know? I'll know now. [*How long does a relationship last . . . is it a one-time encounter? Or does it last three months?*] Well, it depends. . . . Mine usually [last] no longer than two months. The shortest relationship could be, you know, one time. [*Do you get the impression that the women are expecting more out of things than you are?*] Yes. [*So how does that work out?*] For me, right, it's always a conflict. Right now in my life, women, they deal with me because they want to. But they don't really, I'm at the point where I'm like, you know, this is how I feel right now. I'm not trying to be changed. [*So you're up front with them?*] I am. I am. [*And they just have to deal with that?*] And it can get real ugly if you're not up front. It can get real ugly.

Only occasionally did interviewees actually use the label "friend-with-benefits" in our conversations. It's more a term that social observers have elected to use. It simply became obvious that there was no shortage of emerging adults who would have sex—often repeatedly but only for a season—with someone who was not formally understood as their boyfriend or girlfriend. And yet it is presumed to be an exclusive thing. For some who fit its description, taking on the identity of boyfriend or girlfriend seemed too cumbersome, too juvenile (for whatever reason), or implied more commitment than they wanted. Jenna, a 19-year-old from Texas, described how one such relationship worked for a time:

We just kind of hung out together. We went to parties together a lot. I don't know, I guess it [sex] just kind of happened. We were both okay with it. It was very comfortable for both of us. . . . But neither of us were ready to be in a relationship, but we liked the fact that we could [have sex], we had someone to be intimate with and close with, an opposite-sex someone. [*Intimate. Close. I mean, isn't that the definition of being in a relationship? What constitutes being in or out?*] That's a title thing. And we chose not to use any type of title. [*So what were you?*] Friends. [*But exclusive friends?*] No. Like, I mean, sexually exclusive, yes. But otherwise speaking, I think I went on dates and went out with other people. And I'm sure he did the same thing. [*So tell me how this works. So then would you have sex basically every time you got together?*]

Not every time, but almost. . . . [*So did it ever feel weird going out on a date, knowing you'd probably sleep with someone else tomorrow night?*] Ummm . . . uh, yeah. I kind of avoided that topic of conversation with whoever I went out with.

Titles matter a lot to many emerging adults. They're only words, in one sense. But they can be loaded with meaning. They can imply things. They can obligate people. To a generation that has slowed down the process of becoming full-fledged adults, it makes sense that some of them are altering older, more formal titles and what they imply. So while there has always been the possibility of casual sex and short-term sexual relationships that didn't imply romance or commitment, imagining them in their own lives is becoming easier and more attractive.

Despite images of random sex, the most common source for friends-with-benefits relationships is hardly random. They're exes. Sexually active emerging adults seem more apt to settle into friends-with-benefits arrangements with ex-girlfriends and ex-boyfriends than young adults a generation or two ago. While the emotional labor and investment of time in a romantic relationship no longer strikes some of them as worth it, the sexual benefits are retained. Gabriela, who divided her sexual past into five nonromantic sexual relationships and four romantic ones, describes why she had previously resorted to sleeping with an ex-boyfriend:

> I hadn't slept with anybody in a while. Um, you get horny. That's just the way it works. It's easier to sleep with, with someone you've already slept with than to find someone completely new. [*Why?*] Because you can't, I personally can't just like sleep with some random stranger that I met at a bar, that's not the way that, at least now, it's not the way that I work. [*What do you mean at least now?*] Well because I did it before. [*And how does it make you feel?*] Um, you know it's nice to . . . know you have somebody you can sleep with. [*Why is that nice?*] Oh, because it's a lot of work to find somebody else [laughs]. It's kind of like your fall-back. Like I can start dating somebody else, but I, I have a backup plan.

Others elect this pathway, but endure more challenging emotions about it. Cheryl, a 19-year-old from Texas, described a similar postrelationship activity pattern to Gabriela, but with a different ending. Unlike Gabriela, however, Cheryl wanted the relationship to work out and initiated the sex in hope of accomplishing that, despite the fact that her boyfriend made it clear that they weren't getting back together. It went on for five months:

We weren't back together, but it's like we kept the physical part of our relationship. It ended up hurting me in the end because I never like, was never to fully get over him until I moved back home for the summer and got away from him. And that's when I was finally able to get over him. . . . He went out on a couple of dates with this girl and it just hurt me. It hurt me really bad [cries]. . . . I learned my lesson.

It took moving back home for the summer—away from her boyfriend—to sever the sex for good.

For the record, however, the vast majority of emerging-adult exes remain just that: ex, without the benefits.

THE DURATION AND CONCLUSION OF SEXUAL RELATIONSHIPS

Lest we conclude that casual sex and friends with benefits are accounting for a sizable share of all sexual activity among young adults, let us state that this is not true. Most sex—indeed, the vast majority—is still experienced in romantic relationships. However, many of these relationships are fragile and end within six months. Feminist journalist Paula Kamen got it right: what young people now consider to be a monogamous relationship has "become less serious and of shorter duration."[27]

References to economics shape the course and conclusions of many relationships. For example, most emerging adults can identify with what's known as the "upper hand" in relationships: "Whoever cares less has the upper hand," claims Caitlin:

And you want the upper hand. Period. [*Why?*] Because you want to feel like you have control of that relationship. I don't wanna be in a relationship where I'm scared, like, is he going to call me today? Does he like me?. . . . It trades off all the time, because once you start really caring for them, then they might flip it and start caring less for you. It's so messy. [*What's wrong with not having the upper hand?*] They treat you, like . . . I've not had the upper hand at some points, and those moments in my relationships are usually the parts where like, they're treating me bad. What I should do when they're treating me bad is basically ignore them, right? And try to gain back dignity for myself. . . . [*To me as an outside observer, this doesn't sound like a happy state.*] It's not. It's horrible. [*Why try to always have the upper hand? Aren't people trying to fashion a relationship that's mutually enjoyable?*] That's the idea. If I talked about my [future] spouse, it's gonna be completely and utterly like, equal. But ever since I started dating . . . one person has always liked the other person more.

To Caitlin, an 18-year-old from Texas who's had oral sex but not vaginal sex, the addition of intercourse would only add to the drama in an imbalanced relationship. To her it's giving away too much power over the relationship, and would put her at a distinct disadvantage. She anticipates sex would make her want to continue the relationship more, but that would tip too much control in his direction, and that would be a problem: "I'd like to be in control . . . I'd rather be in control than not in control. And I'd rather feel like they're more into me than I am into them. . . . Because sometimes guys like, when they know that they have you, they're done [with the relationship]." The thrill of the chase would be over. Clearly such persistent power imbalances can't work long-term. If he cheats, of course, and tries to woo her back, then the power swings radically in her direction. (Of course, she must manage the script—as well as the emotions—that call for her to end the relationship, because he cheated.) Mutual self-giving must eventually emerge, it would seem, and ideas about upper and lower hands must disappear, or else the relationship is doomed.

Other relationships come to what participants might identify as "natural relationship conclusions." That is, some event—like going to college or moving to a different city to begin a job—precipitates the breakup, which is perceived by one or both partners as inevitable. Justin, 23, moved to Nevada after college in order to coach, teach, and do some skiing. It wasn't intended to be a permanent move, just a part of living out the emerging-adult dream of seeing different parts of the world and doing things he's always wanted to do. This is the time for that, before settling down. Justin has had lots of sex partners, mostly well in the past, and described two "natural" breakups spurred by life events:

> It's not like my relationship with that girl [back East] was worth so much. [*But you were together?*] Yeah, yeah, for a bit. She was my girlfriend in the spring. [*And you guys broke up when you?*] Well, yeah, and I wasn't gonna pay for a ticket to bring her to my cousin's wedding in Spain or anything. And I wasn't gonna be coming back [afterward], so it's like, yeah. [*So that one, and there was the other?*] Yeah, well it was a girl I knew throughout college. . . . We'd hooked up before and then senior year we hooked up more frequently. And then towards the end of the year we got to be like kind of boyfriend-girlfriend for a little bit. But school year ended and that was that.

While interviewees tend to take a passive tone in describing such relationship conclusions, all breakups require action, even if that action is nothing more than a wordless departure. (They're typically more than that.) What is striking, however, is the assumptions shared by emerging-adult men and women about the inevitability of the end. People graduate from high school and move away. Summer flings end just as certainly as August turns into September. Many complete college and pursue jobs in other states. They anticipate such events, and many—though hardly all—react with Justin's sense of inevitability: "and that was that." Indeed, a common theme among interviews with college freshmen is the struggle over boyfriends or girlfriends "at home," often still in high school. They almost never work out. It's as if there's an unwritten script—actually, there is—that dictates that a high school student and a college student should no longer see each other, especially if the college is far from home. It's difficult to thwart this; the logic strikes many as self-evident.

Documenting exactly how long emerging adults' sexual relationships tend to last is challenging, since there is wide variation, and plenty of the longest relationships are still ongoing. But we know several things. Most importantly, it depends on their nature—whether they're romantic or not. Table 3.3 highlights how true this is, and in so doing clarifies the brevity of friends-with-benefits: they just don't last long. Since over one-third of nonromantic sexual relationships last only one day—or more likely, one night—and another 31 percent no more than a month, it's very unlikely that these relationships can be qualified as friends-with-benefits. They're casual sex. The remaining one-third of all nonromantic relationships could be classified as friends-with-benefits: they last at least a month, but seldom much longer. Only four percent of all nonromantic relationships last more than a year. When we tack on romantic relationships, for a sum total of all 17,533 past sexual relationships of emerging adults for which we have data in Add Health, *longstanding friends-with-benefits arrangements amount to just over one percent of all sexual relationships* young adults told us about. When viewed in that light, perhaps it's time to say that the media has overplayed its hand—easy, accessible, and stable sex outside of romantic relationships is very uncommon and far more the domain of fantasy than reality.

Romantic relationships last longer and are a far more stable source of sex. Among both men and women, just about 60 percent of *current* romantic relationships are older than one year in duration (data not shown). These of course tend to last longer in part because

TABLE 3.3 Duration of *Past* Nonmarital Sexual Relationships, Romantic and Nonromantic, in Percent, 18- to 23-Year-Olds

	Nonromantic	Romantic
One day only	35.8	2.5
More than 1 day up to 1 month	31.2	11.7
More than 1 month up to 3 months	16.7	22.5
4 to 6 months	7.0	18.0
7 months to 1 year	5.1	21.7
More than 1 year	4.3	23.7

Source: Add Health

the participants themselves are older, and some of them have acquired a more mature perspective on what makes relationships last. And yet even among this age group, lengthy romantic relationships are uncommon: just over half of all the previous romantic, sexual relationships they reported lasted no more than six months, while only 24 percent of all past romantic, sexual relationships lasted more than a year. Some were extremely short—about 14 percent of all relationships lasted no more than a month, suggesting that one or both partners may have overestimated just how much romance there actually was. So while young Americans don't do commitmentless sex for very long, neither do they keep romantic-relationship commitments for very long, either. Perhaps that's not their intention.

The Centrality of Sex and the Failure of Unstable Relationships

Why do so many emerging-adult sexual relationships fail? Reasons of course are manifold, and for many it's simply part of the script of sex, college (for some), and the natural course of modern relationships. Relationships fail, then, because at some point they're supposed to. Sex columnist Dan Savage reminds his readers that "every relationship fails until one doesn't." While certainly true at face value, this is an observation that can become an imperative: people commence relationships, enjoy them for a time, then await the sure signs of their fatal condition. Alex, a smart, motivated, 19-year-old college student from Missouri, does exactly that. He's been in a variety of relationships—all of them sexual—and has come to the conclusion that he can't be happy in them for very long. It's as if it were a learned behavior. How does he account for it?

> I get attached, but then I feel like, suffocated. It's like, I want more freedom, but then when I get it, I'm pretty upset. It's just like a little six-month mark, and I began to like, not be happy. [*Six months into your relationship?*] Usually. [*What do you think the not happy part is about?*] I don't know. I just don't think I am good at relationships. . . . When you commit that much time to someone, basically you start to doubt yourself. So, it's only a matter of time. [*Until?*] Until you're not happy anymore, because you can't be dependent on somebody else for your happiness.

Relationship norms have a great deal of dos and don'ts to them, as Alex notes. While he doesn't keep close track of time in his relationships, Alex maintains that "there just comes a certain time where it's just, like, I can always sense when a relationship's about to end. I don't know why. I always get a feeling in my gut." Like plenty of emerging-adult men, Alex often lacks the courage to put an end to relationships. Instead, he neglects them until his girlfriends declare them over.

The reasons that Americans of all ages could give for their failed relationships are numerous, but one problem may uniquely plague emerging-adult relationships. It's the role of sex (rather than its presence): many couples lack a clear, shared, and suitable role for the sex they experience within a romantic relationship, especially when sex is introduced relatively early. Many interviewees testify that sex is often difficult to talk about, in part because the partners are still getting to know each other and deep conversation is considered too intimate. Yet sex becomes a clear goal and new priority—the elephant in the corner that demands attention when they're together. It acquires an increasingly central role in the relationship while at the same time other aspects of the relationship remain immature. Compare this to the greater sense of security that a shared residence and bed entail. Having sex with one's college boyfriend in his fraternity house, only to wander home later, can be an emotionally unsatisfying sensation for many women, for good reason. Some eventually solve this dilemma by moving in together. And for many that seems a welcome—if only slightly more secure—step.

Another example occurs in dating. When the habit of going out for dinner, a film, and dessert trails rather than precedes sex, even simple conversations take on a strange aura. After all, such a couple knows more about what each other looks like naked than what each other thinks about school, work, politics, religion, family, or future plans—life in general. Writing in *New York* magazine, Third-wave feminist writer Naomi Wolf wonders if we haven't gotten the order of sex and familiarity mixed up:

> "Why have sex right away?" a boy with tousled hair and Bambi eyes was explaining. "Things are always a little tense and uncomfortable when you just start seeing someone," he said. "I prefer to have sex right away just to get it over with. You know it's going to happen anyway, and it gets rid of the tension." "Isn't the tension kind of fun?" I asked. "Doesn't that also get rid of the mystery?" "Mystery?" He looked at me blankly. And then, without hesitating, he replied: "I don't know what you're talking about. Sex has no mystery."[28]

Communicating with words is thus perceived as a more intimate activity than "body language." Psychologist Jeffrey Arnett notes the irony in which "two people could be unembarrassed enough to have sex with each other yet too embarrassed to talk about contraception."[29] To imagine staying up late into the night feasting on a wide-ranging conversation now strikes many as something one does *after* commencing a sexual relationship, not before. Thus one hallmark of the classic hookup scenario is silence.[30] Talking is perceived as potentially ruinous to the moment. When did talking get to be so sacred? When did honest, verbal communication outpace the meeting of penis and vagina in its degree of intimacy?

In a fascinating *Policy Review* article, Mary Eberstadt notes a shift in language among educated adults of different generations, one that has moved morality away from the domain of sex and into the domain of food.[31] Sound strange? It may be true. Eberstadt asserts that the intense moralization about sex—but utter disregard for food sources and diet—that was a trademark of the 1950s has given way to a reversal of sorts. Today many educated emerging adults obsess about food—its sources, preparation, nutritional value, and ingredients—but care much less about questions of personal sexual morality than their forebears. The older generation consumed "junk" food, which today's cosmopolitans consider nearly immoral. On the other hand, the new cosmopolitans have "junk" sex, placing far less moral weight upon sexual decisions than their grandparents did. Regardless of just how accurately Eberstadt portrays sex among emerging adults—and, to be clear, she didn't intend to—she captures the reticence to associate sex with love and commitment among many emerging adults.

The rapid development of the sexual can obscure other aspects of the relationship that are equally critical, if not more, to its long-term success. One interviewee in another study lamented thus: "We were so distracted [by physical intimacy] towards the end, just to cover our relationship. We drifted apart, and some of the reason we were dragging it out was because of the physical touch. I think that I would have been thinking a lot more clearly without that."[32]

What can we conclude from these observations? Apart from relationship security, familiarity, and a shared domicile, sex has a difficult time playing a supportive role in fostering intimacy and building love. Instead, it wants to be the lead character. But when left to sustain a relationship, sex typically falters. Katie, a 19-year-old from Tennessee, sensed this in her relationship with Daniel, a man with whom she was in a four-year, long-distance relationship (he lived in Arkansas). Only in the past year did the two begin having sex, and—lacking as they were in physical proximity—Katie quickly sensed something suboptimal about it for two reasons, her own moral qualms about premarital sex notwithstanding. First, sex within their sporadic interactions began to claim a place and priority that outstripped its natural boundaries. In most marriages and cohabitations, even in the honeymoon phase, sex plays a supporting role to the mundane activities of normal life. In a relationship where two people are *not* sharing lots of normal life activities—a scenario common among young adults—sex can quickly take center stage.

Katie summarized this bluntly: "I felt like I was dating his dick." Their bonding typically ended with Daniel's inevitable departure. Katie detected that something was clearly amiss and after several months told Daniel she couldn't do it anymore. Most such romantic relationships do not give up sex without breaking apart, and theirs was no different; the relationship ended. Daniel rapidly became sexually active with another woman, while Katie struggled to make sense of it all, wondered about her future, and wrestled with guilt, resolving not to misplace the role of sex again. Keeping that resolution, however, is difficult, since the atmosphere in which contemporary relationships form among emerging adults is heavy with early sexual expectation. Eight months later, Katie and Daniel were back together.

AGE DIFFERENCES BETWEEN PARTNERS

Another hallmark of sexual economics theory is its concern about age—how women tend to be younger than the men with whom they form sexual relationships. While seldom a conscious decision, this longstanding phenomenon—reflected in Table 3.4—coheres to the theoretical claim that women's age is an important relationship asset. Even with the substantial benefits of wisdom and maturity that come with age, youth has long remained a valued relationship commodity, given its correlation with beauty and fertility in women. Note how few young women—less than 4 percent—report being in a relationship with a man that is at least two years younger than they are. Keep in mind that this 4 percent includes such combinations as a 23-year-old woman seeing a 21-year-old man, a pairing that—at face value—doesn't seem exceptionally odd. Except that it is.

Many young women fix an age range of acceptability that prohibits them from being much older than their partner. On the other hand, we interviewed several 18-year-old women who had been in relationships with men in their late 20s and even 30s. Just under 40 percent of young women are or have been in a relationship with a man three years or more their senior. But it just doesn't work the other way around, partly because the physical attractiveness of younger women typically is sufficient to focus young men's attention on peers in their own age cohort, and partly because most women in their late 20s and 30s are no longer interested in the emotional immaturity and lack of resources that characterize younger men, to say nothing of the strong social norms against a wide age disparity.[33]

In men, age is equated with resources like attractiveness, money, experience, and stability, all of which are desirable in a relationship transaction.[34] Age, of course, is only a modest predictor of wealth,

TABLE 3.4 Age Differential from Partner, in Percent, among Nonmarital Sexual Relationships (Past and Current), 18- to 23-Year-Olds

	Men	Women
Respondent is:		
3 years younger or more	10.1	36.6
Two years younger	5.5	15.4
One year younger	10.6	17.1
Same age	28.1	19.1
One year older	22.7	8.1
Two years older	14.4	2.5
Three years older or more	8.7	1.2

Source: Add Health

but it's associated with very different relationship resources among men and women. For women, age is a debit in sexual economics theory, gradually drawing down physical attractiveness and perceived fertility. For men, age is a credit, heightening their access to resources and making them more attractive to women. It's also a more reliable predictor of maturity. Young women are generally more interested in settling into a stable and secure relationship than men of the same age are, and women often presume that older men have already acquired some relationship skills. Lauren, an 18-year-old Texan, was seeing—and sleeping with—a 19-year-old fraternity member. (The relationship lasted around six months.) And yet she remained attracted to men considerably older than that. Why? It was difficult to explain:

> Because they are older. I even think some middle-aged men are pretty cute. [*Did you ever date them in the past?*] No. I dated guys like who are three years older than me. [*You said you are attracted to them because they are older*]. No, because . . . they are just more mature looking and more mature in general.

And yet the age gap in American *marriages* continues to narrow, not widen: marrying men and women were separated by an average of over four years in 1890, about 2.5 years in 1960, and now that number stands below two years. It makes sense: in a postindustrial economy like ours that exhibits modest fertility rates, there are fewer compelling reasons for men to marry younger women. In the past, many did so in order to maximize their fertile years. But today the reverse is true: increasing numbers of men care about their wife's earning potential, which too rises with age.

NEGOTIATING SEX WITHIN RELATIONSHIPS

Young adults occupy a variety of different roles in their lives, all of which entail expectations: sister, brother, child, student, employee, friend, cousin, grandchild, roommate, boyfriend, girlfriend. People are always evaluating their own actions from within the particular moral orders of these roles.[35] What does it mean to be a good son? What would a good roommate do in this situation? How can I be a good friend? But since "being good" in our many different roles invariably leads to role conflict, we find ourselves routinely violating all sorts of moral convictions and normative codes. Indeed, every attempt at rationalizing one's behavior points out the reality of competing moral claims. (Otherwise, we wouldn't need to justify our actions.)

What does this have to do with young adults' sexual relationships? Not only is the price of first-time sex subject to negotiation within an economic and social system in which couples participate, but subsequent sex is as well. All sexual relationships are thickly webbed with moral assumptions, beliefs, commitments, and perceived obligations. Emerging adults spend plenty of mental energy figuring out what a "good" boyfriend or girlfriend ought to do and how a relationship ought to look and feel and transpire. As a learning tool, we ask our students about this in class. Their responses vary little from semester to semester: in keeping with sexual economics, women rattle off a list of valued, if idealistic, resources that are expected from boyfriends (things like honesty, communication, loyalty, and good treatment). The men hem and haw and snicker, not really wishing to hear themselves vocalize what they know to be true: minimally, they want sex.

Given the universal truth that all social relationships entail conflict, sexual relationships of any duration almost never come easily. They require considerable negotiation, given that the partners are—as the theory notes—seeking some different things alongside some common goals. While not true of all sexual relationships in emerging adulthood, there is often a "honeymoon" factor which elevates the frequency of sex at the beginning of a relationship, only to see the pace of sex diminish—as is normal—over time. Sean, the 22-year-old from Alabama, exemplifies this. When asked about how often he has sex with his girlfriend, he reports the common curve:

> When we first started dating, it was several times a day and then, uh. [*How long have you been dating?*] A year and, like, two months. It's been awhile. So like now it's uh, we do, we do it, I don't know, maybe three or four times a week. It's just all I have, it's so busy now. . . . It just really depends on the schedule. Like on the weekends a lot more, if we're not busy or working. Like she'll stay at my house or I'll stay at hers a couple nights of the week. And we'll do it.

Note Sean's very modern remark about the unusual length of their relationship: "It's been awhile."

A fascinating study of German college students' sexual relationships concluded that sexual activity declines in frequency as the duration of the relationship increases. Sexual desire declines, too—and desire for tenderness increases—but only in women. Among men and women who've been in a relationship less than one year, 67 percent said they'd had sex at least seven times in the past four weeks. That percentage drops into the 40s and then into the 30s as relationship duration increases from one to three years and then to more than three years, respectively. While the same pattern occurs with sexual satisfaction as with sexual frequency, it drops off more rapidly—from the low-to-mid 40s (at less than one year) to 27 percent (at 1–3 years) for both men and women. When asked who in the relationship wants to have sex more often, 59 percent of men in new relationships (less than six months old) said "both of us." Such a perception of mutual sexual desire declines in linear fashion until it bottoms out at 23 percent (of men who say "both of us" want to have sex often) within relationships that had already lasted at least six years. While women report a comparable pattern, their own claim that they wanted sex more in the relationship rises in prevalence from 6 percent at the start to 11 percent after seven months and then peaks at 13 percent among women who've been in the relationship between 1.5 and 3 years.[36]

This common sexual pattern can present a problem for emerging adults, since their romantic relationships tend to become sexual fairly early (as Table 3.1 shows). The decline of sexual frequency is felt premaritally, producing the standard complaint of "we never have sex anymore" much earlier than for partners who began having sex closer to—or after—marrying. Again, we recognize that plenty of emerging adults are not seeking marriage when they fashion sexual relationships. Our point is more modest: the early-to-sex pattern erodes the stability of sexual relationships and is likely a reason why very many young adults begin them with little thought to their marital possibilities and why so many relationships fail before reaching a greater level of commitment. There's little mystery—as Naomi Wolf points out—and the relationships "age" rapidly.

None of this is terribly surprising. It's a classic tale that characterizes billions of sexual relationships in human history. Sex is far from a simple pleasure. The human sexual brain is complicated, and women experience sex differently than men. People crave sex, but we also desire romance, and most long for—but may not understand how to accomplish—enduring attachment to another person.[37] And these three systems—sex, romance, and attachment—can act independently. No wonder many interviewees confess "it's complicated" when we probe the nature of their relationships. Megan, the 22-year-old student from Texas, broke up with her first real boyfriend (and second sexual partner) because of this mixing of systems. While she was very attracted to him and enjoyed the sex, her boyfriend "said he was afraid he might get too drunk and end up [sleeping with someone else], because, like, he would get drunk a lot, and make out with random chicks. . . . I mean, that's not cool." He felt romantically inclined toward Megan, yet wanted to have sex with other women in addition to her. She in return displayed the common social, cultural, and interpersonal pressure to channel these three systems toward the same object of affection (him). That is what serial monogamy is about, after all.

Frequency of Sex in Relationships

Overall, the mean frequency of sex (data not shown, from individual self-reports) reported by single, sexually active emerging adults is 59 times per year. By contrast, the mean frequency of sex among married emerging adults is about 100 times per year. Among the unmarried, however, the statistical mean is elevated considerably by the presence of "outliers" (no pun intended) at the top end of the frequency distribution, meaning that a small number of respondents told us they had a ton of sex last year. This suggests that the *median*—which is the middle-most count in the survey—will offer a better sense of the average frequency of sex among emerging adults. When we stick with the median, half of all sexually active young men told us they have sex at least 30 times a year or more, and half told us that number or less. Half of all women said they have sex at least 40 times a year or more, and half told us that or less.

In a remarkable pattern that spans use of both the median and the mean frequency of sex, African American men report the *lowest* average frequency of intercourse (a mean of 38 acts), yet report an elevated number of both lifetime and recent sexual partners (8.6 and 2.7, respectively), suggesting greater instability—as well as possible concurrency—in the nature and/or duration of their relationships, especially among men. By contrast, never-married white men report a mean of 6.8 lifetime and 2.1 recent partners but a mean of 66 sexual acts in the past year. In fact, no other race/gender combination comes close to paralleling the pattern among African American men. Besides the generally high average number of sexual partners for both African American and white men, it is remarkable that the former report an average of 1.8 more lifetime partners but just over half the frequency of intercourse (by the median or mean) that white men do, implying that their sexual activity is less consistent with any one sexual partner. Indeed, any historic stereotypes of hypersexuality among African Americans are patently false. However, the numbers suggest a pattern of sexual behavior among them that is less relational than it is associational, in step with Demetrius's account above. Again, this is exactly what sexual economics theory would expect: Since there are fewer African American men in college, the workplace, or the community, those present have greater power to pursue sex on their terms, with fewer relationship constraints. Interestingly, never-married African American women display a nearly identical mean number of lifetime and recent sexual partners (6.1, 1.8) as do never-married white women (6.0, 1.7) but much less frequent sexual activity (around 30 fewer acts per year).

All this talk of sexual frequency, however, pays little mind to the *context* in which sex occurs among emerging adults. Indeed, it's hard to understand the meaning of medians and means for sexual frequency among this group, since sex for most young adults relies on the presence of some semblance of relationship. Table 3.5 displays the frequency of sexual activity among emerging adults within their previous romantic relationships, sorted by the duration of those relationships. In what amounts to a modest affirmation of commitment in relationships—and in contrast to the German study noted earlier— sexual frequency is actually highest in romantic relationships that last longer. For example, those couples who had sex five times per week or more were the same couples who said they'd been in the relationship for over a year. Now obviously one year is not three or five years, but when we further sorted Add Health couples into relationship duration of 1–2 years, 2–3 years, and over three years (data not shown), it made no remarkable difference: 40–44 percent of each group reported regular sex. The evidence in America, then, suggests that sexual benefits accrue to those who endure within relationships past their first—and likely rockiest—months.

How long they *wait* before having sex obviously matters here as well, since frequent sex will not likely accompany a brand new relationship. Moreover, early sex would be a suboptimal move: young adults that hop in the sack on the first day—or the first week—of knowing someone have only a slim chance at long-term success, if in fact they care about that (and they may not). A year later, only about 14 percent of these fast movers were still in that relationship (results not shown). Waiting even a month or two for sex boosts longer-term relationship success to 26 percent, while 35 percent of people who wait more than six months to have sex are still in those relationships after a year. Let's maintain some perspective, though: 35 percent is not high. The bottom line is that few nonmarital sexual relationships survive. "Selectivity" may be at work as well: those couples who know they

TABLE 3.5 Past Frequency of Sex, by Length of Previous Sexual
Relationships (Romantic Only), in Percent, 18- to 23-Year-Olds

	Had sex only once	Once per month or less	> once per month–once per week	2–4 times per week	5 times per week or more
Dated 1 month or less	45.7	7.2	19.1	17.3	10.7
More than 1 month–3 months	18.8	8.7	20.3	33.4	18.9
More than 3 month –6 months	8.2	9.4	19.7	37.1	25.6
More than 6 month –1 year	5.7	5.8	15.8	38.9	33.9
More than 1 year	3.8	3.8	12.7	37.7	42.1

Source: Add Health

want their relationship to last may have purpose in a slower pace, compared with couples who are less interested in a common future together.

Table 3.5 paints an overall picture of active sexual relationships: among relationships that lasted at least four months, 63 percent of respondents report having sex at least twice a week. That rose to 72 percent and 80 percent among relationships that last seven months to a year and more than a year, respectively.

In reality, a great deal affects the frequency of sex within relationships, especially proximity, work and class schedules, living arrangements, and residence-hall rules. It can also vary widely over time. The Add Health study asked respondents for an average "about how often" portrait of their frequency. It's thus not surprising that young adults in longer-term relationships will recall more frequent sex. When asked about the frequency of sex with her boyfriend, Abby (22, from Colorado) responded "daily." How does it work? Who initiates? What do they do?

I guess intercourse, oral sex, umm [laughing a little], yeah. That's pretty much it. [*Who normally initiates that, and who kinda decides? . . .*] Me! [laughs] [*Oh really?*] Yes, my boyfriend's always really tired or something and I'm like, "Come on, I'm bored." [*Is bored kind of a reason sometimes?*] Yeah, definitely [laughs]. I mean, if I'm bored, or procrastinating, and I'm usually procrastinating, then it's like a good distraction. [*Like "I don't wanna do my homework so . . ."*] Yeah. [*Umm, and what about the different kinds of sex? Are you normally the one who will decide that too?*] No, we're very, I guess we're very equal when it comes to when we're in bed . . .

More commonly, interviewees note a more irregular and erratic pattern. Jalen notes the cyclical nature of his sexual relationship:

I want to say it [sex] is fairly often because it's like I said, we both know that we shouldn't be doing it so it's like [there's] time periods where we just stop. We just be chillin,' you know. [*Okay.*] But when it start, it start, like every other day and finally it be like, "No, we're not supposed to do this," so it's like back and forth.

Others' relationships fail altogether before any patterned rhythm of sexual activity could be discerned. That was the case with Shelby, an 18-year-old from New York whose relationship with her boyfriend ended after she made out with another man: "I wouldn't say it [sex] was regular, but I did it more than a few times." While Table 3.5 suggests a pattern of regular sex for a significant minority of relationships, keep in mind that there are relationships wherein sex is much less frequent and more erratic. Even Megan, who had been in a six-month relationship with a fraternity brother, noted the obstructions to regular sex. She's not having sex currently, since she's not in a relationship: "But when I was, I'd say weekly. [*Once a week?*] Usually. Just because during the week you're kind of busy; you have your stuff you need to do." For plenty of young adults like Megan, sex is a weekend activity. Besides coursework and studying, sexual frequency is often interrupted by distance or work or roommates or other living-arrangement challenges. And since young women are more likely to share a room with another woman than men are with other men, sex is more likely to occur at his place than hers.

Despite popular perceptions about friends-with-benefits, the sex within romantic relationships tends to be considerably more frequent than that experienced within nonromantic relationships, especially if the relationship lasts. In the Add Health study (data not shown), a high frequency of sex—five or more times per week—was slightly more characteristic of nonromantic rather than romantic sexual relationships *until after six months* (itself a very uncommon duration for the former). After that, the frequency of sex within romantic relationships clearly outpaces that of nonromantic ones. We can conclude two things from this: the most rational approach to securing regular access to sex is via an enduring, committed romantic relationship. However, since the frequency of sex within nonromantic relationships remains elevated up until around six months, some sense that a similarly rational strategy is to pursue repetitive friends-with-benefits relationships. These are nevertheless much more unstable and prone to failure. When given the choice, most women choose a romantic relationship. Channing would:

> There is this . . . guy that I kind of on-and-off dated, and we sometimes, you know, go out and then end up having sex, and it's comfortable just because we are friends and we've dated before. . . . But I, yea, like I said earlier, I would rather be in a relationship. So I wish I had a boyfriend.

Navigating Unwanted Sexual Requests

While many emerging adults today who are sexually experienced profess to have few or no regrets about their relationships, reporting satisfaction within them, plenty nevertheless negotiate unwanted sexual requests within those relationships. Indeed, not all types of sexual activity are appreciated or enjoyed by both partners. In the 1992 NHSLS survey, men found 13 of 14 sexual practices more appealing than women did, typically by large margins.[38] Thus plenty of men—and some women—ask for particular sexual acts from their partners, requests those partners would rather not fulfill. Some of them do it anyway, or do so on occasion. Others don't. What is it that they're asked to do? Why do some agree and others nix the request? Is negotiating this aspect of a sexual relationship simply about uneven power dynamics between men and women, or is there more to it than that?

The answer to the first question is easy. The #1 unwanted sexual request made by men to women is for anal sex, while the #1 unwanted sexual request made by women to men is for oral sex (cunnilingus). But the level of distaste for the former far outweighs that for the latter: the majority of men don't report problems in performing oral sex on women, but most women positively detest the idea of anal sex.

Other requests we heard, though far less frequent, included three-somes, unusual sexual positions or locations, and—in one case—a "facial," a practice in which a man ejaculates onto a women's face. (More on that later in this chapter.) While odd sexual requests are probably as old as humanity, vaginal intercourse remains the pre-ferred activity among most. Giving and receiving oral sex as part of foreplay is common among this group, as we noted in Chapter 1. Indeed, while not all men or women have always liked providing oral sex, at least it has possibilities for mutuality. Anal sex largely lacks mutual pleasure for most, at least from what interviewees told us when we asked them about it. And it implies physical risks—since the anal wall is thinner and less lubricated than the vagina—as well as an "ick" factor for many.

Unfortunately, men who are exposed to sexualized media—and that's arguably most men—receive quite mixed messages on the sub-ject of anal sex. One of the most common topics in American men's magazines like *Maxim* is unorthodox sexual positions and locations, even though another common topic—what women want—is largely inconsistent with these practices.[39] Indeed, men's magazines make un-substantiated and incorrect assertions that women want to engage in such sexual behavior as much as men do, suggesting women experience desire in a manner just like men.

Except for sexual positions, nearly all the unwanted requests we heard about came from men. Lots of young men ask their partners for anal sex. Few get it. Among the common responses we heard from women were: "The whole idea just kind of turns me off," or "it just seems painful." They're not alone in their disinterest. Only 15 percent of never-married women ages 18–23 in the Add Health study who had ever had anal sex with their current partner reported liking it "very much," down from 38 percent who said the same about performing oral sex and 83 percent who said that about vaginal sex. That's what the survey data say, but frankly among this age group, we didn't hear a single positive comment about it from a female interviewee. One stu-dent believed he had had anal sex, but claimed he was too drunk to remember it (his girlfriend informed him). Even our most sexually prolific female interviewee disliked the idea. The most optimistic mes-sage we heard was a young woman's comment about a friend, who had gotten used to anal sex:

> One of my friends—she did it maybe multiple times and she said that it
> stopped hurting. But, I don't, I don't think she said anything really

positive about it. Probably just like really neutral like, "Oh yeah, it stops hurting." But you don't have an orgasm from anal sex that I know of.

Women's distaste for anal sex far outpaces men's aggravation with performing oral sex on women—their primary (and yet still minority) grievance. Indeed, 58 percent of young men say they like performing oral sex on their partner "very much," well ahead of the 15 percent of women who say the same about anal sex. Nevertheless, oral sex is a sexual act that not all of them like to perform. Sean, the 22-year-old from Alabama, very much likes receiving but isn't crazy about giving:

> If she does [perform oral sex], I get real turned on, and we go straight into, uh, sex. [*And so do you ever give oral sex to her?*] I have, but I really don't like doing so, hardly ever. [*Do you know, does she, would she like you to do it?*] Oh yeah, she would love it. [*So why don't you wanna do it?*] It's just, uh, I don't know. I don't know if it's just a macho thing or I just, I don't like being down there. Not in my face.

While the majority of men who receive oral sex report liking it very much, only 38 percent of women who perform it say the same. Channing dislikes performing oral sex:

> Um, I have never been forced, but I've felt, like, I felt pressured to, I guess. . . . I haven't really succumbed to it or anything, but I've had, I don't know, like guys sometimes like, try to push your head down, and try to get you to give them a blow job. And I'm not okay with that. That actually pisses me off, and then I'm like, "No, absolutely not," when they do that.

Even Tara, the 20-year-old from Louisiana who reported the most sexual partners of any of our interviewees, dislikes oral sex and won't do anal sex, either. This was also the case with Gabriela, who, despite having a very active sex life with both boyfriends and friends-with-benefits, is not interested in either. But she caves on oral sex:

> Yeah, well, you know you still have to give an occasional blowjob. [*Why?*] You, you have to be reciprocal. . . . [*Okay. So you said you don't want to do that, so, you, would you ask, like, 'Do you want me to do this to you?'*] No, I would never ask. I avoid the situation at all costs [laughs]. But once it gets to be like, 'Come on, please?' Okay, fine. [*They would say that?*] Yeah.

Caitlin, who's avoided vaginal intercourse for religious and personal reasons, doesn't like oral sex but thinks it's just part of the deal in relationships:

I think it's vulgar, but I don't have a problem doing it. I mean, I don't enjoy it, of course. . . . [*Why do you do something you don't enjoy?*] Because sometimes you have to give to someone else in a relationship. [*In order to?*] Be . . . just be a nice person.

So in the realm of navigating a sexual relationship, plenty of women (and some men) are compliant, agreeing to provide sexual favors—both particular acts they dislike as well as more frequent intercourse than they'd prefer.[40] Unwanted sex is not the domain of uniquely poor relationships; it's a reality for many of them. In one study of college students in heterosexual relationships, fully half of all women and one-quarter of men consented to unwanted sexual activity in the previous two weeks alone, suggesting the issue is a very common and recurrent one.[41] There are a variety of potential reasons for sexual compliance:

- direct pressure from a partner (which hinges on power dynamics and the ability to say no),
- perceptions about the script of what a good or loving sexual partner ought to do,
- fear that the partner will pursue sex with someone else if rejected,
- perceptions that it's useless to refuse repeated sexual requests for long,
- the diminished "price" of sex, making saying no seem unreasonable and inexplicable,
- the accumulation of the partner's "credit" within the relationship,
- a genuine desire to satisfy a partner's wishes or to foster intimacy,
- interest in avoiding the conflict or tension that saying no might generate,
- the trading of a sexual favor in return for resources in other areas of the relationship,
- sacrificing for the perceived stability of the relationship, or
- inhibited expressions of reluctance, due to the nonverbal nature of sexual interactions.

Motives for complying with sexual requests also vary with the situation or over the course of the relationship. In other words, it's not always about avoiding conflict or sacrificing for stability or wishing to foster intimacy, but it can be for any of these reasons at any given time.[42] Moreover, compliance isn't inherently associated with negative relationship consequences, and it appears with regularity in nearly all relationships, whether premarital or marital.

And yet there remains a difference between doing something that you find suboptimal—such as having sex when you just don't feel like it—and doing something that one partner considers downright objectionable. Why do some woman agree to anal sex when they dislike the idea of it? People try lots of things once. And to be sure, many women do things for men because they wish to please them, while the reverse seems to be true less often. But doing something you're not crazy about is different from doing something you positively loathe, especially if you anticipate doing it again in the future. The shortest, most practical, and perhaps most accurate answer was offered by one of our interviewees: "They're drunk and their boyfriends really wanted to try it." Certainly there is something to the (mental) lubrication that alcohol affords.

In the Add Health data, 37 percent of the minority of women who've actually had anal sex with their current partner don't expect to do it ever again. That leaves the balance of women who've done it and expect to do it again in the future. Their expectations, however, often have little to do with their enjoyment of the activity. Among those who said they "somewhat" disliked anal sex with their current partner, 45 percent expect to do it again. Among those who disliked it "very much," 10 percent still intend to do it again. Remember, these are *not* people who've been asked to do something, did it, didn't like it, and didn't do it again. This is about women who are repeatedly asked to do something they know they dislike, and yet they still do it. Why? Indeed, in our detailed statistical analysis of such sexual compliance, no demographic, religious, or educational category distinguishes those who will repeatedly comply with an unwanted sexual request from those who won't. There must be a different reason. Some of those listed above for more standard sexual compliance will apply here as well, but power differentials, fear, and submission to perceived norms play a more significant role in this form of compliance. When a boyfriend asked Gabriela to have sex in the bathroom, she refused. But he never forgot it, and she was penalized for saying no: "He, like, brought it up twice after that . . . [*He brought it up?*] Yeah, he brought it up. He was like, 'Well, you know, you didn't do this, so . . . ' [*Was it some sort of sense that you owed him?*] Yeah." In her case, Gabriela felt no regrets about rebuffing his request, but had there been more uneven power dynamics between them, her feelings and actions might have been different.

For all the talk of liberation and freedom to choose in relationships, a minority of women still feel considerably less power and control over their own sexual action-taking. They do things they would rather not, less out of any sense of sacrificial love and quest for intimacy than out of concern for the fragile security of the relationship. Self-giving love tends to grow with relationship maturity, reflecting a sense of security, not generating it.

Finally, an underrated influence here is the cultural script that sexual experimentation or sexual "deviance" is cool, that it's attractive and valuable to be willing to try new things in wanting to please your partner, and that these traits in turn further cement a relationship.[43] Thus some young women agree to sexual requests even though they dislike both the idea and the experience of them, because the goal of being *perceived* as an attractive partner is worth the cost. Perceptions are everything to us humans, sociologists note: in our imagination, we perceive in others' minds some thought of our own appearance, aims, character, friends, talents, and so on. Dubbed "the looking glass self" by sociologist Charles Horton Cooley, young and old remain powerfully affected by it.[44] In other words, what we perceive that others think about us matters a great deal for how we think about ourselves. We spend time and effort honing an image of ourselves, even if it isn't genuine. While it may be cool to be perceived among peers as being open to sexual experimentation, actually feeling open is simply not the reality for most emerging adults. We interviewed dozens of attractive young men and women who revealed genuine sexual conservatism to us but nevertheless work hard at conveying sensuality and perceptions about their sexual skills to others around them. It makes economic sense, after all: advertising is a big deal.

The Boundary between Persuasion and Coercion

Where compliance meets coercion is unclear. Badgering and nagging for sex are common strategies of persuasion and generally aren't considered coercive. In one study of college students, 78 percent of women and 58 percent of men reported that their partners had tried some sort of tactic to push them for sex after they had initially refused.[45] Locating people who would both recognize and recount their own coerciveness is difficult, since it's a socially undesirable thing to admit (even if everyone could agree on what coercion is). Many, like Patrick, have sexual guidelines by which they attempt to abide, and they concern substance use: "Personally I, uh, have like a rule where, like, if the other person is like more intoxicated than I am, that, um, that's kind of off." Better to be legally safe than sorry.

While Bruce, a 19-year-old college freshman in Pennsylvania, declares himself innocent of date rape, he claims the line between consensual sex and a drunken inability to give consent is crossed around him regularly: "It happens all the time . . . they'll [the women] regret it, but like, it's not like a tragedy, you know." Alcohol is almost a prerequisite for girls to hook up, Bruce believes: "I mean, I feel like a lot of people are too afraid to [hook up], like maybe they really want to, but they're afraid and . . . being drunk, like, enhances them to be able to do so." Table 3.6 displays the percent of 18- to 23-year-olds that report having had sex with someone the first day they met them, sorted by categories of their average alcohol consumption patterns. There's definitely something to Bruce's claim.

While the vast majority of young adults never have sex the first time they meet someone, some do, and drinking no doubt helps. It's almost as if most students—especially but not only women—have a visceral aversion to casual sex and hooking up that is only overcome with the help of alcohol. One in three women who drink almost every day reports having had sex with someone the first time they met, a number even higher than their male counterparts (at 29 percent). Among women, the probability of doing so drops rapidly when they drink only socially and occasionally: those who drink a couple times a week reveal much lower rates of first-time sex—only 12 percent of them report doing so. Young men, many of whom are more adamantly looking for

TABLE 3.6 Ever Had Sex with Partner on First Day They Met, by Frequency of Drinking Alcohol in Past 12 Months, in Percent, 18- to 23-Year-Olds

	Men	Women
Never drinks	18.2	11.3
Drinks 1 or 2 times a year	15.3	10.8
1–3 days a month	17.2	13.3
1 or 2 days a week	21.3	12.4
3–5 days a week	24.4	22.4
Drinks every day or almost every day	29.1	33.8

Source: Add Health

sex, reveal a more modest—but still evident—association between drinking and casual sex. While some young Americans find themselves given to falling asleep when tipsy, others get aroused: "When I get drunk, I get horny," noted one young man, while a woman generalizes the same: "When you drink, you usually just get more sexual urges." Alcohol is not necessary, though: 18 percent of young men and 11 percent of young woman who say they never drink nevertheless reported at least one experience of rapid escalation to sex.

Although the Add Health study didn't explicitly ask about sexual coercion within young adults' relationships, data from other studies of college-age adults is illuminating. While men are widely perceived to be more frequent perpetrators of sexual coercion than women—and it's true—the numbers aren't as one-sided as we might expect. A study of college students found 29 percent of men and 14 percent of women admitted to practicing some degree of sexual coercion in their relationships. Nevertheless, women who don't want to take no for an answer tend to use less forceful and persistent tactics than do coercive men. Men are also more likely to attempt unwanted touching, make efforts to get their partner drunk and disrobed, detain them, hold them down, and repeatedly ask for sex.[46] Megan relayed a common strategy of men: they "try to be clever and find some way to get them [women] alone." It happened to her:

> I was at a party. And we had a mutual friend, and he got drunk way too early in the evening, so he went and passed out. And this guy who'd been flirting with me all night, he pulls me off and he's like, "Hey, let's go check on Phil, make sure he's okay." So we go to the room—of course he's passed out—and then he tried something, and it's just . . . [*What did he try?*] He just basically, just kind of threw me down on the bed and kept trying to, just, to. [*Forcefully?*] To a point, and I was just like . . . [*What'd you do?*] I left. I mean I didn't leave, like, I wasn't rude to him. But it wasn't like, he wasn't being forceful, I wouldn't say. But he was really trying to be persuasive. Very, very persuasive. It didn't work.

Notice Megan's efforts to distinguish between real, physical force— which would have been frightening and completely objectionable to her—and the semicoercive, physical banter that this young man attempted on her. His actions, defended by her interpretation of them, lie squarely on the boundary between the powers of persuasion and the force of coercion. He had hoped that his throwing her down on the bed would've worked, that it would've been just the right thing to do at the right time to make the script of a casual sexual encounter work out for him. After all, he must have been thinking, she did agree to go upstairs. That must've meant something, right? Wrong. Sex doesn't happen until she agrees to it. And sex without consent is still rape. Unfortunately, even "consent" can be seemingly coerced. Amelia is an 18-year-old from Wisconsin. Her first sexual experience—with oral sex—was "pretty much forced," in her words. At a party as a high-school sophomore, a guy asked her "to go upstairs."

> [We] started making out. And then I didn't really want to be there, and then I asked, "Well, let's go back down[stairs]." "'No, we're staying. Come on.'" I got up, and then he started getting aggressive. He said, "You're like such a prude. This is so annoying." Then we continued making out, but not really doing much. Then he started taking off his stuff and pushed my head down [toward his penis]. I was, like, really nervous, and I didn't know what to do, so I just did it.

Amelia reflects back now about the emotions of the moment. She was flattered that an older boy wanted to talk to her. She was terrified of the social stain on her reputation that he could deliver to her if she refused. She was young and in a jam. She's never forgotten it, even now with a much stronger sense of self and confidence.

If we could convey a series of key revelations from our in-person interviews with emerging-adult women, one of them would be just how many of them have experienced either actual or attempted sexual assaults, the majority of which were in high school or even earlier. Laura, the 19-year-old whom we met in chapter 1, was molested for two years in middle school by her 35-year-old band director. When she finally worked up the courage to tell her father what had been going on, this authoritative family man "bawled like a baby" over the protection he hadn't been able to provide her. Kate, a 21-year-old, had been carjacked by a man who was preparing to rape her. She escaped. Karen, a 20-year-old, didn't: she had been both molested by her older brother and raped by a stranger. Her subsequent sexual decision-making revealed the lasting influence of those unwanted encounters. There were other stories, too. Make no mistake: while the boundary between legal and illegal sexual activity may be codified, emerging adults often convey a reality that is lot more blurry.

PORN AND RELATIONSHIP NORMS

So far we've offered a strictly supply-side inquiry into why plenty of women (and some men) say yes to unwanted sexual requests. That is, we've wondered why women are giving in when it seems to be against their sexual interests. We've concluded that it's often perceived as in their relationship interest or personal-image interests to do so. But the demand side is also an important part of this story. After all, if no one were asking for anal sex, we wouldn't be wondering about why some women provide it. So, why *are* men asking for it? As we noted in chapter 2, its prevalence has risen recently; either fewer young men requested it in decades past, or else fewer were treated to it. Our bet is on both.

Given that there is no biological basis for preferring anal sex to vaginal sex—and since for the majority of couples, anal sex is either left untried or attempted only once—we're left to conclude that demand for it is largely psychological and the result of a porn-inspired script about the anticipated pleasures of anal sex (for instance, that it mimics vaginal sex with a virgin). The same can be said for other uncommon types of sexual activity that are treated on many popular porn Web sites as just one more option among a sexual cornucopia of possibilities. In fact, locating heterosexual porn depicting vaginal intercourse in the "missionary" position—likely the most common sexual position in modern human history—actually takes some effort. Finding photos and videos of far less common sexual practices—ones many adults have never experienced and would label as bizarre, deviant, and unwanted—is considerably easier. And yet prolonged exposure to such uncommon erotica is known to lead both teens and adults to do several things:[47]

- overestimate the popularity and pleasure of less common forms of sexual behavior,
- presume that sexual exclusivity is both unrealistic and uncommon in real life,
- believe that sexual inactivity is actually bad for one's health, and
- hold cynical attitudes about love, affection, and marriage/family

Porn also provides an alternative—if temporary—universe in which all things sexual seem possible. Alex, the 19-year-old from Missouri whom we met earlier in this chapter, reflected frankly on the mind games that porn fosters:

> I know that porn is totally ridiculous. Like, sometimes I like watching it before I am finished [masturbating] and then after I am finished. It's so weird. It's like you are in a completely different mindset. Like before [you masturbate] you can totally believe everything [you see] and afterwards it's just totally ridiculous.

So is porn an issue among emerging adults? Absolutely. Pornography use is highest among this demographic.[48] In one of the most rigorous and reliable studies of online porn use and norms, researchers interviewed 813 emerging adults—undergraduate and graduate students from six colleges and universities, ranging in age from 18 to 26.[49] Two out of three men agreed that porn use was generally acceptable, while the same was true of half of women. On usage, however, the genders differ significantly. The survey revealed that 86 percent of men "interact" with porn at least once a month, while 69 percent of women reported no porn use at all. Just under half of men watch porn weekly, while only 3 percent of women say the same.

For women, being in a dating relationship—most of which will involve sex—contributes to greater acceptance and use of porn. For men, no such dating association exists. The same is true of both recent and lifetime sexual partnerships: the more of them, the more likely it is that women will not only tolerate porn but use it as well. Again, no such associations exist for men, save for a weak association between porn use and lifetime number of partners.[50]

When we asked Abby, the 22-year-old from Colorado, if she'd ever been asked to do something sexual that she didn't want to do, she answered yes—as plenty of women did. What was she asked to do?

> Well, one boyfriend wanted to cum on my face, which I find extremely degrading. And, um, I refused. And he also wanted to have anal sex, which I considered, but then I was like, "Ooh, I don't like you that much" [laughs]. And we broke up not that long after that.

Although Abby self-identifies as "a huge feminist" and told us, "I freaking hate pornography with a passion," she said she thought that none of her previous boyfriends were into porn. Given his request and the figures noted above, we would beg to differ. Why else would Abby's boyfriend want to ejaculate onto her face? To be sure, there may be a persistent human curiosity about novel sexual experiences—or having sex with new people—but the reason most human beings come back to and settle upon regular vaginal intercourse is because it's widely considered to be the most consistently preferential and mutually pleasurable sexual act in the world.

So we're implicating the Internet as both a sex educator and sexual-activity stimulator, bar none. In contrast to tired Hollywood claims about film reflecting life rather than the other way around, the direction of influence here seems clear, especially among teenagers and young men. Many log on to "learn" sex, or so they think. While almost everyone will acknowledge that of course reality isn't like it is in the pictures and videos, many nevertheless wonder if it *could* be or *should* be. This is the essence of social learning: we're most apt to model others' behavior when the model is attractive and enticing to us, and when we perceive the behavior as possible.[51] So they ask. And some receive.

Gabriela concurs: "Guys, you know, they, [sighs], they expect certain things, and they can only expect them if they have seen them somewhere." Yet the odds of uncommon sexual practices becoming normal habits among average couples are low. The evidence suggests some positions or activities are tried once or twice and then generally discarded in favor of more mutually pleasurable sexual activities, ones that require much less work or convincing.

And yet many emerging-adult women tolerate porn—the central source of new sexual ideas—within their romantic relationships, despite the fact that it encourages infidelity and inspires false impressions about what's pleasurable and what's not. Some tolerate it because they tell us they notice no difference in the way their boyfriends treat them. Most emerging adults wouldn't know the difference, however, since as a cohort they've not known a world apart from easy porn access. Some tolerate porn because they perceive that the world is increasingly hip to such material, and they feel they ought to be too. To protest it would be to appear reactionary or anachronistic, both of which most people prefer to avoid.

Patrick (21, from Oklahoma) looks at porn about once a week, by his estimation. It was how he—and numerous other men with whom we spoke—first learned about sex: "I was kind of surprised what the actual anatomy was the first time I saw it." We asked if he thought porn was a good thing, a bad thing, or neutral:

> You know, I don't know. I don't have a problem with it or anything. Um, I think that, um, like every once in a while, it's like, you will come across some stuff, like, kind of uh, not always friendly to the women. And I think that's kind of weird, but I don't like that. But, um, as long as it's not like that, I don't think there is any problem at all.

While Patrick's ability to discern between types of porn is not uncommon, it nevertheless reveals the reality of what most porn is like: a portrayal of men as sexual aggressors and women as persistently sexually interested and ready for whatever positions men suggest. Perceived sexual hesitation on women's part is just a façade.[52]

When we asked Patrick if porn is a good way to learn about sex, he defended the demand side:

It shouldn't be the only way, I mean. . . . But I don't think it's like, I don't think it's a bad way to get like, additional information. . . . It's what the guys want, I mean, so it's hard to say that porn is creating that [demand]. I think it's just giving people what they already want.

Patrick also believes porn to be instrumental in helping men to *not* cheat on their girlfriends in reality, since they can now do it virtually instead:

Porn is kind of a way to like, have new girls but not actually cheat on your girlfriend, if that makes sense. So I guess in that sense it can actually be helpful for things like that, um, because I think there is a bigger urge for guys to want to, like, um, get new girls even if they already have one. And, um, I think that's a way to get around it.

Patrick's perspective is a very common one among men his age: porn use is not bad, but it's not a great thing or something to be proud of; it might change how people perceive and pursue sex, but it's not the author of some new, profound evil; it's unrealistic but gratifies male thirst for unrealism. It's functional and may help them avoid straying with other, *real* women. What life was like before online porn, they have no idea.

Their girlfriends are increasingly tolerating porn, as the "Generation XXX" study revealed.[53] Welcoming it in their relationships will likely never be common, and a slim majority of emerging-adult women remain uncomfortable with it. Yet many are acclimating themselves to what they see as a porn-saturated world in which they presume men will gravitate toward it. It seems to many the only strategy that makes sense. Megan believed porn to be nearly universal now, and therefore is apathetic about it: "I think it's natural for guys to watch porn." Another added: "I think every guy at some level is hooked on porn." And yet Megan agrees that porn affects people. In her opinion, it changes women: "I think a lot of women think that guys want that [what they see in porn], so they try to [mimic it]." Other interviewees voiced common complaints:

- "I think some people could train their minds to . . . only enjoy things that they see in pornos."
- "I guess it could make it less of an emotional experience and just a more physical one."
- "It gives people false expectations . . . of women and . . . of men, too."

Many women consider porn not so much as threatening but as foolish or stupid. What doesn't bother young women—because they don't realize it—is the effect of online and video pornography on their *collective ability* to begin and sustain romantic and sexual relationships. Earlier we described how women ultimately control the "price" and timing of sex, but they negotiate these not only with their partner but also through observing what other couples around them are doing. The widespread availability and popularity of porn—obviously partnered with masturbation—serves to drive down the price of sex with real women (without their realizing it). It also encourages women as well as men to have sex earlier than they otherwise might have.[54] Sounds crazy, right? It's not. One of the obvious concerns about porn is that it functions for men as a substitute for a real person, and women realize this. It can curb men's ability to relate to women by diminishing their interest—and perhaps more importantly their *patience*—in doing so. As one young woman notes, "Some people . . . have more sexual experiences with porn than with people and then they just have stupid ideas about sex that are difficult to get rid of once you're actually in a relationship with someone." While any person can masturbate and it's as old as humanity, Alex was unapologetic in his love for modern, high-quality, digital porn:

> It's the best. [*Why do you say that?*] I think I like my own "personal time" as much as I like having intercourse. It's just different, but, it's also good. . . . [*Some people would say, 'Wouldn't people prefer the real thing?' Or not?*] I don't, like, I mean, I prefer the real thing because sometimes it's not as accessible. So it's like rarer when you get it. But if I have to choose between never getting to do one [of the two options] again, I don't know, I probably couldn't choose. I like them both.

In an unusual and fascinating published study, a group of men provided researchers with four semen samples acquired via masturbation.[55] Two samples were collected while the participants viewed digital pornographic video and two samples were collected without the porn as a source of arousal. (Each time the men were tested they had gone two days without ejaculating). To get an idea of how satisfying each masturbation experience was, the men were asked to score their level of sexual satisfaction on a 10-point scale. Not surprisingly, the sexual satisfaction the men reported was much higher during masturbation with the pornographic video stimulation than without it. It wasn't just in their imagination, either. The volume of seminal fluid, sperm count, sperm motility, and a marker of prostate function were significantly better in semen samples collected via masturbating to porn. In other words, the ubiquity and perceived quality of digital porn has the capacity to sexually *satiate* more men—and more often—than ever before. Old porn reached a small, self-selected minority of men. New porn reaches the majority.

Together with the study's findings, Alex's admission underscores porn's ramifications for women's romantic relationships with men. If porn-and-masturbation satisfies some of the male demand for intercourse—and it clearly does—it *reduces the value of real intercourse*, access to which women control. Since high-speed digital porn gives men additional attractive sexual options—more supply for his demand—it by definition takes some measure of price control away from women. As a result, the cost of real sex can only go down, taking men's interest in making steep relationship commitments with it. Naomi Wolf detects exactly that in her *New York* article on porn: "For two decades, I have watched young women experience the continual 'mission creep' of how pornography—and now Internet pornography—has lowered their sense of their own sexual value and their actual sexual value."[56] She continues:

> When I came of age in the seventies, it was still pretty cool to be able to offer a young man the actual presence of a naked, willing young woman. There were more young men who wanted to be with naked women than there were naked women on the market. If there was nothing actively alarming about you [as a woman], you could get a pretty enthusiastic response by just showing up. Your boyfriend may have seen *Playboy*, but hey, you could move, you were warm, you were real.

A woman's vagina, Wolf notes, "used to have a pretty high 'exchange value.'" Using frank economic language, she asserts that women were once better positioned to secure relationship commitments in return for access to their bodies. Now, she laments, the same "barely register(s) on the thrill scale." More is needed to arouse men, she observes. One way is the "Brazilian wax job," so popular in contemporary (but not classic) porn: Wolf claims that her 40-year-old peers at the gym all still have pubic hair, while the twenty-somethings "have all been trimmed and styled."

While no survey we're aware of has had the nerve to ask such a sensitive question, Wolf's anecdotal observation rings true with some interviewees' observations. Jill, a 20-year-old college student, estimated that around 80 percent of young woman shave off (or wax) all of their pubic hair. When asked why, she could only vaguely apprehend that "guys like that" and that it had something to do with porn. At face value, porn influence may seem innocuous. After all, what difference does pubic hair make? At a deeper level, however, such change reminds us that while women may remain sexual gatekeepers, the terms of sexual contracts continue to favor men and *what they want* in relationships. While men and women have and will continue to debate the morality of it, porn's practical and market effects deserve more attention than they've received.

CONCLUSION

There's certainly a lot more to sexual relationships than simply tallying counts from individuals about their number of sexual partners or how often they have sex. Indeed, much about emerging-adults' sexual relationships bespeaks an exchange perspective, complete with sexual producers, consumers, prices, conflict, and negotiation. Since their relationships often lack security and commence sex relatively quickly, it's not surprising that most emerging-adult sexual relationships end, typically within a year of commencement. Most Americans of any age disparage the sexual double standard, but such criticisms are unlikely to effect change, since the double standard seems to be a fixture of the sexual economy among unmarried, young Americans. What *has* changed is the price of sex, which has clearly declined. Sex within friendships has emerged as a popular—if still minority—practice. While the sex may be initially frequent within them, it's short-lived, especially when compared to the more stable sexual access afforded to people in romantic relationships. So while emerging adults don't do commitmentless sex for very long, neither are they adept at keeping relationship commitments for long, either. The place of porn in their relationships is increasing, even if women are largely unaware of it. Porn has given rise to requests for unusual sexual practices, plenty of which are one-sided. And yet some women comply, seeking to be perceived as desirable, flexible, and committed to their relationships. All the while, the mainstreaming of porn continues to diminish the price of sex, since it gives men more options for pleasurable sexual experiences.

FOUR

The College Campus

Sex 101?

Oh Lord, make me chaste, but not yet.

—*St. Augustine*

O NE PLACE THAT has been long synonymous with sex is the college campus. It seems to ooze sexuality. And no doubt, sex is
part of the script of college life for many students. Every day,
on thousands of campuses across the country, an untold number of
interactions between students carry a nonverbal, sometimes uncon-
scious, sexual component. Of course 99.9 percent of these interactions
lead nowhere except to places in the mind or heart. Even professors
are not immune to it. Countless sexual liaisons and not a few subsequent marriages have occurred because a faculty member fell in love
with a student. Indeed, divorce and lack of remarriage are more
common among male college professors than men in other types of
work, due—so one study argues—to their long-term exposure to
women in the peak of their reproductive years.[1] While we won't assess
that claim—and we don't intend to contribute to it—we are interested
in evaluating the sexual character of American universities.

Is the college experience really synonymous with sex? Are college
students more sexually active than other young adults? Is the "hook-up
culture" most evident among them, and has hooking up largely
replaced dating as the primary pathway for commencing their

relationships? What role does online social networking play in campus sexual life?

We'll give you a hint about some of our answers: the conventional wisdom about the sex lives of college students in America is wrong. Plenty of collegians are not having sex, at least not regularly, and many of those that are do so within more stable relationships than those who never went to college in the first place. Lots of students are not all that interested in hooking up.

To say that campus couples have gone cold, of course, would be a gross overstatement. Table 2.1 (in chapter 2, p. 16) makes a strong claim about the sexual nature of relationships among young Americans: few romantic partnerships do *not* have a sexual component to them. That remains true about relationships in college as well, although the share of them that are *not* sexual is slightly higher than among the population at large.[2] A truer claim is that there is more diversity on campus in this domain than the conventional wisdom has led us to believe. Many Americans presume that students at four-year universities and colleges are the most sexually active emerging adults, feasting on the sexual cornucopia that campus life provides. But curiously, this is not true. The most active sexual behavior—in terms of more numerous partners, frequency of sex, etc.—is found, on average, outside of college.[3] Interview after interview reinforced this. Emerging adults who never went to college are even hooking up at rates that outpace collegians as well. Perhaps students are actually studying after all.

HOOKING UP: EPIDEMIC OR ALL HYPE?

Much ink continues to be spilled about the notorious hookup, which has created a good deal of concern among parents and even educators.[4] While the data suggest that hooking up is not the most strategic way to begin a long-term relationship—indeed, that's seldom the point— much remains unclear about this relationship form.[5] Defined in lots of different ways by emerging adults, hooking up is best characterized as a paired activity that could lead to sex but is itself not sex. It has become synonymous with college life, though there's no inherent reason for this association. Its simplest and most common portrait involves a bar or party, both partners getting drunk or at least tipsy, friendly conversation, and making out. It can end there—in public. Or it can end privately, with or without more extensive sexual activity.

It's not too difficult to identify and map sexual behavior. Hooking up, however, is a more slippery idea that means different things to different people. Thus getting two people to agree that they did in fact hook up can be a challenge. Some interviewees were only vaguely familiar with what exactly constitutes hooking up, even some who've participated in it. Here are four answers that are typical of what we heard:

- "Depending on the context it can be anything from just, like, um . . . you and a girl paired up and maybe made out or whatever for a while to, like, you slept with him or something. . . . It could be anything."
- "I think it just means having sex with someone."
- "Getting physically intimate with somebody, I would probably say anywhere from making out with them to having intercourse, so anything within that range."
- "That's when random people . . . meet briefly and make out or something. I don't know. Make out, maybe have sex. I don't know. It depends on the situation, I guess. People that don't know each other, pretty much."

The 2000 College Women's Study (CWS), which was commissioned to explore the hook-up phenomenon, surveyed 1,000 women from over 200 four-year, co-ed college campuses. Three out of four respondents agreed with the statement that a "hook up" is "when a girl and a guy get together for a physical encounter and don't necessarily expect anything further" (while a "physical encounter can mean anything from kissing to having sex").

So while hooking up can become sexual, it doesn't start that way. And the majority of hookups don't end in sex. Few keep track of how many people they've hooked up with, unlike their greater clarity when counting sexual partners. Hooking up is more adequately understood as a strategy (for the active) or a pathway (for the passive) that can lead to more overt sexual activity. If there's anything new about it, it's the terminology and perhaps the speed with which two people who don't know each other well proceed to kissing and possibly beyond. To suggest that hooking up is a new sexual form, however, would be untrue. Generations of men and women have pursued relationships with each other in social and conversational settings that were lubricated with alcohol. The sexual ends themselves haven't changed.

Some argue that hooking up has all but replaced dating as the normal means by which romantic and sexual relationships get started.[6] In a *Rolling Stone* exposé of Duke University sexual norms in the wake of March 2006 accusations—later dropped—that Duke lacrosse players raped a paid stripper, the author remarked that "much to the disappointment of many students, female and male, there's no real dating scene at Duke," and that lots of other colleges reflect the same. One attractive Duke student admitted that she'd "never been asked out on a date in my entire life—not once."[7] For her, the script is to hang out, meet men at social functions, hook up, and—if she finds herself with a particular man for an extended period of time—ask him to clarify their status.

This pattern is not the dominant case everywhere. According to the CWS, 55 percent of all women reported having been asked out on more than six dates (during their college years) by the time they were seniors.[8] These numbers are hardly off-the-charts, we admit. Dating as a means to starting a romantic relationship may be an endangered species in some habitats. But it's hardly extinct. Duke, for example, has three institutional traits working against it in this case. First, it's a *private university*: CWS respondents at private schools were one-third more likely to report hooking up than were women at public universities. Second, it's *elite* in its standards: CWS respondents from very competitive schools were 64 percent more likely to report hooking up than women at the least competitive schools (52 percent vs. 31 percent). Third, it has a *Greek system*: CWS respondents on campuses with fraternities were 30 percent more likely to report hooking up. Sociologist Paula England finds similar patterns at Stanford, where sex within long-term relationships is rarer than either virginity or hooking up. In other words, hooking-up-as-the-preferred-way-to-have-sex is not universal across the country but instead is characteristic of students in more competitive schools. There men and women are more apt to extend the already active competition for scarce time to their relationships. They matriculated at Duke and Stanford and other such schools in order to excel and get a jump-start on ambitious careers. The pressure on them is considerable. Sex has to fit in somewhere, so quickly and without strings seems to make the most sense. No wonder the author of *Unhooked* came to such grim conclusions—she only interviewed women at Duke and George Washington University. In the CWS, women attending colleges in the northeast were 50 percent more likely to report having ever hooked up than were women attending schools in the midwest (48 vs. 32 percent, respectively). While hooking up is found everywhere, it's more common in certain places and types of institutions. It's also more common outside of college altogether.

Table 4.1 displays the shortest amount of time before a respondent's relationship became sexual—drawn from their recollection of

TABLE 4.1 Shortest Time to Sex, in Percent, Sexually Active Never-Married 18- to 23-Year-Olds

	Men		Women	
	Not in college	In college	Not in college	In college
1 day	22.2	15.8	15.0	6.9
2–7 days	15.7	14.3	13.1	9.0
1–2 weeks	13.0	10.2	9.7	8.7
2–4 weeks	13.0	10.9	14.9	11.5
1–5 months	17.2	23.8	24.9	32.3
6–12 months	8.8	9.2	11.5	13.3
1 year or more	10.1	15.8	10.9	18.4

Source: Add Health

relationships—and compares those currently enrolled in four-year colleges with those who aren't enrolled in any form of higher education. Among both men and women, it's evident that college students are consistently more hesitant to commence a very rapid sexual relationship and conversely more apt to wait. Collegians don't necessarily wait a lot longer for sex, on average, but it is significantly longer in the statistical sense.

Data from sociologist Paula England's online College Social Life Survey—which has (so far) collected data from over 10,000 undergraduate sociology-course students across numerous universities—reinforces the conclusion that college students may be more conservative than we are led to believe.[9] Her study reveals a variety of things about hooking up among college students:

- 36 percent of them said they'd never hooked up at all.
- The median number of hookups reported by senior year is 4.
- The last time they hooked up, men reported having had an average of 4 drinks, and women reported 2.5.
- Just under half of hookups were the first time with a person; the rest were repeats.
- Nearly half of women and 62 percent of men said they'd have sex with someone even if they weren't in love with them.
- Some hookups go awry: 78 percent of women and 73 percent of men say they've regretted at least one hookup.

- In their last hookup, 42 percent of the men said they had an orgasm, compared with 19 percent of women. On the other hand, fully 38 percent of men *thought* their partner had an orgasm.
- 30 percent of college women said they'd performed oral sex or hand stimulation of a partner to orgasm mainly because they didn't want to have intercourse but felt obliged to provide an orgasm.
- Around half of all men and women reported enjoying the sexual activity (however extensive it was) in their last hookup "very much," while 39 percent said they enjoyed it "somewhat."
- 27 percent of women said "Yes, I was definitely interested" in a romantic relationship after having hooked up, compared with 20 percent of men who said the same.
- 64 percent of men and 66 percent of women said it wasn't awkward to (later) talk to the person with whom they hooked up.
- Men were about 45 percent more likely than women to subsequently disrespect someone who hooked up with them.
- Relatedly, 53 percent of women said they felt disrespected after hooking up, compared with only 24 percent of men.

In keeping with sexual economics assumptions, England and her colleagues note that men tend to initiate hookups more often than women and that men are less likely to damage their reputation in doing so.[10] The results of the CSLS are far more staid than those reported in sensationalist journalism about hooking up. Hooking up is not an every-weekend occurrence. When averaged across students, it's a once-a-year occurrence. And somewhere near half of those events don't involve intercourse. In reality, we suspect the average reflects a significant minority that never hooks up, offset by a slight majority of students among whom it happens a few times a year and a small minority for whom hooking up is a regular practice.

So while experts disagree on just how sexual hookups generally are and how often people engage in them, parents should be relieved to know that not every night out at a bar or party will conclude with their emerging-adult children hooking up and having sex. It's just not that way. Many collegians go out drinking on a regular basis, but as Table 3.6 (in chapter 3, p. 91) reveals, a sexual interaction doesn't result every time.[11] Indeed, casual sex from hookups is rare by comparison, suggesting that popular perceptions of the depravity of the "hookup culture" may be somewhat overstated. Falling in love with someone is a far greater sexual risk than is a night out on the town. In fact, sustained romance is nearly a guarantee of subsequent sex (see Table 2.1, p. 16).

Ambivalence about Hooking Up

Despite perceptions that college students are enthusiastic about hooking up, ambivalence—especially among women—remains a fixture of the sex scene on campus. There's emotional dueling when enthusiasm battles disgust. Such sentiment is captured poignantly in sociologists Laura Hamilton and Elizabeth Armstrong's fascinating and compelling ethnography of women in a university residence hall known to be a "party dorm."[12] They and their research team spent a year living among freshmen women, documenting conversations and interactions involving the students' sexual relationships. They followed up over three years with 64 in-person interviews. All the effort paid off: they uncovered a great deal of nuance that characterizes young women's sexual decision making. The study powerfully reinforces three conclusions of sexual economics theory: first, the sexual double standard remains alive and well; second, any attempts to reduce the double standard are coming from women's efforts to act more like men, not vice versa; and third, imbalanced campus sex ratios work against women's desire to control the course of relationships.[13]

In another in-depth study of hooking up, psychologists Elizabeth Paul and Kristen Hayes evaluated the typical, the best, and the worst hook-up experiences as reported to them by 187 college students.[14] What they found suggests plenty of ambivalence: sexual climax (or orgasm) characterized 34 percent of the worst hookup experiences, compared with only 3 percent of the best experiences; 30 percent of the worst experiences were characterized by "nothing happening with the person" after the hookup was over, compared with 17 percent of the best ones. The authors note that the stories commonly used to socialize students about campus sex are skewed, creating a more positive spin on hooking up that is out of step with the reality of many actual student experiences. When a bad experience with hooking up happens, then, students tend to blame themselves for getting into such a situation. So they hide their feelings, which does nothing to alter popular ideas and scripts about hooking up. Watch how two of Paul and Hayes's interviewees—one a woman and the other a man—each explicitly identify characteristics of the hooking up "script" and make two very different appeals to norms of appropriate behavior:

Woman: "We were at a party but I didn't drink. I tried to talk with him about slowing down and that was seen as abnormal to the guy. I felt dirty, sad, and mad. He didn't respect my requests. He used me for his own physical pleasure. I was mad at myself and lied to my friends and said we didn't have sex."

Man: "She was weird and said some things that you just don't say during a hookup. She wanted to talk about how we felt about each other. Then halfway through she changed her mind about hooking up. It was too late."[15]

This is exactly what psychologist Michael Wiederman would expect when couples pursue such different scripts: "predictability wanes, anxiety increases, and conflict is likely. 'You're not playing by the rules,' might be the spoken or unspoken conclusion," he asserts.[16]

In one study—again, only of college undergraduates—over 80 percent reported having experienced ambivalence about a recent sexual relationship. And half of that group had eventually rejected their partners' sexual advances, primarily out of concern about pregnancy, STIs, too much intimacy given the nature of the relationship, and moral inhibitions.[17] A significant share of women—44 percent—reported being too nervous to accept such sexual advances. Both men and women reported communicating sexual intentions—to engage as well as to refrain—that they admit are not in keeping with their true desires. In other words, ambivalence is not always displayed, understood, or even acted upon. But it's present, and it makes for complicated social interactions, including deception and regret.

Not all who balk at hooking up are sexual prudes. Natalie was a 20-year-old college junior from Maryland, a virgin, and a classic high achiever. She is not particularly interested in remaining a virgin and thinks nothing of having sex before marriage—even her mother ridiculed a virginity standard (which she thought was cool). But she wasn't ready just yet. Natalie didn't date in high school and is only now starting to get boys' attention. She has had two brief boyfriends in college so far, which has functioned to rapidly elevate her level of self-confidence. No longer only a bookish teenager who was never asked out on a date, Natalie seemed newly confident about what she wants and what she will not do. She is not at all interested in hooking up:

I'm not one to like just go [have sex] with a random guy. Like, I know people who have one-night stands and stuff, and yeah, I'm not one of those people. No, it's not my thing. I mean, I know people who do it, and I'm still friends with them, but it wouldn't be me who did it.

What she has learned over the course of two relationships, however, are communication skills for relationships, something that hook-ups typically fail to foster. Like many confident and high-achieving young woman, Natalie told us that her family is very important to her, and she gets along well with them. This is no doubt an understated and long-lasting positive influence on the lives of young Americans—whether they are not only loved by their mother and father but also freely express love back.

Women aren't the only ones who express ambivalence about hooking up, although they do so far more often than men. Nevertheless, some men who seem satisfied with short-term relationships wonder about their wisdom. Bruce, the 19-year-old we first heard from in chapter 3, just finished his first year of college at a state university in Pennsylvania. The son of traditional Asian parents, he plays the prototypical role of a second-generation immigrant child and continues to distinguish himself from that subculture, having joined a fraternity and lived the life of an American jock his freshman year. When we spoke to him at school, empty beer cans littered the sidewalk out front, and lots of half-full liquor bottles rested on top of the refrigerator. In keeping with the jock image, Bruce is a "walk on" to the football team, is majoring in sports management, and has managed a B+ average so far. His mother telephones him every day, stressing the importance of doing better than that if he wants to get into law school.

Bruce also expresses a far more permissive sexual ethic than was handed down to him. In fact, he takes a fairly laissez-faire approach to sex, having hooked up seven or eight times at parties this past year: "You kind of just always go . . . fishing and then hopefully you find that big sea bass," he laughs. But his hookups come with some ambivalence: "Sometimes I feel like that's not how I want to do it. But you know, you do what you gotta do." Bruce seems caught up in living out clichés. He plainly admits that he's been brainwashed into thinking that guys always pursue sex, even if the pursuit leaves him feeling shallow. Interestingly, Bruce repeatedly refers to himself in the third person, as a disembodied "you," as in, "you come to the realization that sex is okay," and "you want the girl to be on birth control." It's as if he was not actually the sexual actor he's describing in his personal accounts. Instead, it's somebody else, somebody who will eventually leave that life behind, find a lifelong mate, and start the life he knows he's meant for and that his parents expect.

Bruce presses forward in spite of his quiet misgivings, because he came to college with the popular intention of pursuing parties, drinking, and sex, and to live the life he had heard about. It's as if he read the "college freshmen script," liked it, tried to memorize and enact it, and yet is aware that the "responsible, mature adult script" of behavior is his to inherit soon as he moves toward his senior year and life beyond college. And despite the socialized pursuit of short-term sex, Bruce actually longs for a real relationship. "True love," as he puts it: "Finding, being in love with another" is the most important thing in life, he claims. But it can wait, because according to the script it's not supposed to happen just yet: "Freshman and Sophomore year, because there's so much, like, partying and opportunity to hookup—people don't want that relationship. That's kind of how I feel. I know later down the road I'll definitely want it."

After the goal of true love, happiness is a close second priority for Bruce, and it's comprised of two key ingredients that could short-circuit his quest for true love—friends and drinking:

> I love companionship. Just, I love people, like, just being around them. I'm always about being with a large crowd. Um, like, when we were ah, we were pretty drunk, we all, at my fraternity, we all had our arms around our shoulders, we were all jumping up and down, just acting like [laughs] like that was like, we look back at that night and we're like, that was awesome, like slapping hands and just being like, you know? [*Is the drinking a particularly important part of it, or does that just happen to be what you do when you are with your friends.*] Um, it happens to bring it out. Sporting events, ah, when you win a game, you know, that's that same feeling. It's that rush, like, 'Yeah!!' Like I love that, truly.

While drinking and true love may not go hand-in-hand, alcohol and sex are almost inseparable colleagues on American campuses. The pair regularly produces so many acts of regret that looking in from the outside one might think there is also a "regret script" that millions of college students similarly rehearse, practice, and repeat.

The Perceived Benefits of Hooking Up

If more women than men dislike hooking up, this prompts the question: What does hooking up provide for women? Obviously there must be some perceived or actual benefits. Otherwise, the practice would never have arisen or would've died a rapid death. There's no guarantee of sexual pleasure, since the odds of mutual orgasm are far smaller in a hookup than in a longstanding sexual relationship.[18] (As the CSLS data infer, many women fake orgasms.) While Hamilton and Armstrong don't directly address this question, they consistently note that many women both enjoy hooking up *and* find it confusing and awkward. Some opt out. The researchers conclude that women's ambivalence about hooking up is best explained by an "institutional contradiction" between social-class and gender concerns that put women into what they call a "double bind." As women, they feel pressure to participate in traditional, committed romantic relationships. Yet the shrinking sexual double standard and the social-class expectations of upper-middle-class women combine to encourage them to enjoy sex by way of hookups that don't threaten to entangle them in romantic relationships (which require a great deal of time and emotion and might pose a threat to their anticipated career paths). To these women, marrying at 22 or 23 is unacceptable, so they feel pressure to avoid letting relationships get too far emotionally. This is indeed happening more widely in America as the median age at marriage for women continues to climb. Naomi, a Duke sophomore interviewed for the *Rolling Stone* article, remarked that "sometimes, girls will be like, 'I'm just horny and I want to have sex. . . . I think you'd be a lot more pressed to find that attitude a little longer ago."

Naomi's probably right. Jenna, a 19-year-old from Texas, has had several sex partners, some romantic, some not. She spoke more about physical and sexual "needs" than did most other interviewees. Fulfilling them was a clear goal of her on-again, off-again sexual-activity pattern:

> I think it [sex] was something that, it's definitely something that makes you feel good. I know for me it's, I don't know if I want to say [it's a] stress reliever, but it's very relaxing. It puts me in a good mood, just all those, like, chemical, science-y things that happen [during sex]. It's true, I mean. [*What chemical science-y things?*] Just, like, I feel great afterwards. Maybe it's just because the people I have been with make me feel really good, but I always feel good and energized.

Jenna can enjoy sex apart from being entangled in formal relationships. She likes that it's possible to do so, yet she too confessed later to preferring a real, romantic, lasting relationship.

The young women in Hamilton and Armstrong's ethnographic study assert that Jenna's path is difficult to successfully navigate in a social and sexual reality that women don't control. Gender traditionalism in the domain of sexuality lags well behind idealism; men still attempt to dictate whether a relationship begins or ends, as well as its course. (Indeed, many men feel entitled to this role, Hamilton and Armstrong note.) Men also control the party scene, a phenomenon common to most American campuses. That party scene spelled the doom of Jenna's most significant, long-term relationship, when she glimpsed a photo on Facebook of her boyfriend making out with another woman.

Like Jenna, most women persistently report feeling like they ought to be in relationships. And for young women from lower-middle-class and working-class homes, relationship concerns trump their career ambitions. In turn, Hamilton and Armstrong witnessed many of them drop out of the hook-up scene and many even out of college; the contradictions were just too great and the ambivalence too profound. Sex, for them, had to be in a traditional relationship.

The CWS sheds considerable light on how women evaluate the dating and relationship options accorded them.[19] Table 4.2 displays the share of agreement among college women with a variety of statements about dating, men, and sex.

The numbers are illuminating and express three themes. First, women say they know how to conduct relationships. They don't necessarily feel pressured to have sex to remain in one, but most will. They don't feel the need to drink in order to be social; they've been warned about the risks of sex; and a solid majority—66 percent—are wary of sex without commitment, at least intellectually. There is an implicit morality to conducting such relationships, they believe. *Implicit* can also characterize the norms and rules about relationships in general: only half of respondents say there are clear, if informal, rules about how to conduct oneself with the opposite sex.

Second, a small majority is pessimistic about their chances at having the kind of relationship they want at the school they're at. Although the men are attractive as partners, most seem disinterested in commitment. And frankly, roughly half of these women aren't really in a hurry to be in such a relationship anyway.

Third, although they don't perceive themselves as sexual free spirits, and most of them hold to a more relational orientation, they wouldn't dream of judging their peers' sexual choices. Just under 90 percent of women in the CWS agreed to the statement, "I should not judge anyone's sexual conduct except my own." Indeed, this is a triumph of twenty-first-century American educational psychology: young Americans are taught—and they have learned—how to get along with each other and how not to get involved in other people's business. What has resulted is profound reticence against judging other people's sexual decision making. Hooking up may not be appealing to a majority of

TABLE 4.2 Attitudes of College Women about Dating, Men, and Sex, in Percent That "Agree" or "Strongly Agree" with Each Statement

	Percent
I have a clear sense of what I should do and not do in my romantic/sexual interactions.	96.2
I should not judge anyone's sexual conduct except my own.	83.0
My parents have told me I should save sex for marriage.	73.5
Sexual intercourse without commitment is wrong.	66.4
There aren't many guys here who want a committed relationship.	60.2
It is hard to meet the right kind of guys at my college.	53.4
At my college, there are clearly understood informal rules about relationships.	50.7
At this time in my life, I am not ready to be serious about romantic relationships.	49.3
I don't find many men at my college who are attractive as potential partners.	40.5
At my college, going out in a group, drinking a lot, and then having sex is common.	39.6
Drinking makes it easier to relate to guys.	26.7
I wish women were freer to have sex with as many partners as they wanted.	19.3
When it comes to sex, there is no right or wrong.	17.8
You can't have a boyfriend unless you are willing to have sex.	4.3

Source: CWS

women, but they feel duty bound to the code of toleration not to press other people to think and act like they do. Indeed, Natalie and many other young adults we interviewed accorded more sexual permissiveness to other people than they allowed for themselves.

This stands in stark contrast to an older code wherein people would hold others to higher sexual standards than they did to themselves, at least in private. While religious and conservative organizations in this country may attempt to construct systematic barriers to sexual involvement, very few young Americans seem interested in expressing categorical barriers for others or for themselves. To do so would violate the code of toleration and would just look prudish. Emerging adults desperately wish to avoid both. As a result, sexual choices become almost entirely privatized, subject to little oversight outside the self. Women who get hurt or who are disappointed by their sexual decisions then typically blame themselves. Men's actions are taken for granted.[20]

I Am Charlotte Simmons

This lack of sexual oversight is certainly evident in Tom Wolfe's 2004 mildly masked novel about the sexual culture at Duke University.[21] Wolfe's book may be partly to blame for generating media hubbub about hooking up. It certainly helped thrust campus sex onto parents' and educators' radar screens. *I Am Charlotte Simmons* is an engaging read, replete with the attention to details for which Wolfe is so well regarded. The plot itself is uncomplicated: Charlotte arrives at "Dupont University" as a bookish but stunningly beautiful virgin from the bumpkin backwoods of western North Carolina. While tolerating a privileged, party culture with which she is entirely unfamiliar, she becomes the recipient of the affections of the hottest fraternity boy on campus, Hoyt. The reader finds Charlotte both repulsed by such rank male sexuality as well as reveling in its attention. Ultimately, she follows Hoyt to an alcohol-soaked fraternity bash, where he finally takes Charlotte's virginity, although not with her volition entirely intact.[22]

The plot to *Charlotte Simmons*, however, plays a back seat to the frank description of primal sexual codes, sexual pecking orders, the alleged power of popular men to bed nearly any woman they want, and to the irony of how some of the most talented, intelligent young women in the country regularly allow themselves to be used by men as they use *them* for social posturing. It's a full-frontal assault upon their mothers' Second-wave feminism. The *Rolling Stone* article on Duke did nothing to dispel the reality of Wolfe's fiction, and—together with a spate of recent articles and books on the subject—turned the topic of hooking up into a national discussion.

And yet it all overreaches: what's portrayed in *I Am Charlotte Simmons* and in the popular imagination of many Americans is *not* normal college behavior. Is there nameless, faceless sex going on? Sure. That is nothing new. But *casual sex is not the norm among emerging adults in college*. Like we suggested earlier, it is more common outside of the college experience than inside it. In other words, emerging adults who never attend college are more likely to hook up. The hypersexual college campus is a fiction, a combined creation of Hollywood, ad agencies, and local businesses who recognize that sex sells well among students.

Casual sex and hooking up as a sexual strategy is instead the preferred option only of a campus sexual elite. This sexual elite is far outnumbered by the more average collegians who may have a sexual relationship or two during college but whose behavior never captures the popular imagination. We're not suggesting that others don't ever hook up but rather that hooking up is the standard operating procedure of fewer students than we've been led to believe. Still, this cadre of students is the popular face of campus life and has long been so. Their weekly search for sex creates the outliers in statistical estimates of sexual partners and frequency.

Bradley is 20 and a junior at a state university in Michigan, a place he calls "a real big party school." He's also a fraternity member and in love with the classic mythological college experience of the sort portrayed in *Animal House*. He's white. All of these are traits of the sexual elite, a minority group on four-year university campuses (whose students are themselves a minority group among American emerging adults). A bit overweight, Bradley has trouble attracting a serious girlfriend (and the access to regular sex that comes with it), but being in a fraternity has its sexual advantages: "There's always people coming to parties." He lost his virginity at 18 to someone with whom he had no relationship and has had several sexual partners since he got to college, but none during the summers when the parties cease. Like the quintessential frat boy, Bradley is not terribly reflective about sex and relationships. He never really plans to have sex; it just happens at opportune moments. So conceiving of sex within a relationship remains something foreign to him. He hopes to get married someday and have lots of kids; children made his parents happy, he notes. How to get from here to there is not on his mind, however.

Bradley is one face of the sexual elite. Never mind that he's not as attractive as his peers. That doesn't matter so much in the world of sexual economics. In the *Rolling Stone* article, Duke undergrad Allison comments on this very thing: "I feel like in the real world, these guys would never be with these girls—they're way too beautiful. And way too intelligent." But Allison incorrectly presumes that in the real world, sexual attractiveness matters equally to men and women. It doesn't.

We regularly ask our intro-to-sociology class to write about the narratives or "big stories" that they live within and enact in their lives, what sorts of social-support systems help sustain their participation in those stories, and the particular scripts that the stories generate to tell them how to act and what to say. Laurie was an attractive sophomore from suburban Dallas, upper-middle-class by her own definition. She was remarkably honest in her attraction to a powerful story about modern womanhood, which she herself claims purveys a "ridiculous standard" and an unflinching set of difficult scripts unknown in the world of men. And yet she so badly wants the stories to be true:

> I daily feel pressured to conform to a certain image. As a young woman, I am expected to be beautiful, thin, poised, elegant, respectful, educated, fashionable, and mature. I should wear certain clothes, shoes, and makeup. I also feel expected to know the latest fashion trends, gossip, and celebrity news. In respect to men and dating, I must be fun, flirty, sexy, and exciting. These expectations and pressures are reinforced through magazines, television, movies, and friends. . . . Together these structures mold the image of the perfect young woman and demand all to conform. Although I am aware of this superficial marketing technique, I still desire to look like the models in magazines and the celebrities in movies. I realize that men are attracted to numerous qualities in women, but I want most to be beautiful and sexy.

These very same traits turned up in the Duke Women's Initiative, a year-long study of the attitudes and concerns of female students.[23] The study uncovered tremendous pressure and relentless hyperactivity, all in submission to maintaining the illusion of perfection in multiple domains of life. Like the Duke women in the *Rolling Stone* article, what Laurie most wants is a convertible skill set—sexiness—that will stead her well even if those men that warrant her affections fail her. Her efforts are common to women as they create "micro prestige economies" in order to distinguish themselves from fellow students. While adults in their later 20s, 30s, and 40s have a wider variety of stratification categories about which to pursue distinguishing themselves from others—such as success in their career, family life, and the accumulation of wealth—collegians have fewer ways to do so. When you're a college student, especially a freshman or sophomore, how do you create prestige for yourself, especially in a new and competitive environment in which you're not known? Sexual attraction is one of the few playing fields—and by far the most obvious—upon which they can pursue recognition and distinction.

At this point, perhaps some confusion is merited. The Add Health data seem to suggest that over 90 percent of people in romantic relationships at this age are sexually active. But the CWS seems to underestimate the prevalence of hooking up (39 percent said they have), at least when contrasted with the online CSLS. Who's right? We realize it may be aggravating to say it, but they each capture a part of the truth about emerging-adult sex. Remember—most emerging adults are not enrolled in the traditional four-year college or university. College students are above average in lots of ways: they take fewer risks (although they drink more), they have fewer sexual partners, and they do less drugs than people who never went to college. They also have less sex: in the Add Health data, 24 percent of traditional college students told us they were still virgins. Only 10 percent of 18- to 23-year-olds who aren't enrolled anywhere said the same thing, a rate less than half that of the collegians. (A good share of college virgins doesn't altogether avoid sexual activity, of course: 45 percent of them report that they have had oral sex before.)

And while most romantic relationships appear to turn sexual given time, plenty of emerging adults are simply slow to enter such relationships. Back in Table 2.1 (p. 16), we saw that around 25–40 percent of emerging adults aren't in romantic relationships. Yet the sex gets all the attention; too few social scientists concern themselves with the decision to avoid sexual relationships in college.[24] College virgins are presumed to be rare, to lack sexual desire, and to be somehow deserving of pity. Such conclusions are unwarranted. They actually tend to be a self-confident and accomplished lot, as Cami, Natalie, and Jerry attest. In each of their cases, the lack of a loving and committed relationship stood out as a central reason for their avoidance of sex. And why shouldn't it? It's a top reason why young women abstain for a season.[25] It's not that they lack for opportunities. As sexual economics theory reminds us, young women never lack for opportunities to have sex, because the demand side (from men) is very stable. While more women than men—by a margin of 31 to 11 percent—rate moral or religious reasons as "important" for staying virgins, it's not the most commonly cited excuse. Indeed, belief that premarital sex is wrong is also hardly a key reason—it ranks seventh among women virgins and eleventh among men. Nor is the absence of sexual desire. That's actually the *least* common reason for abstaining.[26] What remains most important for both men and women is concern that they've not been in a relationship long enough and that they wish to avoid pregnancy.

Even though the majority of college students are either having sex or have had sex, they still overestimate how much sex is actually going on around them. In study after study—as well as in our interviews—emerging adults think that other people are having more sex than they are.[27] In one study of college freshmen, around 30 percent of men and women said they'd had at least four sexual partners in their lifetime, but men estimated that the same was true of 53 percent of other men, while women estimated that 45 percent of their peers had had that many partners. The reverse was true about sexual abstinence: around one in four men and women intended to abstain from sex until marriage, but men guessed that only 13 percent of other men intended the same, while women guessed that 19 percent of other women have such intentions.[28]

In keeping with the code of tolerance, students are also apt to suspect that others are more permissive about sex than they are. A study of 264 college students found that men and women each rate their peers as being more comfortable with hooking up than they themselves were.[29] Men of course were more comfortable with it, and yet both sexes overestimated how comfortable the other was with hooking-up behaviors. This is true about lots of things: we tend to think that other people drink more than we do, aren't as sensible as we are, and are worse drivers than we are. On the other hand, we also tend to think other people "have it together" more than we do, and that they're happier and more successful than we are. This classic phenomenon is called "pluralistic ignorance," a term coined by social psychologist Floyd Allport. Pluralistic ignorance happens when

> within a group of individuals, each person believes his or her private attitudes, beliefs, or judgments are discrepant from the norm displayed by the public behavior of others. Therefore, each group member, wishing to be seen as a desirable member of the group, publicly conforms to the norm, each believing he or she is the only one in the group experiencing conflict between his or her private attitude and his or her public behavior. Group members believe that most others in their group, especially those who are popular and opinion leaders, actually endorse the norm and want to behave that way, while they themselves privately feel they are going along with the norm because of a desire to fit in with the group and exemplify the norm.[30]

This pattern suggests that plenty of college students *think* that they don't have sex as much as other people do and aren't as comfortable with uncommitted sex as other people are, but generally don't wish to appear so. In other words, many college students are more sexually conservative than they prefer to let on. They're afraid to appear prudish, which strikes many as a social kiss of death.

The results of pluralistic ignorance about others' sex lives, however, can "lead one or both sexual partners to act according to the perceived norm rather than to their own convictions." In other words, sex becomes a self-fulfilling prophecy: "The more students believe sexual activity is occurring, the more sexual activity occurs."[31] In a study of over 700 undergraduates, researchers noted that men who considerably overestimated the sexual activity of their male peers were also 11 times more likely to have had sexual intercourse in the past month than were those who underestimated men's sexual activity.[32] When women overestimated, they were four times as likely to have had recent sex. When we spoke with a campus sexual-health educator about her use of *Cosmopolitan* "sex surveys" in their educational efforts, she responded that the statistics were just "fun facts" used to keep the sessions entertaining: "They don't change anyone's behavior or anything," she asserted. We're not so sure. While it's true that not everyone on campus is having sex, if students *believe* they are, then their own sexual pursuits tend to become more urgent.

Our conversations with college students reinforce this. The response to questions about campus sexual activity patterns varied by how sexually active the interviewees have been: one woman who'd had nine lifetime partners believed that "about 95 percent" of her peers had had sex in the past month, and that "65–70 percent" of them had had at least four sexual partners in their lifetime. One man who's had three partners total guesstimated that around 40–50 percent of the campus population has had sex recently—a figure he believed to be higher if you were active in Greek life—and perhaps 30 percent of students have had at least four partners. Another woman who'd only been sexually active with her current boyfriend thought these numbers were closer to 40 percent (who've had sex in the past month) and 15–20 percent (who've had four or more partners). There is a linear nature to this pattern, and it is nothing new. Humans have always been invested in the idea that their own ways of thinking and acting are not that far from normal— even if they are.

MORE BANG FOR YOUR (TUITION) BUCK: SEX RATIOS AND RELATIONSHIPS IN COLLEGE

One remarkable—and largely invisible—demographic phenomenon that shapes decision making is sex ratios within communities. An aspect of sexual economics theory that we only briefly hinted at in chapter 3, a sex ratio is simply how many men there are in a community, compared with how many women there are. It's a demographic and sociological characteristic of which most of us have only the vaguest awareness. People who regularly attend church often notice, if they pay attention, that there are more women in church than men. College students in a nursing class will notice the same gender disparity, while engineering majors tend to sense the opposite in their courses. While sometimes the disparity is blatantly obvious, most of the time sex ratios are a good deal more subtle. If, in a room of 18 people, 10 are women and 8 are men, most of us won't notice the difference. Extrapolate from that to a community of 180 or even 18,000, and very few will take note, because there are plenty of men all around, just not quite as many of them as there are women.

In 1947 there were more than twice as many men on campus as women (245 men for every 100 women). That significant gap dwindled until 1980, when women began outnumbering men in attending college. Since then, the gender gap in higher education has widened appreciably in the other direction. By 1997, the sex ratio on American campuses was just under 80 men for every 100 women. And in 2005, a mere 25 years after the eclipse first began, the ratio stood at 74 per 100, where it remains today.[33] That's a decline in six men per 100 women in less than 10 years. At face value, such news is great for women's continued push for social and economic equality with men. But this educational gap spells something altogether different for their romantic relationships, which have become considerably more difficult to generate and maintain. Why?

The "sex-ratio hypothesis" holds that an oversupply of women on college campuses in the United States gives men there considerably more power in romantic and sexual relationships, which translates into lower levels of relationship commitment, less favorable treatment of women by men, and a more sexually permissive climate wherein women receive less in exchange for sex.[34] All of this rests on the sexual economics theory described in chapter 3—that men prefer lower-cost sex than do women. The foundation of this claim is very old, and it's not just economists who've noticed it: David Schmitt, a psychologist of sexuality whose International Sexuality Description Project has evaluated sexual behavior patterns in over 56 countries, notes how the human reproductive system remains subject to local tweaking:

> The reproductive systems of lust and attachment in humans appear designed to react to features of local ecology. . . . In cultures with more men than women, humans become more monogamous and oriented toward long-term mating. It seems doubtful that the brains of men and women have a different design across cultures. Instead, the human sexual brain is designed to functionally respond to local circumstances and activate the lust, love, and attachment systems differentially depending on ecological conditions.[35]

Here's how it works: power within relationships—a central principle in the sex-ratio hypothesis—is determined not only by such things as the social status and physical attractiveness of the partners but also by surrounding market characteristics. Most pertinent to the sex-ratio hypothesis is the level of a partner's *dependency* within a relationship. All else being equal, the availability of attractive alternatives outside of the relationship yet inside the local market tends to reduce an individual's dependency and result in lower levels of commitment to and investment in a relationship.[36] Alternatives to the relationship are more readily available in markets where there is an oversupply of the opposite sex, or—put another way—where the market sex-ratio is imbalanced: "The individual member whose sex is in short supply has a stronger position and is less dependent on the partner because of the larger number of alternative relationships available to him," explains the authors of one study.[37] The individual in the majority sex may perceive their only alternative as being alone. This places the individual in the minority sex in a position of power within the pair, a position from which they can maximize their rewards while paying only limited costs. When men are in the minority in the sex market, they are thought to be more enabled to pursue sex while avoiding long-term relationship commitments.

The sex-ratio theory is not just an interesting idea when we look at the data. It really works. American women are more likely to marry when there are more men in their marriage market. Data analyses of 117 countries suggest that those with higher sex ratios (that is, more men) have higher marriage rates and lower rates of child-bearing outside of marriage. Even teen-pregnancy rates are higher where men are scarce, given the logic that an oversupply of women leads to a sexually permissive culture.[38] (Keep in mind that's *not* because women are more permissive but because men are.) But we know the theory works not only because other scholars have documented it but because we matched campus data on sex ratios with data from the CWS in order to assess the independent effects of sex ratios on women's attitudes and actions about dating.[39] What we found is startlingly clear evidence in favor of the sex-ratio theory. Women on campuses where they comprise a higher proportion of the student body exhibit certain telling characteristics:

- They express more negative appraisals of men on campus
- They hold more negative views of their relationships
- They go on fewer dates
- They have a lower likelihood of having a boyfriend (or having had one since entering college)
- They receive less (in the way of relationship commitment) in exchange for sex

These significant statistical associations control for a variety of individual and campus characteristics, like class standing, race, church attendance, conservative attitudes about sex, region of the country, campus-enrollment size, the university's academic exclusivity, the presence of Greek life, and whether it's a Christian college or not. After we take all of those into consideration, sex ratio still matters.[40]

As a result of campus imbalances, lots of college women now find themselves in relationships with men that aren't in college at all, creating an awkward—and typically temporary—sexual relationship of imbalanced future directions. (She's busy studying for the MCAT or the LSAT while he's angling for the Xbox.) The gap in maturity they feel with their boyfriends can be profound. Mia, a 19-year-old pre-law student from Texas lamented that she has to tell her live-in boyfriend, who attends a community college, "every assignment he has and then I have to figure out a schedule for him . . . and actually watch him do his homework, [or else] he pretty much won't do it." She's miserable, and he's pathetic, but the gender ratios on campus leave some women feeling like they have few good options around them.

Sex ratios also invisibly shape the sex lives of women (and men, by logical extension) on campus. Table 4.3 displays predicted probabilities of sexual behavior of women in the CWS, sorted by their relationship status and the percentage of women as a share of total campus enrollment. Predicted probabilities are derived from statistical regression models but must be specified to certain "types." Thus we chose to display in Table 4.3 the predicted probabilities that correspond to a white woman who is a junior at a large public university with a Greek system, one that is not located in the northeastern United States, and that reports average levels of religious service attendance, attitudes about sex, and frequency of dating. (A predicted probability of 1.0 would mean that the respondent is sure to have had sex. A probability of 0.5, then, means there's a 50 percent chance of having done so).

The results suggest a pronounced effect of campus sex ratios. While obviously having a boyfriend is the primary predictor of having had sex in the past month, recent sex is far more common—with or without a boyfriend—in colleges and universities that have higher numbers of women. For women who currently have a boyfriend on a campus that is split 50/50, their probability of having sex in the past month is 0.66. But on campuses with only 30 percent women, their probability is 0.50, while on campuses where they comprise 70 percent of all students, their probability of recent sex is 0.79.[41]

Conversely, virginity is far more common where women comprise a smaller share of the student body. For women who haven't had a boyfriend since they've been to a college that has 30 percent women, the probability that they're a virgin is 0.85, well above the predicted average for the dataset (which we suspect slightly overestimates virgins). At the other end of the sex-ratio spectrum, the same woman

TABLE 4.3 Predicted Probabilities of Sexual Behavior and Virginity, by Percent of Women on Campus and Relationship Status

	Sex in the past month			Still a virgin		
	Hasn't had a bofriend in college	Had a boyfriend in past	Currently has a boyfriend	Hasn't had a boyfriend in college	Had a boyfriend in past	Currently has a boyfriend
Percent of Women on Campus						
30% women	.05	.12	.50	.85	.70	.56
40% women	.07	.16	.58	.76	.57	.42
50% women	.09	.21	.66	.64	.43	.29
60% women	.12	.27	.73	.50	.30	.19
70% women	.16	.34	.79	.36	.19	.12

Source: CWS

at a college where women make up 70 percent of the student body has a virginity probability of 0.36.

Suffice it to say that there's something powerful going on here. Changes in American sexual norms have come about not simply because we have decided to think differently about sex and relationships today, but because the traditional sexual economy has witnessed a massive reorganization in the past 60 years. In 1947, 71 percent of college students were men; today that number is about 43 percent. When there are considerably more women on campus than men, it makes romantic relationships more difficult for women to navigate successfully. Ironically, then, being in the numerical majority within the student body is not a good indicator of women's relative power on campus. What scholars describe as the "hook-up culture" may actually be a simple and passive result of this demographic trend—the growing gender imbalance on campuses—rather than any active change in Western sexual culture. While it would be difficult to determine the veracity of this claim with a great deal of confidence, the evidence discussed here favors it.[42]

Different colleges and universities are not the only places that display radically different sex ratios. American cities do as well. According to the Census Bureau, New York, Philadelphia, Baltimore, and Washington, D.C., have the most surplus single women between the ages of 20 and 64 of any metropolitan areas in the country. But sex ratios can show even more extreme variability within cities and at different ages (of inhabitants). In four different zip codes in lower and midtown Manhattan, women comprised 78 percent of 20-year-olds in one location, 63 percent of 22-year-olds in another, 60 percent of 25-year-olds in another, and 57 percent of 30-year-olds in yet another. No wonder Marguerite Fields—a college student who won the 2008 *New York Times* "Modern Love" essay contest—waxes pessimistic about finding a relationship there that will last:

> Sometimes I don't like them [men she has dated], or am scared of them, and a lot of times I'm just bored by them. But my fear or dislike or boredom never seems to diminish my underlying desire for a guy to stay, or at least to say he is going to stay, for a very long time.[43]

Fields reminds readers that "noncommittal is what we're all about." But given what sexual economics theory articulates about men and their sexual and relational preferences—that they prefer a low cost for sex if they can get it—it's just plain hard to get what she wants in New York. So she works at convincing herself that she really wants something else:

I tried to remember that no one is my property and neither am I theirs, and so I should just enjoy the time we spend together, because in the end it's our collected experiences that add up to a rich and fulfilling life. I tried to tell myself that I'm young, that this is the time to be casual, careless, lighthearted and fun; don't ruin it.

Unfortunately, trying doesn't make it a reality. Being casual, light-hearted, and fun are more male sexual values than female ones. Julia, a 21-year-old from Arizona who's been in a sexual relationship for two years, conveys similar frustration with her boyfriend's wishes to "enjoy the moment and not worry about the future." What, she wonders, "is the point of being in a relationship if you don't see a future?" He, on the other hand, thinks such a future orientation "always ruins things."

The Free-Agent Market

Fields laments men's failure to commit and stay. So why don't more men prefer secure relationships as the most rational way to access sex? It is, after all, *easier* to secure sex from a stable source than to repeatedly try one's chances on the free-agent market. Many all-star athletes favor long-term contracts with a small-market team over short-term contracts with the popular club in the big city, because stable cash flow is a valued commodity that accompanies security. The same is true of sex. And yet the free-agent market remains a ready and preferential draw for many men. Why? It's because they can, given the low price of sex on the open market.

If the price of sex remains low—and if variety is valued by men, and we know it is—then it becomes no less rational to pursue the unique and novel pleasure of being a free agent than to sign the long-term contract. Jill, the 20-year-old college student quoted in chapter 3, is caught up in this market snafu. Startlingly attractive, she nevertheless continues to patiently endure her boyfriend's hemming and hawing about the future of their relationship. She's an all-star. If she were operating within a collegiate sexual economy that wasn't imbalanced by an oversupply of women and a low market price for sex, she would not only have her pick of men but could easily secure the "long-term contract" she wishes for: exclusivity and eventual marriage. But so far, she can't get it. Michelle (20, from Oklahoma) was likewise attractive and experienced the same scenario as Jill: "I had an ex-boyfriend of mine who said that, um, he didn't know if he was ever going to get married because he said, there's, like, always going to be someone better. That's what he said."

This quandary won't stop with college-age relationships, either: college-educated women who wish to eventually marry men of similar education—which is most of them—will find this increasingly difficult in the future. If the current ratio remains intact for long, 26 out of 100 college-educated women will have to marry down the educational scale if they want to marry at all. It's not surprising, then, that the sexual decisions of women are looking more like those of men; it's a strategic and rational approach in a sexual and marital economy where women are increasingly *competing with each other* for the affections of increasingly rare high-quality men who are willing to commit. When women compete for men, men win: the price of sex goes down.

SELLING SEX ON CAMPUS

Because they presume sex is on the minds of college students, corporate and retail interests use sex to cater to this demographic. Given that men are the more ready sexual consumers—in keeping with sexual economics theory—advertisers' messages to them are simpler and image-based. Of that there is little doubt. Sexual imagery becomes "the very wallpaper of their lives," as one *New York Times* writer put it.[44] Women, on the other hand, not only consume but are also the primary supply-siders of the equation. Advertising to them within the domain of sexuality is considerably more complicated and subtle. Mixed messages abound, forcing women to negotiate their identity within a narrow range given the stigma placed on both virgins and sluts.[45] There is pressure to be sexually active yet to figure out how to price their sex at a rate that's neither too high nor too low. They're encouraged to be sexual, but not too sexual. This is a challenging directive indeed.

Popular women's magazines tend to err on the side of the sexual. *Cosmopolitan* and *Glamour* are the top two sellers in their category, at a recent circulation of 2.9 million and 2.4 million, respectively. *Cosmo* is the best-selling magazine on campus as well. One in three of its readers are between 18 and 24, and nearly two in three have college experience. Its readers report spending an average of 71 minutes perusing each issue, which—if true—is a remarkable feat in our digital age. Moreover, each copy in circulation is thought to be accessed by five or six women.

To be blunt, women's magazines sell sex. In a textual analysis of women's magazines over time, 45 percent of *Cosmopolitan* cover-story titles featured the word "sex." It's implied in another 17 percent of all cover stories, making for the substance of just under two-thirds of all article content featured on the cover page. When 141 college women were surveyed about *Cosmo* and *Glamour*, the single most agreed-upon statement was that "More than anything else, *Cosmo* and *Glamour* magazines are geared to sex and being single," and the lowest level of agreement came with the statement, "Health is the central theme in *Cosmo* and *Glamour* magazines."[46] Also near the bottom was "I read *Cosmo* and *Glamour* because each magazine sets the record straight about being female." Despite this, millions of young women devour these two magazines. They apparently know that they're being sold a particularly challenging vision of the good life, but it's consonant with their own vision for the same.

Ironically, men's magazines' coverage of sex pales in comparison. *Maxim* was recently the fourth-best seller on campus, just behind *Glamour*. *Maxim* and its competitors take women's sexual interest in men for granted and focus much of their attention instead on other topics, like getting ahead of the competition at work or dressing for success. They don't try to be sex educators for men like women's magazines are for women.[47] They could never top porn for that. Nor could they top online sites—especially campus ones—that specialize in distinctively sexual advice tailored to the local context. Sexually explicit campus publications increasingly afford such aspiring sex columnists the opportunity. While such publications tend to be short-lived, the genre is here to stay. "Everyone wants to be Carrie Bradshaw," notes a student editor in referencing the now widely syndicated star of *Sex and the City*, a television program and film series whose effect on how women collegians think about sex can hardly be overestimated.[48] We're not suggesting that *Sex and the City* directly made anyone do things they might not otherwise have done. But what it accomplished is a popularizing of the narrative of the very eligible, single white female who pursues sex and romance on her own terms. It's an attractive model to millions and has likely helped weaken the sexual double standard (but not sexual economics). Discerning just how these attractive models of behavior filter into human decision making is nearly impossible; but there's surely something to the connection.

On our own campus, there is *Study Breaks*, an ad-heavy, titillating magazine whose stories have included spring-break dalliances of attractive students, an alleged guide to "dating" that is largely about contraception and ways to improve one's sex life, positive perspectives on the porn industry from insiders, ways to keep men from leaving a relationship, and tales of the most unusual places in which students have had sex.

While this type of material is neither new nor unique to college campuses or emerging adulthood, what is notable is the advertising strategies found therein. Well-known companies elect to sell otherwise tame products by using overt—rather than subtle—sexual cues, typically accompanied by suggestive photographs. Some examples have included:

- "Recap last night's debauchery with clarity" (Time Warner Cable and Digital Phone)
- "Who are you sleeping with?" (local apartment complex)
- "The bigger the swell the better the ride" (local bar)
- "Commitments can be scary, but not this one" (local apartment complex)
- "Size doesn't matter but your scores do" (The Princeton Review)
- "Wanna go home with me tonight?" (Budweiser)
- "Get a room" (local apartment complex)
- "Score more" (local apartment complex)
- "Nothing wrong with getting a little nasty" (local bar)
- "We have more excuses for you to come than your boyfriend" (local restaurant)

Such ads aren't just using sex appeal to sell their products; that, after all, is very common. Instead, they're selling particular ideas and norms about sex that are consonant with the hookup model of sexual relationships—the one that only a minority of American collegians actually prefers. Our intention here is *not* to suggest that we find all college-oriented articles on human sexuality somehow unwelcome. Not at all. Rather, it's to point out how in a consumer-driven marketplace like the university, adults give students what they *think* they must want. What results, however, is reinforcement of the message that sex is what gets them noticed and ultimately what counts.

Sandeep, for one, has gotten the message. He just finished his freshmen year at a large university in Illinois. He's been sexually active to some degree and has likely lost his virginity, but he declined to answer the question when we asked it. (However, when asked about any pregnancy scares, he confessed that he was "somewhat worried." Enough said.) The child of immigrants, Sandeep is nevertheless "almost 100 percent Americanized," in his words. He spends a lot of time on video games, drinks several times a week, and smokes pot regularly. For now, he's ditched Hindu temple attendance; he'll pick it up again later. It's time to enjoy the freedoms of college:

> College is like 50,000 kids, and like five adults—but they're only there from 8 in the morning to 5 in the afternoon. And after that, there's no adults anywhere. And then there's just alcohol everywhere, too. So it's just like one big party land with class from 8 to 5. And the dorms are just like, they're like jungles.

College students, Sandeep claims,

> All, like, love each other, and everyone's happy and all that. . . . But then again, there's no like, there's no boundaries to anything you could do, whatsoever. Like you could do anything you want and not have to worry about anyone bothering you there. It's just [there's] somebody else doing it, like, 20 feet away.

While he takes a "whatever is right for them" approach to the sexual morality of other people, Sandeep remains ambivalent about sex, including his own behavior. While people may do what they feel like doing, he wishes the media wouldn't help them along: "I think the media is out of control. . . . They perpetuate it [sex]. . . . I don't really think it's good the way they portray it." Too much air time is spent poring over the sex lives of Hollywood actors, he claims: "They put more emphasis on sexuality and beauty than, like, intelligence and doing well." In a prescient way, Sandeep notes the changes that accompany our present digital era: "We're in a peculiar age where everyone is watching us. Like everything is geared towards us, all the TV channels are geared towards us, basically. Everything. Like all marketing, like, they do so much marketing testing, like, at colleges. So everyone's looking at us."

It's ironic given all this sexualized advertising that in reality many college students are not as sexually active as advertisers are making them out to be. According to our best data analyses—outlined herein—college students are not as sexually active as they're thought to be, and most of the sex that happens predictably occurs within romantic relationships. No wonder they overestimate the sex that their peers are having. In light of this, are advertisers accidentally misinterpreting campus sex life, or do they have a financial stake in the perpetuation of a hookup culture? Do college students actually *like* the use of sex in advertising, even though they themselves are not as keen on casual sex as they're implied to be? We wish we knew for sure. What evidence exists, however, suggests that perhaps they *do* like it: a study of the images in 2,863 magazine advertisements found that ads targeted toward young adults were 65 percent more likely to contain provocatively dressed models and 128 percent more likely to connote sexual behavior than were ads targeted at older Americans.[49] That's understandable, given how Americans have long desensualized the aging process. Sales evidence affirms this. Abercrombie & Fitch—whose trademark name used to be splashed all over the clothing of collegians before it was usurped by Billabong, Hollister, and other more recent brand achievements—saw their revenue grow 30-fold in 10 years after pursuing a more sexually aggressive (and controversial) approach to marketing.[50] All the while, consumers continue to complain about sexually oriented advertising. They say they're less likely to buy such products, but the bottom line suggests that either they're lying, they're a vocal minority, or they're not a target sales market. Americans vote with their feet and with their wallets, and ad agencies know full well that Americans may say one thing and do another. Sex still sells. It's in our country's DNA.

SEX AND SOCIAL NETWORKING SITES

A serious examination of campus sex will come up short without a discussion of the role of texting and Facebook, the popular social-networking site. So far as we can tell, there is no systematic research evidence yet about sex and social networking sites, given the novelty of the latter, its dynamism, and the difficulty in studying the real behavioral effects of online activity. So it's unclear whether online social networking directly contributes to sexual behavior on campus. But we can make a variety of observations. Students rely on Facebook for lots of things, most of which have nothing at all to do with sex, like keeping in touch with distant friends and learning about social events. We claim, then, that its influence is more indirect and subtle. Facebook (and MySpace, etc.) can make persons and social interactions seem more sexually charged than they actually are.

While the cynic peering in from the outside might complain that here is yet more evidence of how public our formerly private conversations have become, online social networking is not simply about making one's personal life public. Instead, Facebook encourages the creation of mythical people: idealized, engaging, busy, attractive people always short on time, long on options, and (for some) persistently on the hunt. And although Facebook doesn't really police the countless digital photographs that users upload to their pages, most of the pictures of college life look the same: Terrence with his arms around his pals; Brittany flirting at a party; Danny chugging beer, lying on a sun-washed boat with friends. This phenomenon is key to how Facebook affects sex—via its collective impression. Seldom does a single page or picture matter much, but millions of pages and billions of photographs of *the same sort of thing* reinforce ideas that emerging-adult life is primarily about fun, flirting, partying, and delaying aging, work, relationship challenges, and responsibility.

Facebook also reinforces "hotness" as a paramount currency and form of stratification among young men and women. Only flattering digital images featuring fun and spontaneity suffice, since what matters is the visual—what can be seen and read about a person. Phone-based digital cameras have become a staple of campus social life, since good photographic material for users' Facebook pages is only a party away. And just like online porn creates the false impression that arousal is constant—since a photograph or video is always live—so Facebook creates the false impression that hotness is constant and the only real attribute that endures.[51] Hotness is even democratized—on Facebook, wealth matters less (since it takes more work to convey it), and power is difficult to discern. Sexiness is a calculable commodity and a primary source of prestige.

Sexualized conversation and innuendo can infuse young Facebook users' pages and conversations. Strategic users can make sure their status updates and wall posts are clever and coy, the sort of comments that require thought and would seldom be anticipated in normal, face-to-face conversation. If users don't like particular posts, they can be deleted. Since in these ways users can alter others' perceptions of themselves, this group of individuals has greater control over the "looking-glass self," the human penchant for viewing ourselves in the ways we believe others see us.[52] It's clear, then, that Facebook provides daily opportunities for emerging adults to live a vicarious life—to *seem* rather than to *be*.

While the visual retains primacy—unlike on Twitter—Facebook is hardly emotionless. Users' ability to update readers frequently—and here Twitter may trump Facebook—is often used not only to convey one's general disposition but to send subtle messages as well. For example, she might signal, "Jane hopes to have a little fun tonight." If she met Joe at a party last night, and they flirted and she's wondering if he's interested in meeting again sometime, she could write on her Facebook something like "Jane had an awesome time last night," with the assumption that Joe will scope out her page to see if she says anything about their interaction. Ironically, that this is all public is thought to *reduce* the embarrassment factor of actually having a face-to-face "are you interested in me" conversation with Joe. If he's not interested, he makes no further contact. On the other hand, if the tenuous relationship will or has ground to a halt, she might post "Jane is moving on with her life," or "Jane is too mature for certain people." Indeed, Facebook and Twitter are easy ways to turn down overtures from interested others, and since this all occurs online, *more of it* is certainly happening now than in pre-Facebook (and certainly pre-e-mail) days, when invitations and rejections had to be made in person or over the phone. The day of the anxious cold call has given way to emotionally "safer" (and yet less intimate) online messaging and texting.

Although we can only speculate here—hard data on this is difficult to come by—we suspect that online social networking contributes most readily to one particular campus sexual norm: the hookup. It's a logical conclusion. After all, social-networking sites are about rapidly meeting new people and maintaining superficial conversations rather than going deeper and growing more intimate with those you already know. This is arguably the very definition of hooking up, sans the sex. Indeed, hook-up options are only a post away. Facebook can also help diminish the awkward factor that exists after a hookup, because it allows the pair to keep in touch with brief wall posts that are neither pursuant of a more committed relationship nor completely disregarding the event.

Indeed, sexual relationships used to largely be over with the formal cessation of the relationship. Today, however, with the advent of social networking and the ease of maintaining "weak" ties online, a part of many, many relationships remains. In particular, it allows people to stay in touch with previous partners even while fashioning new ones. The old partners move on as well, but not entirely. When asked about online social networking, interviewees frequently described maintaining—and monitoring—such weak ties. Changes in relationship status among exes often prompted comments and conversations among exes, no doubt mixing old feelings into new relationships. It's as if connected emerging adults don't have clean sexual or romantic ties, but rather are increasingly interconnected in a web of present and past relationships, with future ones waiting in the wings.

To summarize, then: Facebook doesn't make sex happen. Nor does it *directly* foster a more sexually active campus. Instead we suggest

Facebook's nature—that it allows for rapid information gathering and assessment and the manipulation of others' perceptions about oneself—does nothing to diminish the mentality of the hookup and certainly reinforces the norm of serial monogamy. And it encourages the creation of false impressions, images, and stories about users, events, and relationships as more sexualized and subject to change than they really are or intend to be.

Concluding anything about collegiate use of Facebook or Twitter or other social-networking systems, however, is a temporary accomplishment. Their rapidly changing nature may make our assessment of it moot in just a few short years. Indeed, a very racy advertisement portraying a woman tugging at and peering down the front of a man's jeans recently appeared on our campus, promoting yet another online networking site, this one far less tame than Facebook. Clearly any conclusions on this subject are temporary.

Of course one unshakable reality is that *real* sexual interaction cannot remain online. No wonder real-life meetings that begin online are often disappointments—many of the people that seemed witty and social online are considerably different in person. Real life in a real relationship happens in real time. That this surprises tech-savvy emerging adults is testimony to the human penchant for self-deception and other-deception: we often want to convey to others that we're something we're not. Some of us are pretty good at it. None of us can remain so when it comes to a long-term, one-on-one sexual relationship with another person.

CONCLUSION

College campuses don't lack for sex appeal, yet the conventional wisdom that college students are the most sexually active young Americans is untrue. That distinction belongs to emerging adults who never enrolled at all. They are the most apt to have more frequent sex, to have more sexual partners, and to commence sexual relationships quickly. To be sure, the college hookup scene exists on most campuses, but it is not true that the entire student body is participating. The hookup culture also varies by region and type of campus: it is more prevalent at private universities, especially those in the northeast, than at other places. It's more apt to be found where gender ratios on campus are imbalanced toward more women. And yet media attention has long focused on campus sexual elites—a comparatively small group of students who live up to expectations about them. More students experience more sex in the traditional ways: they wait for the right person, or the right time; they're not so interested in hooking up; they want to feel love first. Despite popular impressions, most college students who are intelligent and ambitious are successful *because* they aren't risk-takers, not in spite of it. All this is not to suggest that the American college campus has gone sexually conservative or that students never hook up. It hasn't, and many do. Students are certainly having sex, but more sex occurs within romantic relationships than all the media chatter about hooking up has led us to believe.

FIVE

No Strings Attached?

Sex and Emotional Health

One half of the world cannot understand the pleasures of the other.

—*Jane Austen*

ELIZABETH IS SOMETHING of an enigma: She enjoys living in Boston, likes clubbing with her friends and meeting guys, and is flirtatious and fairly permissive in her sexual attitudes. There's just one complication—she doesn't like hooking up. She wants something deeper: "I want a serious relationship. I've, I mean my longest relationship was like, two months. Honestly. Which is nothing. That's not like, a relationship." Elizabeth even considers hooking up a nationwide social problem. Though she took a pledge of sexual abstinence in high school, she now thinks people who want to marry their first sexual partner are shortselling themselves: "You need to branch out a little bit, see what else is out there."

Elizabeth's coupling of permissive sexual attitudes with a principled objection to relationshipless sex is quite common among young women. They are not opposed to sex, and many of them are not virgins. But sex is largely unwanted apart from an emotional connection. Many have tried to have sex without emotion and found it impossible to sustain. Elizabeth *has* hooked up with men before, but she avoided having sex with them: "I mean, I would hook up with random, stupid people at clubs and, you know, whatever. And it's just stupid." She recognizes that having sex with them would have changed everything:

"When you go that far, it just brings it to a new level. . . . People get into a weird state and now they expect things."

By "weird," Elizabeth might actually mean "normal," since that is what happens to very many people after sex. They want more: more relationship, more sex, more security. People are connectional beings. And while we don't wish to reinforce simplistic stereotypes here, it seems obvious to us that emerging-adult women are more interested in such connections than men. Women are more conscious about sexual relationships and tend to romanticize them more than men do.[1] On average, women want more depth, exclusivity, maturity, and stability in their romantic relationships than men. Like many emerging adults, Elizabeth both pines for such connections and yet is sufficiently socialized into contemporary cosmopolitan gender norms to verbally disparage the idea of them. When asked whether a relationship is the optimal setting for sex, she opines:

> I don't know. I think maybe it's a better idea, because then there's emotional attachment and all that other bullshit [laughs]. Because then you start getting attached and all that other stupid stuff, so I think it's better when you are involved with somebody. But if you don't care, then go right ahead.

The challenge, of course, is getting one's heart to care less. Even in high school, girls who become romantically involved (with or without sex) are more likely to become depressed over time—and at rates that exceed those of boys—than are girls who don't, according to one study. The trend was so clear that the authors of the study aptly titled it, "You Don't Bring Me Anything but Down."[2]

After age 18, as we noted in chapter 3, most romantic relationships become sexual ones as well. But regrets don't disappear with age. A tally of interviewee-reported sexual regrets in one study of emerging adults reveals that 75 percent of those who reported no regrets were men, while two-thirds of those who did were women.[3] In terms of their own reflections about sex, then, women and men are not the same. Psychologists Elizabeth Paul and Kristen Hayes note women's mixed emotions in their study of casual sex and regret: "Although some women may have experienced positive emotions during the sexual encounter (i.e., feeling chosen, noticed, attractive), they are more likely to feel ashamed and regretful afterwards."[4] More likely, that is, than men.

Some young women get used to having sex without an emotional connection, and a small minority seems to prefer it this way. Traditional dating, meanwhile, seems an endangered species. Considered quaint and culturally conservative—certainly out of step in a cosmopolitan setting—dating implies a growing interest in a long-term commitment that one or both partners may fear. And dating, admittedly, takes time, which Elizabeth lacks: "I wish there was more [to my love life], but it's just like I have too many other things on my mind to do." So Elizabeth, like many young women, doesn't really date. And she, like many women, doesn't know what else to do. There is no script or standard operating procedure that men or women unequivocally like. There's no master narrative that has so far usurped the old story about generating and sustaining romance.

Researchers have published a great deal about the effects of clinical depression on sexual functioning but very little on the emotional-health consequences of sexual decision-making. Many scholars are no doubt concerned about appearing conservative or antisex. So entrenched is the solitary fixation on the physical risks of sex, that most researchers haven't even bothered to ask about negative *emotional* outcomes.[5] On the other hand, very many sexually active emerging adults know exactly what we're talking about, because they've felt it. Their negative emotions vary widely but can include guilt, regret, temporary self-loathing, rumination, diminished self-esteem, a sense of having used someone else or been used, a sense of having let yourself down, discomfort about having to lie or conceal sex from family, anxiety over the depth and course of the relationship, and concern over the place or role of sex in the relationship.

Others experience more intense versions of these, which can include obvious depressive symptoms, crying more than normal, difficulty shaking "the blues," and extreme anxiety over the future of the relationship. While the former, milder symptoms are important in their own right—and many give voice to them at some point in their emerging-adult years—our focus in this chapter is on the latter, the more obvious signs of sustained emotional trauma.

Of course, not everyone experiences negative emotional consequences from regretted sexual decisions. And among those who do, plenty exhibit no long-term effects. Dahlia, a 21-year-old from New York, has had three sexual partners since we last spoke with her (at 18, when she had had none) and seems comfortable navigating sex without involving her heart: "I don't think sex is such emotional stuff. For me, I never really thought of it that way." The majority of emerging adults navigate their relationships without bringing inordinate amounts of emotional pain or guilt (or pregnancies or STIs) upon themselves or others. But a significant minority suffers lasting emotional problems, and this chapter is about them.

DEPRESSION IN EMERGING ADULTHOOD

Adult use of antidepressants nearly tripled between the early and late 1990s. They are now the most prescribed drugs in the United States, exceeding even blood pressure medication.[6] While some see this as simply meeting a need, others see more ominous signs—the medicating of problems that may have a social or behavioral source rather than a chemical or biological one.

Among women aged 18–23 in the Add Health study, 16 percent have been diagnosed with depression at some point in their lives, and 8 percent say they are currently taking prescription antidepressants. These figures are two and three times higher, respectively, than young men. Some think the disparity is even greater, while others suspect men's depressive symptoms are underdiagnosed.[7] It's not just about gender differences in diagnosis, though. Even economists note that measures of women's happiness exhibit a sustained decline (compared with men's) that spans datasets, demographic groups, and countries.[8]

Understanding *why* young women are more depressed than young men is a challenge. Some of it no doubt involves how men and women experience and navigate romantic and sexual relationships. Plenty of it does not. And later in this chapter, we review the research about which direction the causal arrows seem to point—do sexual decisions breed emotional pain, is it the other way around, or is it both? The bottom line is that lots of people have emotional issues for lots of reasons—including sexual ones—but even if they're not about sex, problems can spill over into the sexual domain with little difficulty. Relationships are a major playing field upon which other life contests and struggles get worked out.

Why so many references so far to women's emotional responses, and almost none to men's? Because the central story about sex and emotional health is how powerful the empirical association is for women—and how weak it is among men. As we noted in chapter 3, women and men commonly experience sex differently. One of those differences is in how they process and exhibit emotional reactions—both positive and negative—to sexual experiences. There are of course no fixed, gendered ways in which people experience their relationships. But there are robust patterns that emerge from survey data analyses. These associations are probabilities, not certainties. We don't expect interviewees to always reflect the statistical associations. But they do help us understand the patterns that emerge.

THE EFFECTS OF SEX ON EMOTIONAL HEALTH

Table 5.1 displays simple associations between four sexual-action patterns and five emotional-health outcomes. When we examine simple connections between recent and lifetime sexual partnering, frequency of sex, and a variety of emotional-health indicators—including depression scales, self-reported episodic crying, life satisfaction, depression diagnoses, and current use of prescription antidepressants—it quickly becomes apparent that having more numerous sexual partners is associated with poorer emotional states in women, but not men. There's a linear association between both lifetime and recent partners and indicators of poorer emotional health, and women who report the greatest number of partners display the clearest symptoms of depression. Although earlier we noted that 16 percent of emerging-adult women said they'd ever been diagnosed with depression, among those who reported more than 10 lifetime partners, 32 percent had been diagnosed. Depression diagnoses run just under 50 percent among those who'd had more than 10 partners *in the past year*.

It's not just the high-end category of sexual partners that exhibits emotional-health problems, though. Women who report having had 2–5 or 6–10 partners—either in their lifetime or in the past year—also reveal poorer emotional health than do women who report zero or one partner. More of them currently take antidepressants, have ever been diagnosed with depression, say they're less satisfied with life, and score higher on the CES-D depression scale. At the same time, some women seem fine with this relationship style; after all, 70 percent of young women who report more than 10 recent partners are *not* on antidepressants.

The age at which women first had sex is also associated with emotional health. Like in journalist Paula Kamen's study, women in our study who had lost their virginity at a comparatively young age "stood out from the rest of the interview sample as having more regrets and confusion about their recent behavior."[9] The figures aren't nearly as striking as those related to numbers of partners, but they are robust across the five measures. The frequency at which men and women report having sex, however, is largely unrelated to emotional-health

TABLE 5.1 Emotional Health Outcomes by Sexual Activity Patterns, Never-Married Women / Men Ages 18–23

	Average depression scale score[a]	% Cry every day or almost every day	% Satisfied or very satisfied with life	% Ever diagnosed with depression	% Taking antide-pressants
Lifetime Number of Sex Partners					
0	4.5 / 4.2	2.0 / 1.2	86.2 / 86.6	10.3 / 4.7	4.0 / 3.1
1	4.8 / 3.8	5.2 / 2.1	85.4 / 86.2	11.5 / 8.1	6.7 / 4.4
2–5	4.6 / 4.1	5.3 / 0.7	84.9 / 83.3	14.4 / 6.8	7.0 / 2.4
6–10	5.4 / 4.2	5.2 / 1.4	78.6 / 79.3	18.4 / 7.7	10.3 / 3.4
11+	6.2 / 4.2	8.0 / 0.3	73.5 / 81.7	31.6 / 10.6	15.3 / 3.0
Number of Sex Partners in Last Year					
0	4.7 / 4.1	2.8 / 1.2	84.2 / 83.8	11.7 / 5.7	4.9 / 3.5
1	4.6 / 3.9	5.9 / 1.1	85.8 / 86.7	15.0 / 8.1	6.9 / 3.2
2–5	5.4 / 4.4	5.3 / 1.2	77.7 / 80.0	19.5 / 7.2	11.6 / 2.8
6–10	5.9 / 4.6	3.1 / <1.0	72.3 / 73.5	19.6 / 10.3	11.8 / 1.4
11+	8.6 / 2.9	13.0 / <1.0	56.1 / 86.6	48.1 / 11.4	29.3 / 3.0
Frequency of Intercourse in Last Year					
0	4.7 / 4.1	2.8 / 1.2	84.1 / 83.6	11.6 / 5.5	4.8 / 3.5
1–3	5.3 / 4.8	6.6 / 2.4	85.8 / 81.9	18.6 / 9.5	9.7 / 4.1
4–15	5.2 / 4.2	5.5 / 0.3	78.2 / 81.9	13.5 / 7.4	6.0 / 3.7
16–40	4.8 / 3.8	4.4 / 0.7	82.2 / 85.4	14.0 / 5.0	8.8 / 1.7
41–75	5.1 / 4.1	7.0 / 0.6	82.5 / 81.9	17.0 / 10.3	8.1 / 3.2
76–100	4.8 / 4.1	5.6 / 2.5	87.4 / 82.7	22.4 / 8.0	8.9 / 3.4
101+	4.8 / 3.6	6.7 / 0.2	81.1 / 84.4	21.5 / 9.8	13.1 / 2.2

TABLE 5.1 (continued)

	Average depression scale score[a]	% Cry every day or almost every day	% Satisfied or very satisfied with life	% Ever diagnosed with depression	% Taking antide-pressants
Had First					
Sex before					
Age 16					
Yes	5.6 / 4.5	7.3 / 1.3	76.7 / 80.1	22.0 / 8.7	9.4 / 2.6
No	4.6 / 3.9	4.0 / 0.5	85.5 / 84.6	13.0 / 6.7	7.2 / 3.2

Source: Add Health.

[a]*The Add Health depression index is a shortened version of the common CES-D depression index. It's calculated from agreement with the following set of survey statements, using "during the past seven days" as a metric for the respondent: "You were bothered by things that usually don't bother you," "You could not shake off the blues, even with help from your family and your friends," "You felt that you were just as good as other people," "You had trouble keeping your mind on what you were doing," "You were depressed," "You were too tired to do things," "You enjoyed life," "You were sad," and "You felt that people disliked you."*

outcomes in either direction. So the story is not about the sex, then. We will revisit this claim shortly.

Men's sexual partnership and behavior patterns, on the other hand, display no clear associations with any depressive symptoms, except having been diagnosed with depression. Even this link is far weaker than among women. Among those who report the highest number (more than 10) of lifetime or recent sexual partners, just 11 percent say they've ever been diagnosed with depression—three to four times fewer than among women. Besides that, no other obviously linear association exists between sex and emotional health self-reports among emerging-adult men. This is not to suggest that no young men feel badly about sexual relationships gone awry or hookups they've regretted. Some do, and we'll discuss men's emotional responses later in this chapter. But such men are uncommon, and in a general analysis of data across thousands of men like them in the United States, their experiences don't stand out. Sure, some men exhibit diminished life satisfaction, are diagnosed with depression, and take antidepressants. They just don't generally do so as a result of sexual decision-making patterns or relationship histories.

Emotional health is a deep well, and plunging its depths is complicated. It certainly involves both things that happen to people as well as things they choose to do, things from the past as well as more immediate actions. As scientists, we can only make inferences from the facts we've gathered. And from what we've learned so far, adding sexual partners seems more destructive to a woman's sexual well-being than is the act of intercourse itself—which generally appears neutral or even positive. But sexual partners and sexual practice go together. How are we supposed to sort out this phenomenon, apart from simplistic claims that more partners mean more pain? And what about all the baggage that people bring forward into their relationships? In order to address these concerns, we built and tested a comprehensive conceptual model (Figure 5.1) of the effects of sex on emotional health. The model suggests that current sexual-activity patterns may directly affect emerging adults' emotional-health status but may also be themselves shaped by—and perhaps overshadowed in their influence by—the experience of sexual trauma (such as self-reported childhood sexual abuse) and early adolescent sexual activity. Other factors believed to be associated both with current sexual-activity patterns and emotional health include individuals' own appraisals of themselves as popular, intelligent, attractive, and overweight (or not) as well as demographic, family, and other unalterable influences (like race/ethnicity and age).

Tables A5.1 through A5.3 (in appendix A, pp. 259–62) detail results from more advanced statistical models that predict emotional-health problems in women as a function of a variety of sexual and demographic effects.[10] For the sake of brevity, we will only highlight them here. We don't report results for men, because as Table 5.1 suggests, there's nothing much there to talk about.

In the simplest models—the ones exploring only the effects of number of lifetime partners, recent partners, recent sexual frequency,

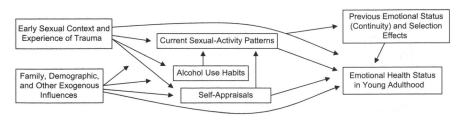

FIGURE 5.1 Conceptual Model of the Effects of Heterosexual-Activity Patterns on Emotional-Health Status.

and age (as a control)—the results suggest a stable pattern: The more lifetime partners women have had, the higher their depression-scale score and likelihood of diagnosis, the more crying they report, the lower their life satisfaction, and the more likely it is that they're currently taking antidepressants. Only on life satisfaction does an independent effect of *recent* partners appear.[11]

When we add a set of other variables—including drinking frequency, ever having had an abortion, sexual abuse by a parent or other adult, sex before 16, and self-reported same-sex attraction, the association between emotional health and lifetime sexual partners remains significant for three of the five outcomes (depression-scale score, diagnosis, and crying). Frequency of sex, however, becomes significantly *positive* in its effect on a lower depression score and greater life satisfaction, confirming that there's something to the theory about the positive effects of intercourse.

The introduction of a large set of demographic effects (in the third and final set of models) as well as a measure of the outcome at an earlier wave, as a way of predicting stability and change in emotional-health outcomes over time, suggests that the number of lifetime sexual partners appears to affect emotional health largely through earlier indicators of emotional health. In other words, a significant share of the emotional problems incurred from having previous partners arguably happens earlier in the emerging-adult life course. That makes sense. The long-term effects may not go away, since we see their association with *present* emotional health in earlier models and in Table 5.1. But the damage was done earlier, when those partnerships were formed, or—more likely—when they were ended.

While our purpose in this chapter remains largely to assess the effects of partner counts and sexual frequency on emotional health, it's worth noting that these more *common* experiences seem to alter emotional health less reliably than do the more *uncommon* events or experiences like abortion, same-sex attraction, and sexual abuse. These remain firmly associated with emotional-health difficulties even after accounting for other indicators. Having experienced an abortion remains associated with a higher depression-scale score, while past abuse predicts both that as well as depression diagnosis and lower life satisfaction. Same-sex attraction is significantly associated with all five outcomes.[12]

Other studies certainly concur about childhood sexual abuse; it is powerfully associated with adult-onset depression for both men and women. Americans know viscerally and intellectually that sexual abuse is a terrible thing, and they call vehemently for its punishment. It can leave in its wake a pathway to emotional brokenness, self-destructiveness, and poor sexual decision-making. A history of such abuse is more common for girls than boys; the ratio of girls to boys as victims of sexual abuse is as high as 12 to 1. Most studies estimate an overall incidence rate in the population of between 6 and 15 percent, depending on how it is defined.[13]

Sexual Types and Emotional Health

In lived reality, there are lots of different sexual relationship styles and experiences, and people mix and match them. In one three-year span, for example, Jane Doe might have had a one-night stand with one man, a week-long fling with another, and a six-month-long relationship with another. And then she may be presently in the middle of a year-long relationship. The one-nighter likely involved only one or two sex acts, the week-long fling perhaps several, and the pair of longer relationships would no doubt exhibit varying frequencies of sex and might not have become sexual until weeks or months into them. Advanced statistical models like those we just discussed pick apart each of the different aspects of a sexual and personal history and evaluate their *independent* effects: the existence of sexual relationships, how many of them, the frequency (or lack) of sex in the past year, etc. But people experience all these things in a bundle. To only pull them apart and assess their independent effects—like we just did—would artificially force clear distinctions among real people's experiences where such boundaries don't typically exist. More useful, then, is a presentation of sexual *types*. We created eight types of *common sexual actor patterns* that treat people as unities and yet capture variation in four major experiences:

1. More distant sexual partner history
2. Recent sexual partner history
3. Current relationship status
4. Frequency of sex (if currently in a relationship)

Although the possible permutations of sexual histories are endless, we settled on these eight in part because of what we learned from Table 5.1—that multiple partnering is suboptimal for emotional health (especially for women) but that sexual frequency and current relationship status might well alter the negative consequences of multiple partnering. Specifically, we have created and defined for analysis these groups:

Group 1: Virgins (have not yet had vaginal intercourse) not currently in a relationship

Group 2: Virgins currently in a romantic relationship

Group 3: Those with one or two lifetime sexual partners, but none in the past year

Group 4: Those with one or two lifetime partners, who are currently in a sexual relationship that has lasted at least one year, having had sex at least 30 times in the past year

Group 5: Those with 5–9 lifetime sex partners, including 2–3 in the past year, but none currently

Group 6: Those with 5–9 lifetime sex partners but who are currently in a sexual relationship that has lasted at least one year, having had sex at least 30 times in the past year

Group 7: Those with 10 or more lifetime partners, at least two in the past year, but none currently

Group 8: Those with 10 or more lifetime partners but who are currently in a sexual relationship that has lasted at least one year, having had sex at least 30 times in the past year

Not every 18- to 23-year-old in the Add Health study fits one of these groups, of course, but over 4,600 do. And there's much about emerging adults' sexual history to which such a simple typing cannot do justice, including things like how long until a relationship becomes sexual and how long it lasts. But by creating such categories that blend the past and present with the actual experience of regular intercourse, we can bring clarity and an alternative perspective to the "independent effects" evaluation of sex and emotional health in Tables 5.1 and A5.1–A5.3.

Taking advantage of this perspective, Table 5.2 reinforces the conclusion that a *sustained pattern* of serial monogamy—implying a series of failed relationships—hurts women far more than it hurts men. The results also suggest that women who are either virgins or who are currently in a sexual relationship (with no more than one other previous partner) that has so far lasted at least one year are the most emotionally stable types. The former report the fewest recent experiences of depressive bouts and crying. The latter exhibit the lowest scores on the depression scale, least antidepressant use, and the highest levels of life satisfaction.

Among those with a more extensive sexual history, there's nothing about having had seven sexual partners that necessarily makes one feel worse than having had six, or 12 versus 10. Rather, as our analyses indicate, it is in the general adding of partners that the problem lies;

TABLE 5.2 Emotional Health Outcomes by Sexual Partnerships and Behaviors, Never-Married 18- to 23-Year-Olds

	Mean depression score	Percent depressed at least some-times in last 7 days	Percent ever diagnosed with depression	Percent taking antide-pressants	Percent cried every day or almost every day in last 7 days	Percent satisfied or very satisfied with life
Men (Groups 1–8)						
Virgins not in a relationship	4.40	21.5	5.8	3.7	0.9	85.1
Virgins in a relationship	3.65	17.1	0.9	1.3	2.5	91.7
1–2 partners, none in past yr	4.16	23.0	8.6	4.9	1.1	78.4
1–2 partners, one current	3.06	14.5	8.0	2.9	0.6	87.7
5–9 partners, 2–3 in past yr	4.30	29.2	4.8	2.0	<0.1	78.9
5–9 partners, one current	3.75	23.7	11.4	0.6	<0.1	87.3
10+ partners, 2–3 in past yr	4.21	27.4	9.9	2.7	0.4	79.9

10+ partners, one current	4.74	30.7	5.3	2.5	2.8	74.8

Women (Groups 1–8)

Virgins not in a relationship	4.48	19.4	9.8	3.8	2.0	86.2
Virgins in a relationship	4.61	19.3	12.2	4.9	2.0	86.2
1–2 partners, none in past yr	5.59	34.6	19.7	8.3	3.0	80.6
1–2 partners, one current	3.91	22.8	10.0	3.7	2.6	90.1
5–9 partners, 2–3 in past yr	5.67	44.6	22.2	17.1	7.6	74.4
5–9 partners, one current	4.94	27.8	15.6	6.0	7.0	83.0
10+ partners, 2–3 in past yr	6.11	39.7	26.9	14.1	7.3	68.1
10+ partners, one current	5.44	34.4	34.7	17.4	4.4	81.2

Source: Add Health.

amassing sexual partners betrays a lack of relationship security. There is no magic number of partners to avoid other than "more."

And as mentioned before, not all women consider sex without security a negative experience. A minority of emerging-adult women exhibit a set of personality characteristics that shield them from the pain other women may feel with uncommitted sex. Scholars have distinguished types of women who engage in casual sexual relationships, including the *Ludic* and the *Eros* types. The former pursue sex for the game-like competition of it and the experience of conquest, mimicking the "alpha male," while the latter pursue it for the powerful physical attraction and anticipation of emotional connection.[14] The former feel considerably less emotion over failed sexual relationships than the latter; they appear to enjoy sex as a recreational activity more than a bonding one. The latter may form short-term relationships but generally think they shouldn't; a longer relationship is really what they wish for.

Carlita, a 20-year-old student at a state university in Pennsylvania, is ambitious, brash, defiant, and unreligious. She has witnessed the trauma that poor sexual decision-making has reaped in the lives of her friends. As a result, she's become exceedingly planful about sex and is no longer in such a hurry. Carlita didn't always think this way: she's had several sex partners but none in the past three years. So extensively have her friends been hurt by their sexual decisions that Carlita thinks unprotected sex is wrong in and of itself. Now she dates but is just not interested in sex. Her early experiences lacked mutual pleasure, which is often a casualty of relationships that are quick to sex:

> If you're not with someone that you actually like, then the sex is gonna suck, you know. Um, especially when you have sex when you're younger; nobody really knows what they're doing. It's gonna suck. Like, I wish somebody would have told me beforehand [that] you're really not in for much, you know. . . . Like what the hell you getting all excited about?

If Carlita could go back and do things differently, she would:

> Yeah, I would have just not done it. Okay maybe like once or twice. But you can't really pick like, "Oh, he's gonna be fun." Or, "He's not." So you would have had to give it a try. So I guess the bad experience was like, "Well, you're gonna suck, I can tell already. This isn't worth my time." But yeah, I probably would have just not done it.

Our data and other studies concur with Carlita's observations: emerging adults who engage in shorter and more frequent sexual relationships exhibit lower self-esteem and more guilt than those who are either abstinent or sexually active only within the confines of a sustained romantic relationship.[15]

Even getting married—deciding to settle down with only one sex partner for good—doesn't erase the emotional challenges for women who've had numerous sex partners in their lifetime. While no association with depressive symptoms is apparent among now-married young women who've had up to four sex partners in their lifetime, problems appear among those who've had 5–10, and even more among those who've had more than 10 partners (results not shown). On all six outcomes, such women display more intense emotional difficulties. Among those who've had more than 10 partners, 41 percent report being depressed at least some time in the past seven days. Just over 14 percent are actively taking antidepressants, and only 79 percent say they're satisfied or very satisfied with their life. So while the security of a marital relationship can diminish sex-related emotional-health problems, it doesn't often take them away.

What about men? What does the "types" analysis tell us about them? Very little that we didn't already learn from Table 5.1. Few patterns are discernable, and those that are remain weak when contrasted with the women's patterns. No group of men exceeds a depression-scale score of five, whereas four of the eight women's groups do. It appears that men with fewer lifetime partners report less frequent recent depressive bouts, and men currently in a sexual relationship report better emotional health, regardless of the number of previous, failed relationships.

SEXUAL SECURITY AND EMOTIONAL HEALTH

Sexual relationships in emerging adulthood, often removed several years from more enduring relational commitments like marriage, tend to wrestle with the subject of security. Many wonder how much commitment is "enough" to merit a sexual component in a relationship. Both conceptual and actual answers vary widely in the minds and actions of emerging adults, but the subject of security itself recurs with regularity. In analyzing interview transcripts, we were struck by the language that many young adults use to convey their ambivalence over their sexual relationships—their meaning, their stability, and their future. They don't wish to be "tied down" to one person for the long run, but they do enjoy the company and the sex. When deeper feelings emerge from only one partner, it's often cast by the other in language like, "He was getting a little possessive," or "She started getting clingy." On our campus fraternity members recognize such symptoms and declare their girlfriends as having a problem: "they're crazy," one asserts. We're not so sure. Maybe their response to sex is *not* abnormal.

What happens next can compound the problem. A common scenario in many emerging-adult sexual relationships evolves like this: "I think probably one of the reasons I broke up is that . . . we were having issues, and I didn't feel that we were a married couple, so I didn't feel the need to work them out." This quote comes from Shelby, an 18-year-old from New York, who is very independent and confident, the (new) classically competitive young woman. She was making reference to the universal experience of conflict in romantic relationships, yet barring a higher level of commitment, she felt little impulse to work through the conflict. Notice her remarks are deferential to marriage—it's a big deal, and it's where and when conflicts really have to be worked out and solved. But a late-teen relationship isn't marriage, and so there's no pressure. Such a model works for Shelby, who seems no worse off emotionally for concluding the relationship. Others don't fare nearly so well. When we asked Sean (22, from Alabama) if he thought he had ever hurt anyone emotionally, he knew the answer:

> Yeah, that one I left. [*Oh right, okay. . . . How did you know that?*] Uh, well, I broke up with her. That was my freshman year and I was partying a lot and like, doing some drugs, and I was kind of in for the ride. And uh, yeah, I broke up with her, and she cried a lot, and she was really sad, I could tell. I think that she had been kind of hurt before and uh, so she, when we were dating, she was real scared [about] commitment. So I mean I know when I broke with her it hurt her. [*So do you think like, if you had just been dating and not been having sex, if you'd broken up with her, it would have been the same?*] Ah, it would have been a lot easier. [*What do you mean, for her, or for you, too?*] Yeah, I still, there's one thing. Once you've had sex with someone, it uh, it kind of takes the relationship to a whole other level whether you think it does or not. Especially as far as a girl is concerned. So that's, I think it's kind of a plus if you break up with someone you haven't had sex with.

Sex apart from security can be fun. Some, especially men, say it's more erotic than relational sex.[16] Carlita emphatically disagreed. Minimally, it creates awkward moments. More likely, it ushers in uncertainty and anxiety about the status of the relationship, which leads to either a persistent lack of clarity about its status—an unsatisfying state to many—or to clarification, or to conflict. And relationship conflict in the absence of security often seems more easily dealt with by ending the relationship, as it did for Shelby and Sean.

An increasing number of young men and women are having a difficult time discerning exactly *how* to generate a secure relationship and what it might look like. When we talk about marriage in the classroom and describe its relative security, most—especially women—like what they hear. They want it for themselves. But how they get from where they're at to where they'd like to go is often a big mystery. And most young men have no interest in helping them find it at present. Journalist Jonathan Zimmerman, writing about the gender gap in satisfactions with hooking-up, notes how the absence of a dating script plays to men's interests: "I've heard plenty of my 40- and 50-something male peers complain that they were born several decades too early [and thus missed out on hooking up]. But I have never, ever heard a woman say she'd prefer today's hooking-up system to the dating rituals we grew up with."[17]

So what is it that is hidden deep underneath the thrill of the chase, the endless conversations among friends, and the relatively rapid consummation of relationships? We suggest there lies a very human desire to matter—and a quest for security. The problem is that we have purchased the expensive idea that security is found not in human relationships but in personal accomplishments and appearances. It's been a costly acquisition. "I think the ease of hooking up has, like, made people forget what they truly want," says Naomi, a Duke University student interviewed in a *Rolling Stone* article about the lacrosse scandal.[18] "People assume that there are two very distinct elements in a relationship, one emotional and one sexual, and they pretend like there are clean lines between them." She concludes that women's hard-fought values aren't easily recognized in the sexual decisions she sees around her: "There's a big difference between the global values and feminist ideals we think we should be subscribing to and the behavior a lot of us exhibit. And I do it too," she confesses.

Journalist Paula Kamen notes that of the women she interviewed, "Even those with the most promiscuous pasts gave the sexual revolution of the 1970s (and 1980s) a very mixed review, inclined toward the negative." One remarked frankly, "I see more freedom staying with one person who I feel I can explore all the possibilities with than from going from bed to bed to bed. . . . I think the sexual revolution was a big joke. I really do." Another asserts, "We separate love from heart, from thought, from God—and that's not organically [what] we as human beings are."[19] While orgasms can be had, truly satisfying sex remains elusive. Women, on average, don't want to *have sex with*. They want to be made love to. The results bear this out: the partnership findings reveal that *having sex with* puts the focus on the partner, who it is, the nature of their relationship, etc. Being made love to implies a secure relationship and puts the focus on the benefits of the act.

THE SEX ITSELF IS NOT THE PROBLEM

The act can indeed pay benefits. Table 5.2 also reveals that, partner history aside, nonvirgin women's emotional health is better when they're in a relationship than when they're not. The bottom four rows of very experienced sexual types are distinguished only by the fact that groups 6 and 8 are currently in a relationship that has lasted at least a year, whereas groups 5 and 7 are not. The emotional health of groups 6 and 8 is consistently better than that of groups 5 and 7. Even still, the effects of past decisions are evident: group 8 has considerable experience with antidepressants and previous depression diagnoses, and they still cry more than average. Thus women who report being in a relationship, regardless of how many previous partners they've had, typically exhibit better emotional health outcomes than women who've had *comparable numbers* of previous partners but aren't currently in a relationship.

The story, then, is not so much about avoiding sexual relationships but *sustaining* a relationship rather than cycling in and out of them. Women who've never started such a relationship seem quite content to have avoided the drama of them. Women who *are* in one are in better shape than women who *were*. This suggests that it's not the sex per se that causes the (emotional) problem. Indeed, the sex is operating as it tends to—bonding persons, deepening relationships, and fostering greater interpersonal intimacy.

Carlita complained about the bad sex that often characterized her relationships and resolved to charge a much higher "price" next time. Her grievances make good biological sense. The hormone oxytocin is released during orgasm in both sexes; inside the brain, oxytocin is involved in social recognition and bonding, and it may also contribute to the formation of trust between people. It's the same hormone that is released during breastfeeding, which bonds mother to child. Mutually pleasurable sexual relationships generate more orgasms, more oxytocin, and more bonding sentiments, intentions, and emotions. It's not that orgasms can't be had in uncommitted relationships; they most certainly can. But as we saw in chapter 3, such relationships are inherently far more fragile than romantic ones. They really can't be stable, given what we know about sex. And you can bet that women end them far more often than men, not because they dislike the sex or perhaps even the partner, but because they can't tolerate the instability. "No strings attached" language is ubiquitous in contemporary sexual scripts, but it's largely a fiction. For most women, the strings are what makes sex good.[20]

Holly, the 19-year-old from Oregon we first met in chapter 2, characterizes the push and pull of sexual relationships with surprising candor. Even now, after obvious and recent emotional pain, she still misses the thrill of desiring and being desired. She now counsels patience— waiting to have sex—after she herself had four partners in the past 18 months: "I was happier before . . . 'cause I didn't have sex until I was 18, and I was probably happier before it. Before I knew what I was missing." Sex with her first partner, a boyfriend named Josh, felt secure and good. Indeed, sex in a romantic context is not often associated with depressive symptoms for women, while expressions of love and commitment reduce instances of regret for both men and women.[21] But the relationship with Josh ended, and the sex that Holly's had since then has attempted to recapture those feelings, with little success. Three of her partners were friends (with each other). Drinking made it easier, both to accomplish and to forget:

Even though I feel like you're coherent enough to make choices most of the time, you don't remember everything that you did. Not all of it, at least not in detail. And so I've seen on a couple of friends' [online] profiles a couple of times some really not flattering video footage [of me]. But for the most part I just laugh, and I'm like, "Well, I brought that on myself." [*But you regret that?*] Oh, definitely. It was just a really bad call. I didn't care about him. He did not care about me. And I hurt myself a lot more than I helped myself by doing that. I didn't feel that liberation or that freedom that supposedly comes from that. [*How did it hurt you? Emotionally? Is it that?*] I would say just for a while after that I just didn't feel like I deserved to have any self-respect. 'Cause I hadn't done anything [to merit self-respect]. [*So you violated a standard that you once held yourself to?*] Yeah, that's something, one of my own core beliefs that I completely and totally disregarded for fun. . . . And you should always look past the moment. You always should. And I totally didn't. So then when you have no respect for yourself over something like that, it doesn't bother you as much when people don't have respect for you, because you know that they're right to think that. And I think the thing that finally snapped me out of it was when . . . I slept with him and then a couple of his other roommates were, like, sort of hookups, but not really . . . and so I mean it was just not a good situation. [*So you were sort of hooking up with some of the other people in the same place?*] Yeah. [*That could be a problem.*] Yeah, and I mean nothing that big of a deal, but still. And one of the roommates—this was all in the house, this all happened in the same house with the same group of five guys—and one of them called me a party favor. . . . And I think that that's finally what snapped me out of it a little bit. . . . See, I have a lot of trouble since Josh of looking past the moment. Because you know exactly where it can go and how great it can be, and both people have already been there. Before either of you have done it, before you've ever done it, it's so easy to not do it, because you don't know. It's such a big deal, because it's the first time. And now that you've been there, it's there, and it's available. And do I really feel that great, the fact that I did? Not really. . . . At this point, I'm rebuilding my self-respect. . . . I do have these core beliefs that are so easy to say. But then when I'm actually faced with it, I have a lot of trouble. I really do. I have a big problem. . . . [*So is it more an intimacy, relational thing, or is it just sheer pleasure?*] Well, with Trevor and with Darren, it was definitely like we really felt like we were going somewhere in our relationship. Like me and Trevor were very misguided, but we really thought that we were building something amazing. And with Darren, it was just he was this really great guy— how could I not fall in love with him? It'll come, right? And so with them, it was definitely misguided. It was a conscious choice. But I was like, "Oh, well I'm gonna be with these guys for awhile; this is someone who I can see a future with," even as misguided as it was. And see, that's the problem with calling the shots so early in a relationship is that you have no idea. When you're past puppy love, there's no telling. And I guess that's the only way that I know that I'm right in saying what I do about waiting and stuff like that, because I've been there, and I've made the wrong choice.

Going somewhere. Building something. Finding a future with someone. Even though Holly bedded four men in 18 months, each encounter was built on the hope of making something more permanent develop. Given emerging-adult women's interest in security, it's a noble sentiment. It just doesn't work. Many women who agree to sex early in a relationship hope for a degree of "appreciation" in return, but sex bargained for too little—as we documented in chapter 3—seldom generates something so ambitious as a commitment to fidelity and security. Holly's trio of friends appreciated her, but only as a party favor.

On the other hand, when it's within a stable, romantic context, sex is seldom associated with depressive symptoms. In that case, it displays either positive or neutral emotional-health outcomes. Apart from any ideals about it, relational sex functions for many partners (though not for everyone) to deepen and secure a more enduring interpersonal bond. Patrick (21, from Oklahoma) notes this trait:

> Somehow, if we have sex or something, that [conflict] kind of goes away. And it, I don't, I don't really understand it, because I don't understand girls and how they think, but um, it does seem to, it does seem to make things like that better. Um, if it's in like a, um . . . good situation, like I said before.

The trick is in deciphering when one is in a good situation. Unfortunately, many emerging adults are mistaken when they interpret both the seriousness and the security of their relationships. Like no shortage of interviewees, Michelle (20, from Oklahoma), whom we first met in chapter 3, underestimated the security of her first serious romantic relationship and began having sex as a way to solve problems. But her plan backfired; it was *not* a romantic experience, not by a long shot. A year and a half later, the two aren't together but communicate almost daily. He has a new girlfriend, with whom he's sexually active, but Michelle remains fond of him and admits wondering if they'll eventually get back together. She claims to feel a connection to him that words fail to express. Indeed, intercourse bonds. So it's not that sex cannot help women solve relationship problems. It can. But it typically requires a far more significant level of relationship security than they are led to believe. Unfortunately, romanticized myths circulate widely in both media and conversations among peers. Channing (22, from Texas) describes this genre of interpersonal conversation about sex without security:

> We always tell each other the same thing when it happens, and just kind of, things like, "That happens, and there is no use feeling bad about it. It's, you know, at least you were safe," and "If you don't want to talk to the person, you don't have to." And just kind of, we always just talk each other through that, those sorts of situations.

Channing's group of confidantes represents a plausibility structure, a network of friends and acquaintances that tacitly, subtly, and sometimes even nonverbally affirm some ideas and scripts as good and others as bad. But in cases of sex without security, the structure is not enough to stave off the symptoms their minds and bodies are emitting. As one interviewee confessed, "It's one of those things where you convince yourself that you're okay with it, but you're not, not at all."[22]

Semen: An Antidepressant?

The neutral-to-positive association between sexual frequency and emotional state in women (as noted in Tables A5.1 through A5.3, pp. 259–62) suggests there just might be something to the connection recently noted between the absorption of semen and better emotional health in female young adults.[23] In a study of college students' sexual habits, women who had sex without a condom (though perhaps with another form of contraception) were significantly less depressed than were women who were altogether abstinent or women who had sex with a condom, regardless of sexual frequency or relationship duration. It's a provocative thesis, no doubt. But it's one worth exploring. Depressive symptoms among women who used condoms were proportional to their consistency of condom use: the more they used them, the more depression they report. Moreover, women who didn't use condoms reported having sex twice as often as women who always used condoms.

Unfortunately, the study didn't explore the context of the sexual relationships. It is very possible that the lack of condom usage in a relationship is a sign of trust, itself a builder of positive emotion. The authors do, however, note the science that may be partly responsible for their results: semen may have antidepressant properties, because it contains several mood-altering chemicals, including testosterone, estrogen, follicle-stimulating hormone (FSH), luteinizing hormone (LH), prolactin, and prostaglandins, which are more readily absorbed into the vaginal wall than into the skin (or the mouth).

Anthropologist Helen Fisher notes this connection between hormones and emotion as an explanation of why hooking up can hurt. Sex, she writes, can stimulate attachment as well as sentiments of romantic love. But casual sexual arrangements bank on a way of human functioning that seems dissonant with natural biology—people (especially women) just don't work that way:[24]

> Many young adults have had sex with "just a friend" and never fallen
> in love. But it can happen, perhaps because increasing activity of

testosterone associated with the sex drive can elevate the activity of dopamine, one of the neurotransmitters associated with romance. . . . Hence teens and young adults who copulate with "just a friend" are biologically susceptible to falling in love.

Humans are complicated animals, notes Fisher: "Despite the interactions between these three brain systems—lust, romantic love, and attachment—these mating drives can also act independently. You can feel profound attachment for a long-term partner *while* you feel romantic passion for someone else *while* you feel the sex drive for a range of other individuals." But breaking bonds to pursue sex doesn't often work out well: in one study, 21 percent of casual sex partners were actually cheating on someone else at the time; such infidelity itself is linked with depressive symptoms.[25]

Here again, women think and feel differently than men do: In the study of casual sex among college students that we've highlighted several times in this chapter, 18 percent of women but only 3 percent of men believed that their most recent casual sexual encounter was "the beginning of a romance."[26] It's an ironic thing that many who seek sex without strings—in the hope that it *won't* complicate their life or generate emotional vulnerability within them—get exactly that: complicated feelings and hurt.[27]

Masturbation doesn't really cut it as a replacement to intercourse, either. It relieves pent-up sexual tension, of course, but it's hardly the same sense of emotional connection as paired intercourse. There's a physiological reason for that, too: research into orgasms notes that prolactin—a hormone that serves to diminish arousal and thus provide sexual satiety—is released following intercourse at a rate *five times* that following masturbation.[28] Thus intercourse is more satisfying than masturbation, something most adults already know but can't quite explain.

ABORTION AND EMOTIONAL HEALTH

Robin, a 19-year-old high-school dropout from New Hampshire, freely confesses to feeling old despite her age. Although she dropped out of high school, she hopes and intends to enroll in a local community college soon and then eventually transfer to a school of arts in a different city. Raised Catholic, she attended Catholic school for a time. But the subject of religion is distant to her now. She "used to go to

Mass all the time," but now finds the Bible "kind of far-fetched." She reads it only "for shits and giggles." Some of her religious antagonism, and some of her general malaise, may have to do with her abortion. Robin had had one since the last time she was interviewed; the subject came up unsolicited when we asked whether she had been involved in any things that she thought were wrong:

> Yeah. And I don't like feel comfortable telling you this, but I had an abortion . . . which I think is definitely wrong. But I definitely knew I couldn't take care of it so . . . [*Kind of a lesser of two evils kind of thing?*] Yeah. [*Okay, so why did you think it was wrong? Was it some belief you had?*] Probably because it probably deserved to live, like, you never know who it could have been, you know? [*How did you decide what to do?*] Basically my boyfriend. He really, he wasn't like mad about it, obviously since he was involved in it. . . . He said it was my decision really, obviously. But he said he'd rather not have it and he wants to like keep his money growing and stuff. And he didn't feel like neither him nor I could take care of the kid, so.

Robin told us she struggles with "depression and like insomnia and stuff. Like really, I have like, chronic insomnia. I've been taking sleeping pills for like, a year and a half now. So that's kind of bad, I guess." She's currently on medication but no longer seeing a psychologist, and she spends most of her time just sitting at home, smoking, watching TV, playing video games, and occasionally hanging out with her boyfriend, who is employed. What caused her depression and sleeplessness?

> Just thinking about the past actually, like what I've done to myself or what I've done to other people, stuff like that. . . . I actually had to end up going to like, a mental hospital, because I was actually getting better at that time, but my mom found some poetry that I wrote that she thought was bad, so she gave it to my psychologist, and I had to go to a mental hospital. Like I got out the next day, but it really scared me. It was really creepy; people in there are actually really gone.

She's getting better, but Robin is not happy with her current life. Why not?

> Just my laziness, like I said before. I can't really get anywhere, get up and get going. [*What's been the most significant challenge you've faced in the last couple of years?*] Probably the deciding whether or not to have the baby or not. [*And we've talked about how you dealt with that step.*] Yeah. [*Has it affected your life since then?*] No, I try not to think about it.

One need not be a social scientist to find Robin's "no" unconvincing. Data in Table A5.1 (pp. 259–60; and to a lesser degree, Table A5.2, pp. 260–62) suggest that abortion may contribute to depression in emerging adulthood, independent of sexual-behavior patterns. After listening to accounts of abortion, we can assert that the average woman who pursues an abortion certainly doesn't treat it lightly. And most get over the experience. But for plenty, an abortion results in emotional pain, guilt, disappointment in oneself, and a diminished sense of self—all of which can give rise to long-term depressive symptoms and to barriers in forming enduring sexual relationships. (Those who have had abortions tend to report higher numbers of lifetime partners.) We don't wish to overstate the results; not every young woman who gets an abortion reports such experiences. There is certainly plenty of self-selectivity here, too, meaning that some types of women are able to weather the emotions of abortion better than others. But for a significant number of them, it is a serious challenge. For some, it triggers a downward spiral. While the existence of a postabortion syndrome is debated, civil minds can recognize that the act can weigh heavily on the consciences of women. Some struggle with the decision for a brief period of time afterward, and some for much longer.[29]

Robin's postabortion experience may or may not be normal, but her struggle for emotional health mimics other interviewees who've made the same decision. Jamie is a 21-year-old woman from Louisiana who has been in and out of three different colleges in just over three years. She's on a prescription of antidepressants, but she says that her doctor has not yet been able to accurately adjust them to generate stability in her emotional health. Some of her troubles, however, are distinctly relational, stemming from her habit of forming sexual relationships before she forms deeper and enduring emotional ties to the men she has slept with. When asked if the man she is now seeing loves her, she said she didn't know. Blushing, she confessed she couldn't bring herself to ask him; it would be socially inappropriate and embarrassing. Besides, if he loves her, that means that the topic must be addressed, something she's not sure she wants to do. She waxes and wanes between wanting him to love her and worrying that maybe he does. It's a strange place to be and an impossible place to stay.

Jamie confesses to missing her first boyfriend, her first love, the man who impregnated her. She had an abortion, largely upon the insistence of her mother. Here again, we're not going to draw a direct line from the abortion to her emotional-health challenges and sexual decisions. But to suggest that the abortion didn't matter in her struggles just doesn't make sense, according to the data.

That Jamie withholds the question of love from her current sexual partner actually reinforces her connectional qualities, in spite of what she may wish to convey. (She's definitely an *Eros* type, not a *Ludic*). There must be *something* held back until a deeper relationship is established. That something for many just isn't sexual intercourse anymore. As chapter 3 revealed, it is engaged in earlier in a relationship than in the past, on average—and we're not glorifying the past, just making an observation. Perhaps emerging adults are lonelier than we think and are convinced that sex, with its connectional characteristics, is the glue that will cinch together something good and create a relationship that ought to endure—even if it doesn't.

SEX AND EMOTIONAL HEALTH: A TWO-WAY STREET?

By now it should be obvious that there's a gender distinction in how young men and women experience sex, especially sex without security. Men generally don't mind it, but it leaves many women dissatisfied and sometimes emotionally injured. Perhaps sex and emotional health is a two-way street: women may get hurt by some sex decisions and feel regret, but hurting women may also be more likely to have sex apart from security. When we discussed partner numbers with Megan (21, from Texas), we asked her if there was a number that was too high for her age.

> Probably . . . five or six. [*Do some of your girlfriends have more than that?*] Mm-hmm [yes]. Some of my girlfriends that have more than that are the ones who I know like, have really bad self-esteem issues, too. [*Do you think it's that the self-esteem causes the search for sexual partners or that sex diminishes their self-esteem?*] It could be both. It could be that meaningless sex diminishes their self-esteem. [*Do you think that's true?*] Probably. I wouldn't feel good about myself if I kept having sex with [different] people. [*Is it the sex itself, or is it a partner, or having multiple partners?*] It's probably more the way the partner treats you afterward.

What social scientists call "selectivity" may be responsible for some of the apparent association between sexual-partnering patterns and emotional status. We certainly see it with drinking patterns: drinking lowers inhibitions and increases perceptions of your own and others' attractiveness. This distortion has been called "beer goggles." Drinking "medicates" depression for many Americans yet is itself a depressant. The same may be true for disconnected sex. To be sure, the statistical models we discussed above reveal a complicated story that has only partly to do with recent sexual decisions and certainly plenty to do with things that happen much farther back in women's pasts. One study of casual sex in college notes that the most likely pairing is between self-confident men and distressed, depressed women.[30] The avenue no doubt runs in both directions, then; depression can breed casual sex as well as the other way around. But no matter the direction of influence, the simpler tables tell a compelling story—that where we see a pattern of many sexual partners, we are far more apt to find emotionally struggling women.

Other scholars haven't been so guarded in their claims about directionality. A study of teen virgins found that those who subsequently experienced first sex within a romantic relationship exhibited far fewer depressive symptoms and delinquency than did those whose first sex was casual.[31] Denise Hallfors and her colleagues, also using the Add Health data, found that depression did not predict sexual behavior (contradicting the notion that it is a two-way street).[32] Their 2005 study found that sexual behavior patterns came before depression, not after them. Girls with multiple sex partners were about 11 times more likely than virgins to report elevated depression symptoms. And the instigators differed between the sexes: teen girls' depression increased with substance use or sex, while boys' depression increased with substance use or binge drinking. Even "experimenting with sex" generated greater depressive consequences for girls than boys.

The evidence doesn't stop with one dataset, either. In a study of college women, psychologists note that women with depressive symptoms are more likely to masturbate than pursue paired sex, further suggesting that depression doesn't cause young women to (socially) seek out sexual partners.[33] Instead, it's more likely a cycle for women: a sexual relationship doesn't work out, which depresses them modestly. After a while, they pursue a new relationship. If the process repeats itself enough, a minority of women come to think they're depressed and some are clinically (and perhaps medically) treated as such. But women who exhibit sustained or severe depression are more likely to withdraw from seeking sexual relationships than pursue them. Thus while we're content to suggest that there is certainly something to selectivity concerns—that sexual decisions and depression can be a two-way street—the evidence certainly leans more in the direction this chapter presumes, that certain types of sexual decision-making can bring about emotional difficulties for women that they might not otherwise have experienced.

MEN, SEX, AND EMOTIONAL HEALTH

We've established that regardless of the direction of association, a significant minority of women who report having had a lot of sex partners are quite unhappy. Men who recount the same experience, however, tend to respond very differently. In a study of casual sex among college students, researchers found that men who engaged in casual sex reported the *fewest* symptoms of depression but women who did so, the most symptoms.[34] These results couldn't be more polarizing.

For social or psychological or biological or evolutionary or some other set of reasons—scholars may never adequately conclude—young men seem to endure far less emotional wrangling about sexual relationships than do young women. But why the *positive* emotion among promiscuous men? David Buss—evolutionary psychologist and our colleague at the University of Texas—wagers that men pursue casual sex encounters simply because they can.[35] How's *that* for a satisfying explanation? But many men can identify with it. Part of the common sexual script for young men and women is that men are "supposed to" want sex and minimize relationships, while women are "supposed to" value relationships more than sex.[36] Given the robust findings described earlier, however, there's more to this story than just a script. Men don't always recognize an emotional component to sex. Jalen, the 18-year-old from Boston quoted in chapter 3, had to take cues about this from watching women: "I guess sex is an emotional thing, because I notice that a lot of girls get attached. Even if they say like, 'Oh, I'm not,' they do."

We don't wish to convey that *no* men feel down or depressed after hookups or failed relationships. Or that *no* men find themselves interested in pursuing a deeper relationship with a sex partner. Or that all men always *like* their sexual contact with women. None of these are true. Some men do fall hard and struggle to recover from failed relationships. Sex makes some desire a deeper emotional relationship. Plenty of others who don't seem to be depressed nevertheless experience emotional disappointment or longing that gets channeled into drinking, minor violence, or—in college—slumping grades. In other words, some men experience problems after short-term sex that is *not* reflected in guilt or sadness but in other ways, such as isolation and loneliness.[37] We may not easily recognize this because men are socialized to channel and express their feelings in ways quite different from women. In a study by psychologists Pamela Regan and Carla Dreyer, one 18-year-old man noted both the power of sexual desire as well as a lingering sense of dissatisfaction with himself:

> All I wanted to do was to have sex with her. . . . This is the socially accepted thing to do in my social circle. Maybe I'm more of a man because I'm able to say that I conquered this woman. I don't know, I feel kind of depressed about it now.[38]

Abby (22, from Colorado) seems able to have sex with no strings attached. As noted in chapter 3, she's had just under 10 sexual partners and seems no worse off for her experiences. Nevertheless, "there's definitely a few in there that I wish that I hadn't slept with," she notes. Some were more into her than she was into them. That made ending the relationships easier, she asserts. When remarking about a New York fling that went south, she adds, "Oh, well, I can't feel as bad as he does [laughs]." She then recognizes that she's gone a bit off-script for a woman: "I know it sounds evil, but it's true." That failed relationship wasn't the only one where her partner fell harder than she did. Another one—this time at home in Colorado—did likewise (note the economic language of resource comparison Abby uses in describing him):

> Well, I was dating this guy who was like, I guess, he wasn't like ugly or something, but he was like not *that* attractive. And he was really nerdy, like super geek and a computer programmer and umm . . . just like insanely intelligent and really funny. And we had a really good time together. But he was way too into me, and I just remember, we went to this Mozart symphony one night, and he just like, would not stop kissing my neck and like, touching me. And I was like, "Would you just get *off* me?! I'm trying to listen to the freakin' symphony!" And so . . . the next day I broke up with him. And he was like . . . completely not expecting [it], which I was surprised at, because I had been irritated with him for like, I dunno, a week or something. We only went out for maybe five weeks. . . . He reacted much more strongly than I thought he would. Because it had only been five weeks, but I think that actually he was like, umm, he told me afterwards that he thought that he was in love with me and stuff. And he really, really took it hard and wouldn't leave his house for a while. And all his friends were calling like, "What did you do to him?" and I was like, "I don't know! I didn't do anything!

I just broke up with him!" [*Were you already sexually involved?*] With him? Yes. [*Do you think that had anything to do with his attachment? I mean sometimes it is for a guy, but maybe not as often.*] Yeah, I think it probably was. He was really sensitive.

Abby's boyfriend didn't expect her to offer sex so soon in their relationship, and he misinterpreted what it signaled (in reality, not much). To most women, of course, it signals more.

Gary

As with Abby's boyfriend, Gary too takes sex seriously as an important signal not to be pursued lightly. A slight young man from Michigan first featured in *Forbidden Fruit*, Gary seemed uncommonly sensitive about how his first sexual partner had emotionally experienced their relationship. That was two years ago. Now 19 and a college sophomore, Gary has had a few more partners (a total of four in his lifetime) and is sexually active with his current girlfriend. Nothing very surprising. But he expressed considerable remorse over one of those encounters—a one-time fling with an old friend from middle school when he was sloshed at a party he didn't even want to attend. Unlike many young men, the hookup bothered him a great deal, and it does to this day.

> I forget what [the party] was for. But she asked if I wanted anything to drink. There was like a pint of Jim Beam. I get there and I'm real uncomfortable, because her former fiancé is the only other person there. They were supposed to get married—had the invitations bought and everything. She backed out, [said] "I'm not gonna marry you." He still lives nearby; he still comes around. She invites me over, and he's there, and I'm real uncomfortable with the whole situation. So I go, "Oh, did you have that pint?" And she says, "Oh, they didn't have a pint so I got you a fifth." So I'm like, "Oh jeez." So I just started drinking out of sheer nervousness, and I just want to go. I don't want to be there. And people start showing up and [I had] nothing in common with anyone, so I just separated myself from everyone, just drinking. And I drink way too much bourbon, went and lay down, woke up, and she's there. In the bed with me. And I'm like, "Oh jeez, what's goin on?" And then we ended up having sex. [It was] a real bad, uncomfortable situation. I woke up and I was like, "I'm going home." How I woke up was her ex-fiancé pounding on the window, right by my head. And I wake up, and he's staring at me in bed next to her. [*Oh, no*] Yeah, so we haven't really talked. It wasn't like we got in an argument or anything. . . . It's just like

that never happened. And I think she's kind of put it out of her brain, but when I think of that, it's like a real low spot for me. . . . [*And what is it about that, do you think, that really felt like it was wrong?*] The fact that I let myself have sex with her, get physical with her, without having any sort of regard for her. I mean I like her, I think she's a neat person, I like her a lot. But that was . . . that could've been anybody and I let myself, let my inhibitions go enough to let that happen without putting a check on and saying, "Wait a second." And the fact that I let the alcohol do that to me, which has never really happened. I've never been in that situation before. So the fact that there was not even really a time for judgment and consideration, that I just said, "Screw it" and let it happen. I feel like it was really damaging to have sex with someone like that, who I really had no relationship and now really have no relationship with. It was damaging for her, damaging for me, just a bad situation to be in. . . . I mean for me, it doesn't feel right if you don't have like, a mutual understanding between the two people beforehand, some sort of relationship preceding, some sort of understanding and discussion after the fact. . . . I mean ideally, I think there should be other emotions involved before sex. . . . There should be a buildup to that interrelationship, building up some kind of foundation before that happens. In my mind that's just infinitely better, a better situation that way than [what I did] . . . 'cause like now I could never . . . see myself having any sort of close relationship with her ever again, be it a romantic relationship or just a close friendship. Just because that was there, and we would really have to talk about that a lot before. We would have to sort of work backwards from that, which is sort of difficult to do.

Uncharacteristically for many men, Gary notes the damage he may have caused his friend, even though she was a willing partner and seemed more interested in sex than he was:

I don't know what her relationship is with any other man or her ex-fiancé, so I'm sure that, if not damaging, [it] severely complicated anything that was going on in her life at the time. For me, I had just broken up with Randi [ex-girlfriend], but she was still sort of resenting the breakup . . . was less willing to buy into it than I was. So then I told her about it. I didn't keep it from her, you know. We were broken up but talking, and . . . it bothered her [Randi] a lot, because we weren't broken up very long, and it bothered her to see me with a lack of self-control. So it was damaging in many ways with our relationships with other people and potentially damaging healthwise.

If sexual practices among emerging adults are ever to change for the (emotionally) better, it's not likely that men—who are less affected—will be leading the charge. But they are neither monolithic nor beyond responsibility. Their sexuality is generally less malleable than women's, but that does not mean change cannot or does not occur. It did for Gary, who's no longer interested in hooking up yet remains fine with the idea of sex within the boundaries of an established relationship. In hindsight, he recognizes the swath of destruction he helped create—a threat to his own health, the chance of pregnancy with a woman he barely knew, the harm it caused their tenuous relationship, the added blow to the woman's ex-fiancé, and the disappointment he fostered in his own ex-girlfriend—all for a sexual event that he can barely remember. All this bothered him, enough to resolve never to do it again.

Why exactly Gary seems more sensitive than the average emerging-adult man is hard to say. He does, however, have a remarkably open relationship with his mother, with whom he has shared much about his relationships. Most young men don't do that. And most mothers would rather not know. Perhaps he is close to his mother because he shares some feminine traits, or perhaps his persistent relationship to his mother opened his eyes to "the other" in a relationship. We don't know. But clearly sex is not emotional only for women.

Justin

That wouldn't be an accurate assessment of Justin, however. From an upper-middle-class suburb of Providence, Rhode Island, Justin could hardly be more different from men like Gary. He was in as bad a mood for his second interview—when he was still in college—as he was when we first interviewed him. Why? Because it had been two weeks into the new semester and "I still haven't banged a chick." To make matters worse, "some fucking freshman chick didn't return my calls last night." Justin spends much of his time trying to access alcohol, marijuana, cocaine, and sex—all while maintaining a passing GPA at a respectable private university. In fact, Justin had already earmarked the $40 we paid to each interviewee for their time toward cocaine: "Yep. I'm gonna, there's this grad student I wanna like, bang, who loves that shit. So tonight, I'm gonna call her up, spend the 40 bucks." If he could change anything about his life, it'd be to increase his ability "to get like, more bitches and shit." While physically he's not the most attractive young man, Justin estimates that he's had 25 partners, "maybe a few more than that," displaying again the rounding up that men typically do when estimating partner counts. Given the variety of stories he tells us, he's probably not off by much. His emphasis is on variety, not reliability or security. He has what many students call a "fuck buddy," a reliable source of straightforward sex: "Once you get it once, like, you can keep going back. . . . I don't have relationships, but I do kind of like go back [to them]." But he's never as interested in his reliable source as much as he is in the *next* sex partner.

Now Justin is a 23-year-old living in Nevada; we wish we could paint him in a better light, but we can't. He is the type of man whom the vast majority of American fathers would never want laying a hand on their daughters, and the fact that 25 young women would agree to have sex with Justin is a statement itself about the poor quality of sexual judgment in emerging-adult America. But there's a lot we can learn from listening to Justin. The fact that he responds to sexual issues with bitterness and frustration may betray how some young men respond to poor sexual decision-making. His are not *fulfilling* sexual encounters. Sex is not a source of real, sustained happiness in his life. Nor is it a precursor to depression or regret. He simply can't see sex any other way than as transactional, self-focused, and brief—a monkey on his back that demands regular satiation but one that doesn't afford him satisfaction. While remarkably, he speaks of marriage in his future, he's not interested in a secure relationship, and it's unclear whether he could ever be faithful. He's too interested in numbers—increasing the variety of people with whom he has had sex. How common Justin is among young men in America is not clear. We suspect that—once you remove the crude language and raw calculation—his sexual style is more common than we'd like to admit.

Unlike Justin, most men aren't opposed to long-term relationships. And yet most relationships still end, and typically within a year. Add in a few hookups, and it's no surprise that many men report several sexual partners before age 23. And yet they navigate the termination of those relationships—or their complete lack of a real start—with greater aplomb than the average woman. The potential reasons for this ability are many, but it is not entirely a social construction, as some sociologists might assert. Real differences characterize the sexual experiences of average men and women. Women might be taught—by friends, peers, media, or even teachers—that they can have sex "like a man," but it's just plain hard to accomplish and sustain that practice in reality. Evolutionary psychologists might assert that our social-control issues and our guilt impulses—especially in women—are very old and that our brains still presume a world without safe and effective forms of contraception. One such scholar states it plainly: "Women do not seem well adapted to casual sexual encounters."[39] We don't know much about evolutionary psychology; evaluating the lives and decisions of emerging adults is difficult enough without including speculation about our distant past. But try as they might to feel like men, women's greater ambivalence about sex and their more poignant experience of its emotional consequences are a stable heritage and an enduring component of the stubborn double standard.

CONCLUSION

Sex is far from a *simple* pleasure. The emotional pain that can linger after poor sexual decision-making, at any age, suggests a complex morality inherent to human sexuality. Some—more men than women—prefer sex without security, which tends to damage others—more women than men—on the inside. Others seem emotionally able to handle relationship instability in their sex lives better than the majority; our interviews confirmed this. Simplifying and disenchanting human sexuality, however, nets few gains across the population, and is instead more apt to leave unhappiness and fractured relationships in its wake. Investigations into the consequences of sex have long tended to focus on the physical health consequences of sexual activity. As a result, sexual-health efforts tend to target unwanted pregnancies and STIs. Far fewer inquiries concern the emotional-health consequences of sexual decisions and patterns. The reality, however, is that most emerging adults will *not* experience an unintended pregnancy or an STI, but have already and will continue to experience regrettable sex.[40]

SIX

Marriage in the Minds
of Emerging Adults

*It isn't tying himself to one woman that a man dreads when he thinks of marrying;
it's separating himself from all the others.*

—Helen Rowland

SOME OUTSIDE OBSERVERS look at the relationship scene among young adults, consider it entirely about short-term hookups, and presume that the majority of emerging adults are avoiding lasting and meaningful intimate relationships in favor of random sex.[1] While certainly the times have changed and so have our sexual norms, there's no evidence to suggest that emerging adults are disinterested in relationships that last, including marriage. In fact, they want to marry. In our interview study, in the online CSLS, and in lots of other studies, nearly all young women and men tell us they would like to get married someday.[2] We're not talking half or even 80 percent, but more like 93–96 percent. Most just don't want to marry *now* or any time soon. They feel no rush. The slow-but-steady increase in average age at first marriage—to its present-day 26 for women and 28 for men—suggests that the *purpose* of dating or cross-sex romantic relationships is changing or has changed. Most sexual relationships among emerging adults neither begin with marital intentions nor end in marriage or even cohabitation. They just begin and end.

Reasons for their termination are numerous, of course, but one overlooked possibility is that many of them don't know how to get or stay married to the kind of person they'd like to find. For not a few, their parents provided them with a glimpse into married life, and what they saw at the dinner table—if they dined with their parents much at all—didn't look very inviting. They hold the institution of marriage in high regard, and they put considerable pressure—probably too much—on what their own eventual marriage ought to look like. And yet it seems that there is little effort from any institutional source aimed at helping emerging adults consider how their present social, romantic, and sexual experiences shape or war against their vision of marriage—or even how marriage might fit in with their other life goals. In fact, talk of career goals seems increasingly divorced from the relational context in which many emerging adults may eventually find themselves. They speak of the MDs, JDs, and PhDs they intend to acquire with far more confidence than they speak of committed relationships or marriage. The former seem attainable, the latter unclear or unreliable. To complicate matters, many educated emerging adults are skeptical of possible relational constraints on their career goals.

We should admit here that we think the institution of marriage remains a foundational good for individuals and communities, even if all of us have plenty of anecdotal examples of poor and failed marriages. Even the best marriages endure regular challenges. Yet many Americans—and westerners in general—underestimate the *collective benefits* of marriage at their peril. Most would still agree that it's the optimal setting for child-rearing. Married people also tend to accumulate more wealth than people who are single or cohabiting. Marriage consolidates expenses—like food, child care, electricity, and gas—and over the life course drastically reduces the odds of becoming indigent or dependent on the state. And since the vast majority of single emerging adults still hope to marry someday, how they think about marriage in their future seems like a topic worth exploring here.

Since emerging adults esteem the idea of marriage and yet set it apart as inappropriate for their age, waiting until marriage for a fulfilling sex life is considered not just quaint and outdated but quite possibly foolish. It's certainly not a big deal anymore. Sex *outside relationships* might still be disparaged by many, but not sex *before marriage*. And yet creating successful sexual relationships—ones that last a very long time or even into marriage—seems only a modest priority among many in this demographic group. Jeffrey Arnett, the developmental psychologist of emerging adulthood, notes the absence of relationship permanence as a *value* in the minds of emerging adults:

Finding a love partner in your teens and continuing in a relationship with that person through your early twenties, culminating in marriage, is now viewed as unhealthy, a mistake, a path likely to lead to disaster. Those who do not experiment with different partners are warned that they will eventually wonder what they are missing, to the detriment of their marriage.[3]

Arnett's right. The majority of young adults in America not only think they should explore different relationships, they believe it may be foolish and wrong not to.

Instead, there is value placed upon *flexibility*, *autonomy*, *change*, and the potential for *upgrading*. Allison, an 18-year-old from Illinois, characterizes this value when she describes switching from an older, long-term boyfriend (and sexual partner) to a younger one: "I really liked having a steady boyfriend for a long time, but then it just got to the point where it was like, 'Okay, I need something different.' It wasn't that I liked him any less or loved or cared about him any less, I just needed a change." Many emerging adults—especially men—conduct their relationships with a nagging sense that there may still be someone better out there.

SETTLING DOWN: IS MARRIAGE THE DEATH OR THE BEGINNING OF REAL LIFE?

Despite the emphasis on flexibility and freedom, most emerging adults wish to fall in love, commit, and marry someday. And some already have. (More about them shortly.) The vast majority of those that haven't married believe themselves to be too young to "settle down" yet. They are definitely *not* in a hurry. In a recent nationwide survey of young men, 62 percent of unmarried 25- to 29-year-olds (and 51 percent of 30- to 34-year-olds) said they were "not interested in getting married any time soon."[4] While their reticence could be for good reasons, their widespread use of this phrase is an interesting one, suggesting a tacitly antagonistic perspective about marriage. "Settling down" is something people do when it's time to stop having fun and get serious—when it's time to get married and have children, two ideas that co-occur in the emerging-adult mind. In the same national survey of men we just noted, 81 percent of unmarried men aged 25–29 agreed that "at this stage in your life, you want to have fun and freedom." (Even 74 percent of single 30- to 34-year-olds still agreed.) That figure would have been even higher had they interviewed men in their early 20s.

Trevor, a 19-year-old virgin from North Carolina, agrees whole-heartedly with this sentiment. He would like to marry someday. When asked if there were certain things people should accomplish before they're ready to marry, he lists the standard economic criteria. But he also conveys a clear understanding that his best days would be behind him: "I'd say before you're married, make sure you have a place to live. Don't have a child before marriage. . . . Have a decent paying job, because, I mean, it's only going to get worse."

Sex is for Singles

A distinctive fissure exists in the minds of young Americans between the carefree single life and the married life of economic pressures and family responsibilities. The one is sexy, the other is sexless. In the minds of many, sex is for the young and single, while marriage is for the old. Marriage is quaint, adorable.

A key developmental task, then, for Juan, a 19-year-old from southern California, is to consume his fill of sex before being content with a fixed diet. His advice would be to "get a lot of stuff out of your system, like messing around with girls and stuff, or partying. . . . Once you get married, you won't be able to do all that stuff." When and whether the task of "getting it out of your system" can be successfully accomplished is anyone's guess. (A look at the continuing sexual dalliances of politicians suggests it may not be so easy.)

Likewise, Megan (22, from Texas) doesn't conceive of parenthood as a sexual life stage, the irony of it aside. She captures what very many young men and women believe to be a liability of marriage: the end of good sex. The last omnibus sex study of Americans—issued in 1994—disputes Megan's conclusion,[5] as do our interviews with married emerging adults. But the power of surveys and statistics are nothing compared to the strength of a compelling story in the minds of so many people. We asked Megan whether married life would be less sexual than her single life:

> Probably. [*Because?*] Just, as you age, your sex drive goes down. [*Okay.*] I mean not because you want to be less sexual, that could be the case, but I won't know till I'm older. [*Um, so some people say when you get married, you settle down, like it's literally a settling down. Do you look at marriage and married sex as being like, "That's off in the future; it might be a disappointment. Now I'm having a better time"?*] Yeah. [*Do you?*] Yes. [*Why?*] Why do I think it might be a disappointment? [*Sure.*] Um, just

because of the horror stories of getting married. Nobody wants to have sex anymore. [*Where do you hear these stories?*] Movies, other people. . . . [*Like what? Can you think of one?*] Um, there's plenty. Like the movie that just came out—*License to Wed*—there's this one scene where the guy is sitting on top of a roof with his best friend talking about how his wife doesn't want to have sex anymore.

Although Megan enjoys sex for its own sake and predicts a declining sex life in her future marriage, it's not the death of sex that frightens her about marriage: "It's living with a guy that freaks me out." Author Laura Sessions Stepp claims that today's young adults are so self-centered that they don't have time for "we," only for "me." They begrudge the energy that real relationships require.[6] If that's true—and we suspect that's a journalistic overgeneralization—Megan should get together with Patrick. While he's so far slept with six women, Patrick informed us that he cannot imagine being married, and yet he too plans to do exactly that someday:

Well, I don't want to get married now. I guess, like, I do want to find a girl but I just can't see myself being married. . . . [*And you can't see yourself getting married or being married because?*] Um, I guess I just don't like the idea of being real tied down.

His current girlfriend is someone to hang out with, have sex with, and generally enjoy her company. Imagining more than that frightens him: "You sacrifice like so much stuff to be in a relationship that, um, that I guess I'm just not ready to make that huge sacrifice yet." Nor is Gabriela (23, Texas):

Once you get married, your responsibilities change. It's no longer, "Oh, I want to go to China next year. I have to save up money." No. Now you have to pay for the house. . . . or you have a job and you have, you can't just leave, because your husband can't get that day off. And things like that. It doesn't just become you, it becomes you and another person." [*So what do you think of that?*] I think that it's fine when I'm older. [*Which will be when?*] At least 30.

For many emerging adults, the idea of marriage is a sexual letdown—something to do only after they've sampled the cornucopia of flesh that's out there. After that, sexual vitality and freedom must be traded for the different pleasures and pressures of family life. It'll be worth it, they believe. Eventually. Amber, a 22-year-old from Arkansas, notes that someday, along with a marriage, she would like to have children, because they're "what makes your life like, full, after like, you are done with your life, I guess." Marriage and children would then become her life.

Devon, a 19-year-old from Washington, does most of his peers one better. Getting married—which he too eventually plans to do—is not just about "settling down" from the vibrant sex life of his late teen years. It signifies a death, albeit a scripted and necessary one. When asked what he wanted out of marriage, he said, "Just to have a good ending to my life, basically." Chen, a 20-year-old from Illinois, agrees: "I don't really plan on getting married for a while, or settling down for a while. I'd like to do all my living when I'm young. Like, save all the rest of life—falling in love, and having a family—for later." He does wish to marry, though, because he doesn't expect his current self-focused life to satisfy him forever:

> I don't want to die alone. That's the number one thing. It's like, especially after I'm done living my life, that would be like the worst thing for me. I'd like to have a kid eventually, but there's always time for that later on. I'll settle with a kid when I'm 40, 45. . . . The time to live a selfish life is while you're young, and the time to live a giving life is when you're older, when you have kids. I'd rather live for myself while I have the time to.

Such perspectives fly in the face of lots of empirical evidence about the satisfactions of marriage. That is, marriage tends to be good for emotional intimacy as well as sexual intimacy.[7] Married people have access to more regular, long-term sex than do serially monogamous single adults.[8] But that doesn't *feel* true to many emerging adults.[9] Many perceive their parents as having modest or poor sex lives, and movie sex largely features singles. Indeed, relational instability and immaturity are perceived by some as *sexual values*. That is, sex is thought to be better when a relationship is new or tenuous, when it might not exist in the future. It's an erotic thought to some, including Tara (20, Louisiana), whose relationship with David was currently on the rocks. When asked if they were still sleeping together, even as she made plans to move out of the apartment they shared, she not only replied affirmatively but also noted a heightened quality to their sex: "It's actually been better, too. [*Why?*] I don't know. Just more like, passionate, I guess you could say. [*Why?*] I feel like it's mainly because of me . . . I am more into it than I was."

Not every emerging adult pictures marriage as a necessary but noble death, of course. Elizabeth (20, New York) likewise saw her 20s as about having fun. But her 30s (and marriage) would not be simply about settling down; they would be the time "when your life is really gonna kick into gear." We suspect that contemporary male and female perspectives on marriage, sexuality, and fertility are indeed different, on average—that many men anticipate the institution as necessary and good for them, but with less enthusiasm for it than women express.[10] For emerging-adult men, the single life is great, and married life could be good. For women, the single life is good but married life is potentially better. Ironically, after years of marriage, men tend to express slightly higher marital satisfaction (on average) than women.[11] Moreover, marriage seems to be particularly important in civilizing men, turning their attention away from dangerous, antisocial, or self-centered activities and toward the needs of a family. Married men drink less, fight less, and are less likely to engage in criminal activity than are their single peers. Married husbands and fathers are significantly more involved and affectionate with their wives and children than are men in cohabiting relationships (with and without children).[12] The norms, status rewards, and social support offered to men by marriage all combine to help men walk down the path of adult responsibility.

No wonder the idea of marriage can feel like a death to them. It is—the demise of unchecked self-centeredness and risk-taking. Plenty elect to delay it as long as seems feasible to them, marrying on average around age 28. That's hardly an old age, of course, but remember that age 28 is their median (or statistical middle) age at first marriage, meaning that half of all men marry then or later. Their decision to delay makes sense from a sexual economics perspective: they can access sex relatively easily outside of marriage, they can obtain many of the perceived benefits of marriage by cohabiting rather than marrying, they encounter few social pressures from peers to marry, they don't wish to marry someone who already has a child, and they want to experience the joys and freedoms of singleness as long as they can.[13]

WHO MARRIES EARLY AND WHY

A good deal more is known about why people are *not* marrying in early adulthood than why some still do. And yet a minority marry young— and even more wish they were married—despite the fact that cohabitation and premarital sex are increasingly normative and socially acceptable. While the majority of emerging adults have no wish to be married at present, more than we expected actually harbor this desire. Just under 20 percent of unmarried young men and just under 30 percent of such women said they would like to be married at present. Understandably, religious emerging adults are more apt to want to be married. And those emerging adults who are in a romantic or sexual relationship are nearly twice as likely to want to be married right now than those who aren't in a relationship. Cohabiters are more than *four times as likely* as those who are single to want to be married. In fact, just under half of cohabiting young women and 40 percent of cohabiting young men said they'd like to be married right now.

Those who marry younger face a variety of hurdles, no doubt, including potential impediments to their educational attainment, a more economically modest beginning, and possibly becoming parents ahead of their peers. Among all the 18- to 23-year-olds in the Add Health study's third wave—the group about whom we've been talking in this book—19 percent of women and 11 percent of men report having ever been married. This is a snapshot of emerging adulthood taken at one point in time. However, since plenty of 18- to 19-year-olds will get married before the end of their 23rd year, we have to reach beyond this age group to get a better, retrospective portrait of just how many emerging adults actually marry before they turn 24, and what they're like. According to Table 6.1, 31 percent of women and 23 percent of men reported being married before they turned 24. We'll call this marrying "early," since the median age for men and women is 28 and 26, respectively.

Marriage in early adulthood is clearly patterned by race: only 15 percent of African American women marry before age 24. White and Hispanic women have the highest rates of early marriage at 36 and 30 percent, respectively (although Hispanic women are not significantly more likely to marry by this point than are Asian women). Among men, African Americans are likewise the least likely to marry young, at 15 percent, compared with 22 percent of Asian men and 24 percent of white men. Hispanic men are the most likely to marry early; nearly three in ten of them are married before the end of their 23rd year.

Given the historical proximity of the institutions of religion and family, it's no surprise that religion continues to distinguish earlier marriages from later ones. In the Add Health as well as other studies, the results are similar: on the later end of the age spectrum are Catholics, Jews, and the religiously unaffiliated. Mainline Protestants appear in the middle, and evangelical Protestants and Mormons are the most likely to marry young.[14]

TABLE 6.1 Percent of Young Adults Married before Age 24, Split by
Gender, 24- to 28-Year-Olds

	Women	Men
Overall	30.8	23.1
Race/Ethnicity		
White	35.7	24.4
Black	14.8	15.1
Hispanic	30.3	29.9
Asian	29.4	21.7
Region		
Lives in the South	38.4	29.7
Lives outside the South	26.2	18.5
Urbanicity		
Lives in urban area	28.6	21.9
Lives in suburban area	27.9	21.2
Lives in rural area	45.1	31.3
Parents' Educational Attainment		
Resident parent(s) have college degree	13.4	11.3
One parent has college degree	23.1	16.6
No parent has college degree	35.8	26.1
Structure of Family of Origin		
Biological parents married	29.9	25.3
Single-parent family	28.4	16.4
Stepfamily	32.8	26.4
Other family structure	36.0	22.1
Religious Affiliation		
Conservative Protestant	48.8	36.2
Black Protestant	16.2	14.3
Mainline Protestant	38.5	22.6
Catholic	20.5	19.4
Mormon	53.7	30.7
Other religion	40.9	31.9
No religion	27.8	18.5
Educational Attainment		
Earned high-school diploma	31.5	23.9
Did not earn high-school diploma	26.9	19.2

continued

	Women	Men
Family Income (from family of origin)		
Family income below $30,000	33.4	24.1
Family income $30,000 or higher	29.9	22.8
Parent's Age at Marriage		
Parent married at age 18 or younger	42.7	31.5
Parent married at age 19 or 20	34.0	25.7
Parent married at age 21 or 22	27.6	15.4
Parent married at age 23 or older, or never married	19.2	15.3

Source: Add Health

Note: *There were too few Jewish young adults to establish a stable estimate.*

Parental socioeconomic status (SES) is a major factor in younger marriages. Only about 13 percent of young women with two college-educated parents, and just about 11 percent of such young men, marry before turning 24, compared with 36 percent and 26 percent of young women and men (respectively) with no college-educated parent at all. Indeed, educated parents may be quicker to socialize their daughters to wait for marriage than they are their sons. Young women who come from a household where neither parent earned a college degree are 167 percent more likely to marry early than are women from households where at least one parent has a college degree. Among men, the difference is 131 percent, suggesting that, whether intentional or not, parents' class-based wait-to-marry messages may resonate more with women than men.

Emerging adults whose families seem best poised to financially assist them are the very ones most disinterested in marrying relatively young. In one sense, it's ironic: those who could, don't. (It's an extension of the demographic-economic paradox we noted in chapter 2.) On the other hand, their choices make perfect sense and bear witness to the power of social learning or mimicking: because one's parents have succeeded economically, they're more apt to nudge their children toward the best possible routes for their own economic success. And marrying in the early 20s is seldom part of that formula.[15] Maximizing education and focusing on individual skill-building, however, is.

Another example of mimicking is the connection between parents who married young and children who do the same.[16] Given the increasing age at first marriage, this connection is becoming more tenuous over time. Most emerging adults getting married today are doing so later than their parents did. Indeed, about two out of three Add Health respondents who married before age 24 still married later than their parents did. But a strong link remains, and it's nearly linear in effect: the younger a respondent's parents were when *they* married, the more likely the respondent was to be married themselves.

Other predictable characteristics of marrying young also emerge. More than 38 percent of all women who live in the South marry before turning 24, as do about 45 percent of those from rural areas. Considerably fewer rural men marry by then—31 percent—but still far more than their urban or suburban counterparts. Sonja, a 23-year-old from Missouri, married when she was 19. Why so young?

> It was one of those things where we would [either] get married or live together without being married, and neither wanted to do that. Out of high school, I went to college for a year, and he went off to basic training. And he was coming here, so we just got married.

Since Sonja's answer isn't very illuminating, we let the variables do the talking. She fit a variety of types that marry when younger: she's Hispanic, from a military family, and lives in a small town. Her parents were supportive, not oppositional. Sonja does, however, fracture at least one stereotype about early marriage—that it's poisonous to higher education. She completed her bachelor's degree in nursing both after marrying and in a timely manner.

None of this is terribly surprising. For all the rebelling that emerging adults think they're doing against their parents, parents are having the last laugh. They appear to be very successful at transmitting their ideas about marriage and appropriate marital timing—whatever those ideas are—to their children.

EARLY MARRIAGE: GUARANTEED DIVORCE?

As obvious as it might sound, getting married introduces the risk of getting divorced. And that very specter remains a key mental barrier to relationship commitment among emerging adults. Six in ten unmarried men in their late 20s—who are already beginning to lag behind the median age at marriage—report that one of their biggest concerns about marriage is that it will end in divorce.[17] Thus getting married young is increasingly frowned upon not just as unwise but as a *moral mistake* in which the odds of failure are perceived as too high to justify the risk. This conventional wisdom is at work in journalist Paula Kamen's interview with a

24-year-old woman who claims she knows her boyfriend far better than her parents knew each other when they married. But would she marry him? No: "Like, are you stupid? Have you read the statistics lately?"[18]

Emerging adults claim to be very stats-savvy about marriage. They are convinced that half of all marriages end in divorce, suggesting that the odds of anyone staying married amounts to a random flip of a coin. In reality, of course, divorce is hardly a random event. Some couples are more likely to divorce than others: people who didn't finish high school, people with little wealth or income, those who aren't religious, African Americans, couples who had children before they married, those who live in the South, those who cohabited before marrying, and those who live in neighborhoods that exhibit elevated crime and poverty rates. Lots of emerging adults have a few of these risk factors for divorce, but most don't exhibit numerous factors.[19] And yet the compelling idea in the minds of many is that any given marriage's chance of success—however defined—is only 50/50, and worse if you marry early. In fact, most Americans who cite the statistics argument against considering marriage in early adulthood tend to misunderstand what exactly "early marriage" is. Most sociological evaluations of early marriage note that the link between age-at-marriage and divorce is strongest among those who marry *as teenagers* (in other words, before age 20).[20] Marriages that begin at age 20, 21, or 22 are not nearly so likely to end in divorce as most Americans presume. Data from the 2002 National Study of Family Growth suggest that the probability of a marriage lasting at least 10 years—hardly a long-term success, we realize, but a good benchmark of endurance—hinges not only on age-at-marriage but also gender.

- Men and women who marry at or before age 20 are by far the worst bets for long-term success.
- The likelihood of a marriage (either a man's or a woman's) lasting 10 years stably exceeds 60 percent beginning at age 21.
- Starting around age 23 (until at least 29), the likelihood of a woman's marriage lasting 10 years improves by about three percent with each added year of waiting.
- However, no such linear "improvement" pattern appears among men.

To reiterate, then, the most *significant* leap in avoiding divorce occurs by simply waiting to marry until you're 21. The difference in success between, say, marrying at 23 and marrying at 28 are just not as substantial as many emerging adults believe them to be. And among men, there are really no notable differences to speak of. While sociologist

Tim Heaton finds that teenage marriage—and perhaps marriage among 20- and 21-year-olds—carries a higher risk of marital disruption, he too notes that "increasing the age at marriage from 22 to 30 would not have much effect on marital stability."[21]

Still, to most of us, marital success is more than just managing to avoid a divorce. It's about having a *good* marriage. Sociologist Norval Glenn's study of marital success, where "failure" is defined as either divorce or being in an unhappy marriage, reveals a curvilinear relationship between age at marriage and marital success.[22] Women who marry before 20 or after 27 report lower marital success, while those marrying at ages 20–27 report higher levels of marital success. The pattern is a bit different for men. Men who marry before age 20 appear to have only a small chance at a successful marriage, while those who marry between ages 20 and 22 or after age 27 face less daunting—but still acute—challenges for a successful marriage. The best odds for men are in the middle, at ages 23–27. In a meta-analysis of *five different surveys* that explored marriage outcomes, researchers note that respondents who marry between ages 22 and 25 express greater marital satisfaction than do those who marry later than that.[23] In other words, the conventional wisdom about the obvious benefits (to marital happiness) of delayed marriage overreaches. Why it is that people who wait into their late 20s and 30s may experience *less* marital success rather than more is not entirely clear—and the finding itself is subject to debate. But it may be a byproduct of their greater rates of cohabitation. While relationship quality typically declines a bit over the course of marriage, the same process is believed to occur during cohabitation. If so, for many couples who marry at older ages, the "honeymoon" period of their relationship may have ended *before* they married, not after.

All these findings, however, are largely lost on emerging adults because of the compelling power of the popular notion in America that marriages carry a 50 percent risk of divorce. End of story. Indeed, what matters most is what people *think* reality is like, not how reality really is. Human beings think and act based on what they *believe* to be true, often with little regard to alternative possibilities that may stick closer to empirical accuracies. They have faith in the conventional wisdom about marriage—and especially about early marriage. Consequently, marriage is considered off-limits to many emerging adults, especially those in the middle of college or building a career. Thus while research suggests that adults who are married and in monogamous relationships report more global happiness, more physical satisfaction with sex, and more emotional satisfaction with sex, emerging adults don't believe it. Such claims just don't *feel* true. And why should they? When's the last time you watched a romantic film about a happily married 40-year-old couple?

REASONS FOR THE RISING AGE AT FIRST MARRIAGE

Among today's emerging adults, the story of marriage is a narrative that begins in and belongs to the late 20s and the 30s. To thwart that notion—either by marrying much earlier or much later—is to go off-script and face social sanctions from peers and parents. A faculty friend of ours who married at 19 (after her freshman year at an elite private university) shared with us how much of a pariah figure she became:

> We got married when we were both 19, the summer after our freshman year . . . and I can't tell you how many people gave us—especially me—a hard time about it. Very few people took us seriously. And when I announced my engagement, instead of congratulating me, many people asked, "Are you pregnant?"

As a result of social pressures, then, most emerging adults don't veer off-script. They wait.

Before we describe the different imperatives embedded in that script, we should recall the economic state in which emerging adults currently make decisions about sex and marriage. In general, the economic situation in America and the West is a good one, all recessions aside. The American higher education system is extensive, very forgiving, and widely accessible. The share of women in the labor force is remarkably high by historical comparison. The times are good, relatively speaking. And when times are good, delaying marriage will strike many as a rational decision. Since marriage for many implies children—and children are no longer producers so much as they are consumers—and sex is widely available outside of marriage, the dominant impulse will be to delay marriage as long as makes biological and fiscal sense. And that is exactly what Americans have done. However, such mundane motivations to hold off on marriage are often couched in a variety of cultural claims and stories. It's to seven of those that we now turn our attention.

Can't Afford It

Putting off marriage makes a good deal of practical sense in our modern information economy, especially given how educationally intensive it is. Strapped with debt, however, college-educated emerging adults nevertheless report that it's important for them to be "financially set" before they marry.[24] In a nationally representative survey of 1,003 young adults ages 20–29, 80 percent of unmarried respondents asserted that educational pursuits and career development take precedence over marriage, and 86 percent affirmed that a person "must be economically set" before marrying.[25] In other words, many believe they can't afford marriage yet.

This can be a steep challenge, given elevated expectations of financial security. So some frame marital readiness as arriving once schooling is finished and they have a steady job. When asked to share his ideal age for marriage, Vincent—a 22-year-old from New York who's clearly in love and sexually active with his girlfriend Jennifer—voiced the common narrative of economic stability yet also its competition with his romantic desire to be wed. All of it came haunted by family divorces he's known, resulting in evident struggle over the answer:

> Before I'm 30. But probably like 28 to 30. I don't want to rush. Like, obviously if I stay with Jennifer, it'll be younger than that, because [we'd marry] probably as soon as we get out of school and get jobs. We'll wait a long time, because she's got a lot of school ahead for her still, but if we stay together, it'll be sooner than that. But I've seen my [extended] family. . . . Two are divorced. And one's remarried. . . . I don't want to get into a relationship that ends up going sour. But I don't think that I would. . . . Some people say the reason . . . divorce is so common is people don't stick with it as much. They don't give it as much [effort], but I do see that people weren't, just weren't right for each other. They definitely were not, especially in the one case, they weren't right for each other. Just, I don't know why they decided to get married, because they were just so not compatible.

Darci, a 22-year-old from Arizona, definitely wants to get married, but like many emerging adults, "just not yet." She admires her parents' marriage—which, statistically speaking, is a good omen for her own future—and wants "that American Dream kind of" marriage. When would she prefer to marry?

> For myself—it's when I feel I'm emotionally and financially prepared. So I would say in my late 20s. [*And why that age in particular?*] Just because I would be older than I am right [now], and I would be completely done with school, my spouse would be done with school, and we would both be in stable jobs and both know where we're at in life.

Ben, a 22-year-old from Pennsylvania, concurs. He hopes to marry in his "late 20s, early 30s." Why then? "Because then I would feel like I was at a good point to where I'll have a job and be able to travel a little bit before I settle down." Here we have four key elements in one sentence: the right timing, a steady job, after traveling, and time to settle down.

Most emerging adults are exactly like Ben—they want to put off marriage until later in their 20s or early 30s. They feel no rush. For most, education and work take priority over marriage. They anticipate that these priorities may shift, but their presumption about this shift is entirely passive. It will just happen. They believe, too, that postponing marriage will ensure a better shot at eventual marital success.[26] Rushing to marry means a shorter search and heightened odds of a poorer match.

Be Your Own Person

The 20s—and to a lesser extent, the 30s—are a time to figure out *who you are*. This is another cultural mantra in marital decision-making. Figuring this out takes time, and marriage feels like it would be a full-time job, one stacked on top of career concerns. To marry before one knows what one "really wants" feels profoundly foolish and short-sighted. Clara, an 18-year-old from Oregon, for whom marriage seems understandably distant, articulates this identity-formation argument well:

> I think that [the] main thing is making sure that you are your own person, because I know people who are getting married and this is their sophomore year of college. I'm like, "You are not your own person, and you are going to have some major changes." And, you know, you don't know if at the end of 10 years after this if they're going to be the same person you married. [Or] if you'll be the same person. So just make sure you're your own person. That way you are ready to present yourself to someone else.

What exactly it means to be "your own person" is unclear, given the intensively individualist world we already live in. What is clear, however, is that emerging adults expect to *change* what they think and feel and want as they move through college and their early adult years *and* that such change will move them from being who they are now—the product of their parents and peers—to who they'll become: their true selves. Jane, a 23-year-old from Maine, concurs: "I think when you're like, this young, you're still trying to find out who you are and what you want, and it will change by the time you're five years from now." To commit to a relationship *now* would seem to them to foolishly promise *not* to change. Change, it's clear, is perceived as inherently damaging to marriage.

Darci senses this concern: "I feel like at this age, I'm still changing and still learning so much about myself and about people around me that it'd be difficult to have someone be dependent upon me to not change or to stay the way that I am now. So I feel like until [your] late 20s, you're still learning so much about yourself that it would be difficult to be married." Natalie, whom we met in Chapter 3, concurs: "I've been with some really awesome people, I think, that I really got close to, and I learned a lot about different things and just experienced different people and different situations." However, the 20s have no firm grip on the "figuring out who you are" phase. Nor do singles. Cindy was nearing her mid-20s and had an 8-month-old daughter when her husband decided he was better off apart from marriage and fatherhood. He said he wasn't sure who he was anymore. What did that mean? It's a mirage, she says: "It means nothing. It means starting the same thing over again and making the same mistakes, thinking you'll get different results."

It's a very powerful story, however. Emerging adults think about their 20s in a very different way than they conceive of what their 30s will be like. Now is the time for experimentation; then will be the time for settling into a stable set of preferences. Now is for self-discovery and experiencing things; then involves other people. Now is for change; then is for stability. Now is for self; then is for others. How exactly this shift happens, however, is a mystery. (For many, it won't occur smoothly because it was never advocated or modeled.) And if marriage is about stability and other people, it's certainly not something to consider in the present.

It's Too Soon to Have Children

The prospect of children born too soon is also a big deal to many emerging adults. Indeed, the thought of marrying early is often rejected because of the limits that marriage is believed to place on personal freedom. And yet a marriage that doesn't add children for several years is conceptually no more of a restriction on personal freedom than is cohabitation or a series of sexual relationships. Again, however, the power of the compelling story is what's important here. Marriage and parenting are a *package deal* in the minds of many, including Meredith, an overachieving 21-year-old from Florida who's already on her way to graduate school:

> People don't realize . . . that your life changes when they have kids. . . . When you have a kid, it's downhill from there, if you're too young. [*In what ways?*] Oh man, it's just, you don't get to live your life. You have to worry about somebody else. And, like, their life becomes your life. So if you're not mature enough, you haven't experienced enough, it's not a good situation.

Numerous interviewees responded to our question, "Why do you want to get married?" with an answer that included "because I want to have kids." Natalie, now a 22-year-old, thinks a good age to marry is in her late 20s: "what's the difference, really, if you wait a little longer? Because I don't want kids for awhile, so if I don't want kids, I don't really need to get married right away." And Dahlia (now 21): "I think marriage comes with wanting to have children." That many middle-class emerging adults equate marriage with children suggests that an older precontraceptive era mentality dies hard. The pill "opened up opportunities for new aspirations to be fulfilled prior to parenthood," note demographers.[27] Although sex has become decoupled from marriage, fertility has not for this group. It's what marriage is for.

Especially in the minds of the middle and upper-middle classes, marriage means children, stability, a mortgage, and responsibilities.[28] Avi, a 20-year-old from Pennsylvania, equates marriage with the burden of worry and pressures to succeed. So he'd like to marry in his late 20s. Why then? "I don't have to be worrying about a kid, or my wife, or something like that. I can be focused and a little bit more devoted so that I can maybe be a little bit more successful by the time that I have a kid, [and] provide more." The story of marriage assumes a variety of intensive responsibilities about child-bearing and parenting.

Nevertheless, it's a biological reality that women's fertility plateaus at age 20 and stays there for less than 10 years before beginning its slow decline just prior to age 30 (and then a more rapid decline around age 35). This aggravates many emerging adults who would much prefer peak fertility to range from 30 until 40 rather than from 20 until 30. So distasteful are these facts that many emerging adults are not even told them. In our introduction to sociology course, most students guess older when asked about peak fertility. Accompanying generalized ignorance about fertility is strong faith in science to reverse fertility problems that arise—in part—from ignoring peak fertility. A nurse at an obstetrics office remarked how ironic it was that "we spend our college years doing everything we can to avoid pregnancy, only to spend our 30s trying to do the exact opposite." Feminist writer Kristin Rowe-Finkbeiner laments that "fertility isn't taught in sex education; birth control, not babies, is stressed in college health centers."[29] It's as if emerging adults really would like to separate the generation of life from the act of sexual intercourse. The two don't go together in their minds, and they wish they didn't go together in reality.

As a result, many women think they can have a baby so long as they are still having periods. This is rarely the case. But fertility ignorance remains remarkably high, given how much emerging adults seem to know about sex. Thankfully, fertility problems don't haunt *most* women, especially those who marry around the median age at first marriage. If they want to have kids, they still have ample time for the two children that comprise the typical family size in America. But fertility struggles hamper far more women today than a generation ago: one in five women aged 40–44 is childless today, compared with just one in 10 a mere 30 years ago.[30] To be sure, some women don't wish to have children. But that number certainly hasn't doubled in 30 years. As far as our bodies are concerned, perhaps the 20s are not too soon to have children after all.

The Travel Narrative

Lots of interviewees referenced their own desires to travel in their early-to-mid 20s and indicated that marriage would hamper that quest. Emerging adults were less clear about how exactly the desire to travel would necessarily interrupt or undermine a romantic relationship on its way to marriage. The travel ideal was seldom accompanied by references to particular places they wished to go. It's just the idea of it that's appealing. And the assumption is that marriage nixes one's travel possibilities. It's as if marriage means children, work, a mortgage on a house in the suburbs, and the end of all things creative and spontaneous—things like world travel. Trevor, the 19-year-old from North Carolina quoted earlier, intends to follow the advice of his father's friend, who adamantly advised him not to marry until he's past age 25:

> Funny story on that age. Back in 9th grade maybe, my friend's dad— who's from Britain, and he's like a typical dude who traveled around— he didn't get married until he was 30. He told me, he was like, "Once you get out of college," he's like, "you'll be making the money." He's

like, "Do *not* get married until you're after 25." He's like, "Once you're making that money, you'd be surprised how great your life really is, when you have that kind of money and you can just spend it on your-self." . . . He said, "You can travel. You have the money to do it. You can do whatever you want." He's like, "Do that for a couple of years until you meet that right person, and then go for it."

Such travel discourse is not limited to those with the means, either. "I want to experience traveling and seeing the world," dreams Martha, a 22-year-old retail-store employee from Virginia who told us she lives "paycheck to paycheck." Indeed, the travel narrative is a classic piece of emerging-adult lore, even if many of them don't actually travel very far or very often. The logic doesn't always compute, and the experi-ences don't always turn out like Trevor's adviser asserts. In reality, marriage often expands access to shared financial resources, while re-ducing or splitting expenses. But the image of the freewheeling trav-eler is still a vivid one in the minds of many, even if *where* all the time and money needed to travel extensively comes from is seldom specified in their stories. Given the modesty of most starting salaries and the need to work hard to build a career, the travel narrative may be more imagination than reality for most.

Parental Resistance

While the emerging-adult ideal of marrying in the later 20s is consid-erably later than when many of their own parents married, most of their parents aren't balking at their wish to delay. On the contrary, they're applauding it. Darci told us her parents agreed with her about the right age to marry: "mid-to-late 20s, even early 30s, just at a time when they would want me to be fully settled and just confident in life and financially [and] emotionally ready for that."

Most of the emerging adults with whom we spoke didn't suggest that their parents had become jaded about the institution of marriage, even if it hadn't worked out well for them. Many parents do, however, warn their children of the hazards of considering early marriage. Like turning 18, getting married remains a strong symbolic move toward indepen-dence. It's the strongest one, in fact: among all emerging adults (from intact, two-parent families) who are living on their own, those who marry without ever having cohabited are the *least* likely to receive subse-quent financial assistance from their parents. (Single women are the most likely.) Laura, a 19-year-old college student from Texas, recognizes this very clearly. She is very much in love with her boyfriend and would like to be married right now but equates talk of marriage with staging a family rebellion. Her parents "want my full attention on grades and school because they want me to get a good job," she reveals. To pursue marriage would mean giving up their help with rent, tuition, and a car. Vincent, the 22-year-old from New York, told us that his parents discouraged him from considering marrying Jennifer just yet: "No, my parents are the opposite [of encouraging]. . . . My mom's like, 'Be careful.'"

As many parents reflect upon their own economic successes (or dreams of such), a common piece of advice to their children is to finish their education, to launch their careers, and to become financially independent. Dependence feels like weakness to them. As a result, parents counsel their children, "Don't rush into a relationship," "First loves don't last," "You can't bank on a mate," "You have plenty of time." Even parents who married young and are still together find themselves readily dispensing such advice. It's what they're supposed to say. It's in their script.

Such parental warnings tend to work, too. In her evaluation of data from 341 women aged 27–30, sociologist Monica Gaughan notes that with each incremental increase in the mother's preferred age for her daughter's marriage, the odds that her daughter would actually be married at the time of the interview dipped 23 percent.[31] Clearly parental expectations are not only conveyed but obeyed. And since the majority of emerging adults don't actually wish to be married just yet, marriage is a domain in which parents' and children's attitudes are in consonance.

The Pursuit of Sexual Chemistry

In the age of online-dating personality algorithms and matches, emerging adults have become well acquainted with the cultural notion that getting the right fit in a partner is extremely important. "Chemistry" is the new watchword as emerging adults meld relationships with science. Such chemistry is not just about how well two people get along, the conversations they enjoy, the hobbies they share, their religious or political commitments, or their shared visions for a common future. It's also about how complementary they are in the bedroom. Is there sustained erotic attraction? Does she do what he likes? Does he know how to please her? Are their sex drives comparable?[32] According to Jenna, sexual chemistry is "the automatic feeling you have with someone. It's just, you feel right with them. You feel good."

Such an automatic feeling stands in contrast to the *learned* nature of sexual intercourse and its various potential positions, habits, and methods. Many emerging adults wish to get the learning stage out of the way early, so that they may acquire a transferable sexual skill set and be considered "good in bed." Although sustained sexual chemistry actually takes time and requires conversation, many believe the idea that good sex should emerge rapidly and silently with the commencement of a sexual relationship. (It seldom does.)[33] If it doesn't—or if the sex is awkward or if a partner doesn't like the same things you like—it's often perceived as a sign that sexual chemistry just isn't there. "If you experience more people, you may be able to know what you like when it comes to romance," said one interviewee.

While not all emerging adults anticipate having such a sequence of relationships—hoping for one permanent one instead—others simply assume that they will, given the powerful norm of serial monogamy, their young age, their professional interests, and their ideal age at marriage (still several years in the future).

When we talked with Ben back in high school, the 22-year-old Pennsylvania native was considerably more sexually conservative than he is today, fresh out of college. Four years ago, he was hoping to retain his virginity until marriage, not for religious reasons but just for accomplishment's sake. He never did sleep with his girlfriend of six years. They grew tired of each other and broke up. Shortly thereafter he met his current girlfriend. The two of them are sexually active, and he no longer perceives value in avoiding sex. On the contrary, "I think that [sex] is a major part of making it [a relationship] work, and if you're not compatible, then it would be a huge problem. . . . I've become more accepting of sex, and it's become something that I feel is important in developing a relationship."

Naturally, figuring out whether you have sexual chemistry with someone precludes waiting very long to have sex. Ben waited about three months. The presumption is that if the sex is bad, it may not get better, and continuing a relationship could end up being a waste of time. That's why Kara, a 21-year-old from New York, believes it's a profoundly bad idea to avoid sex before marriage:

> Because then you get married and then you've already committed to being with one person forever and you, I mean, there's definitely like, sexual compatibility that can exist between two people or not exist between two people. And I also think that like, once you're in this marriage, suddenly it changes everything. And I think, I mean like, if you

have the stresses of like, say, getting a new house or whatever and at the same time you're trying to like, discover how to know each other sexually, it probably stunts it rather than that being able to be like, in the initial puppy-love stages, when that's probably the best time to experiment with sex.

Thus many emerging adults, excepting the most religious ones, sense that abstinence is actually risky. To wait and see about sexual chemistry may reveal that it doesn't, and perhaps can't, exist. To abstain until marriage could reveal—and seal—poor sexual chemistry. Such a marriage would be doomed, they believe.

The sexual chemistry argument dovetails well with what family scholars call "search theory," an explanation of delayed marriage that suggests women are not opting out of marriage so much as they are engaging in a longer search process.[34] This search process, however, involves a good deal of sex, given that serial monogamy is the cultural environment in which most emerging adults pursue romance and sexual relationships. But is there such a thing as too much experimentation to ensure sexual chemistry? Sociologist Monica Gaughan's study of 341 women in their late 20s revealed that the search-theory explanation of marital timing may not always work out so well in reality. In fact, women who had more numerous sexual relationships during their early adult years, who spent more time in such relationships, and who had additional sexual liaisons besides their romantic relationships were all less likely to be married at the time of the interview. Gaughan concludes that "more is not better," if the goal of relationships is to search for an optimal marital match.[35] That isn't every woman's goal, of course. But if it is, the chemistry-search strategy doesn't work as well as many believe it does.

On the contrary, evolutionary psychologist David Buss notes that the number of premarital partners is a good predictor of infidelity within marriage for both men and women.[36] Others concur. In an article highlighting research on the cheating behavior of married 20-somethings, Naomi Riley notes that serial monogamy is hard to simply drop after a pair weds.[37] But as age-at-marriage rises, previous sexual relationships are what we will most certainly have. The problem is that "settling down" is a likable idea but a challenging reality. In sum, more information about romantic opportunities—by way of experiencing a series of monogamous relationships—does *not* lead to greater confidence in the marriage market.

But in the era of electronic communication, Facebook, Twitter, and Web porn, heightened personal information about *everything*—about potential romantic or sexual interests, about opportunities for social interaction, and about sex itself—is what we have. Too much information, perhaps. Repetitive relationships—including repetitive experiences with cohabitation—don't lead to better marital odds.[38] They just lead to more sex. Sexual economics, a theory Gaughan doesn't directly consider in her study, would predict as much.

Deflated Confidence in the Institution

Growing numbers of American emerging adults—in consonance with their European peers—are simply less optimistic about the idea of marriage and place less confidence in the institution itself. In the National Marriage Project survey of men cited earlier, fully 55 percent of 25- to 29-year-old unmarried men agreed that "there are so many bad marriages today, it makes one question the value of marriage." And given the legal ability to extract resources from men, some have given up the idea altogether. DeMarcus, a 20-year-old from New York who might otherwise have married for religious reasons, will have none of it: "[There's] a lot of legal ramifications when you consider marriage, bro. See Michael Jordan? He's about to get half taken from him. It's crazy."

Some demographers have nevertheless suggested that traditional economic answers for delaying marriage are increasingly insufficient for explaining contemporary shifts in family formation. Instead, many sense a concomitant *cultural* shift in marital decisions toward very individualistic ones based largely on personal freedom, taste, and fit.[39] Criteria like seeking an emotional or spiritual connection make more sense today than in generations past. The vast majority of emerging adults—94 percent in one survey—want their marriage partner to be first and foremost a "soul mate."[40] Meredith echoes these values when asked about marrying someday.

> If I do, it'll probably be in my late 30s. Middle-to-late 30s. But I don't know if I want to do it. [*And what makes you uncertain?*] I think my parents' marriage, even though they're fine, I think they would be better off sometimes by themselves. And just having to account for other people, and like, you can do anything you want if you're single. You can take off tomorrow and not have to worry about anything. So it's just freedom and independence.

Emerging adults have great expectations about marriage, and many of their parents didn't live up to them. Meredith questions her own parents' marriage, "even though they're fine." Indeed, many of the interviewees we spoke with revealed a palpable sense of entitlement around marriage—it has to be very good, or it won't be worth trading their independence for. As a result, marriage can wait until they're more certain about it.

To some, then, marriage just doesn't make sense—certainly not until later in their 20s or 30s, if then. Cultural motivations for marriage still resonate, but more modestly than ever. The growth rate of nonmarital parenthood among 20- to 24-year-olds in America illuminates this well. While historically this age span was a peak period for marriage, today the pattern of nonmarital births therein is pronounced, climbing from 20 percent in 1980 to 60 percent in 2007. That's not a gentle slope. That's a mountain of change, suggesting a wholesale drop in consumer confidence in marriage.

Jenny told us she wants to get married around age 30. Why then? "Because it's far enough away that I don't have to think about it," confides this 18-year-old college freshman from small-town Texas. We might presume that the dating-and-marrying culture in which Jenny grew up would have had more influence on her. But it doesn't seem to. She's been seeing an old high-school friend for the past 16 months. They go out on a date—the classical kind, where he pays for dinner and a movie—about once every two months. But she spends numerous hours a week at his apartment, where she estimates they have sex about three times per week. Although Jenny rejects the wisdom of hooking up, she slept with her boyfriend for the first time a month before they recognized each other as being in a relationship. However, Jenny isn't optimistic about a future with him, or anybody else for that matter. She doubts they'll be together a year from now:

No. [*Because why?*] I've never seen a relationship last that long. [*Seen a relationship among other people, or yourself?*] Myself. Family. Parents. Every single [one]. [*So what do you think about that? Do you ever wonder what it takes to get and stay married, or not?*] I have no idea. I've never seen a relationship last more than five years. . . . I don't think it's possible.

While popular images of going it alone might conjure up 30-something professional women fed up with noncommittal men and electing to pursue a child by artificial insemination, nothing could be further from the norm. The drop in confidence in marriage is in fact most evident among poorer and less-educated Americans. So an institution that can help keep Americans from being indigent and dependent on state assistance is being shunned by the very group that would most benefit from it.

On the other hand, emerging adults may so esteem the institution—as Kathryn Edin and Maria Kefalas argue in their urban ethnography, *Promises I Can Keep*—that no relationship they experience ever feels like it could live up to what marriage is "supposed" to be. Indeed, many idealize marriage, expect a great deal from it, and are refusing to settle for what they perceive to be less than the ideal. The bar for a sexual relationship is lowered—for lots of reasons, several of which we outlined in chapter 3—and even the bar for childbearing is lowered, allowing for increasing numbers of nonmarital births. But the bar for marriage is never lowered. It remains very high, higher than they are able to reach. For others, it is simply higher than they are willing to climb.

MARITAL MENTALITIES AND THE MILITARY

One option, however, seems to stem the diminishing confidence in marriage among Americans who don't attend college after high school—military service. Apart from its core purposes, the military is a conservative cultural institution. Since enlistment is by choice, and has been so since 1973, military service is increasingly considered one of two things—it's either the only sensible option for many emerging adults or it's a statement of the enlistee's identification with culturally American values like service, duty, honor, and tradition.

We began to wonder about whether being a soldier made a difference in how young Americans anticipated marriage, another conservative institution, when no shortage of university students—mostly women, of course—noted to us that their boyfriends, or fiancés, or exes were in the military. (Remember the sex ratio difference in campus enrollment statistics?) In conversation with several of them, we detected a very different ideal timetable for marriage. Whereas the men we interviewed and the students with whom we interact daily seem in no hurry to cinch a mate, the soldiers we heard about did. Following a class lecture on family formation patterns, Juanita, an 18-year-old college student from Texas, became curious and wrote:

> I experienced a long distance military relationship for one year and my ex-boyfriend would always ask me about marriage or a possible

engagement. We ended our relationship because I wouldn't say "yes." (Of course, I was only 18!) Now, after six months of meeting another girl who he works with, he is now engaged. My question is: why the rush? Do these kinds of relationships last? I am constantly surrounded by people who meet a military man and are suddenly madly in love with him and ready to get married. I just don't understand.

Is her experience just an anecdote from a more conservative state (Texas), or is there something systematic going on? Unfortunately, there's not a lot written about social processes and patterns in the military, in part because sociologists are typically antagonistic toward the institution and the craft of war. And it's certainly true that we study what we find interesting or compelling, or that reflects our ideals of the world. As a result, very little study of the military occurs among our peers. Sociologist Jennifer Lundquist, however, studies the family formation patterns among soldiers, and what she's found is illuminating. First, she reminds us that the military's historic association with the institution of marriage has *not* been linear:

> This was not the case for enlisted troops historically, who were discouraged from marriage, hence the old Army adage, "If the Army wanted you to have a wife, it would have issued you one." In most companies, enlisted men had to receive permission from their company commanders in order to marry. . . . The volunteer-era military, on the other hand, acknowledged that stable families were key to retention and, thus, prioritized support for soldiers' families.[41]

But socially *supporting* families is different from tacitly *encouraging* their formation. What do the data say? While such a "total institution" like the U.S. Army is imagined to be incompatible with family life—and long deployments certainly take an emotional toll on families—the military actually boasts more and larger families and at earlier ages than the rest of the emerging-adult population. Lundquist notes that marriage rates in the U.S. military are comparatively higher than in the civilian population, and at younger ages. In 1999 data, nearly 50 percent of white and 45 percent of African American military personnel were (or already had been) married by age 22, compared with around 30 percent and 18 percent of white and African American civilians, respectively.[42] While we suspected social-class values may have been driving this, her results hold while controlling for social-class indicators, self-reported conservative values, a rural past, and being raised by a single mother—all classic indicators of early weddings.

The same pattern she documents for men holds true among women as well. Women in the military marry earlier and have more children than their civilian counterparts. The vast majority of married military women (86 percent) were wed to fellow soldiers.[43] Given what we already know about male-tilted sex ratios (from chapters 3–4), that women soldiers could find a spouse—indeed they could even be choosy—and begin a family earlier than their civilian counterparts isn't surprising in the least.

Lundquist isn't the only one who's detected these patterns. Sociologist Jay Teachman reports similarly, revealing that 11 percent of 18-year-old white male soldiers reported being (or having been) married, compared with four percent of white civilian men. At age 25, he notes, 66 percent of white male soldiers had been married, compared with 51 percent of their civilian counterparts. Among African American men, the contrast is even more striking: by age 25, 57 percent of them had married, compared with only 25 percent of their civilian counterparts.[44] Being on active duty is significantly associated with *getting* married, despite ideas about deployment and responsibilities that take men away from both existing families and potential spouses.

In the end, our student's hunch was right—men in the military want to be married. So do women. Whether they are seeking the security of a stateside relationship, are simply mimicking their peers, want someone to miss them when they're deployed, fear missing out on opportunities civilians will have for seeking mates, or are just plain in love—and the truth probably draws on these answers and more—the military unwittingly builds, rather than undermines, confidence in the institution of marriage.

DIVORCED BY 23

About 18 percent of those emerging adults who reported having ever been married had already split (either separated or divorced). While marrying young is widely understood to be the best predictor of being divorced by 23, as an explanation *for* divorce, age is profoundly unsatisfying. *Age at marriage cannot cause a divorce.* (It's like saying being wealthy causes people to be Republican). Rather, a young age at marriage is often an indicator of an underlying immaturity or impatience with marital challenges of the sort that most others eventually figure out how to avoid or solve without parting.

Overall, a total of around 9 percent of women and men in the Add Health study who had been married by age 23 told us they were now divorced. What are young divorcees like? Table 6.2 displays the characteristics of emerging-adult divorcees. When compared with their counterparts who remain married, divorcees are more immature, more attractive, more self-centered, more independent, more likely to be from nonintact families of origin, and more sexually experienced. They had sex earlier in their teen years, and they were less religious as teenagers. Half of the population of married emerging adults are southerners, as are over 70 percent of divorced emerging-adult men. It is also clear that those with an associate's or bachelor's degree or who are enrolled in four-year colleges are less likely than others to divorce (not shown in Table 6.2).

While demographic factors are notable, young adults' own assessments of themselves as popular or immature seem to affect their probability of divorcing. Early divorce is especially more common among those who think of themselves as very attractive. This makes a great deal of sense and is what sexual economics would predict. Attractive mates are the most apt to wonder whether they "settled" too easily and too early, especially given their own recognition of their continued elevated value in both the sexual and remarriage market. And when in relationships, including marriage, physically attractive young adults are more likely to be the targets of "mate poaching."[45] Thus, predictably, more of them opt out of marriage and back into the pool.

Table 6.3 provides a more stringent test of this: It connects respondents' own perceptions of their physical attractiveness with the interviewer's perceptions of the same. The logic behind this test is to assess whether others' perceptions of attractiveness could be considered as a proxy measure of *remarriage market value* (in considering whether to divorce or not) independently of one's own perceptions of attractiveness. That is, people who think of themselves as attractive may perceive they have a good chance at finding someone better if they were to divorce. Nevertheless, plenty of people tend to underestimate or overestimate their own attractiveness. So others' perceptions of their attractiveness can help us out here. Table 6.3 largely reaffirms the link between attractiveness and perceptions of remarriage market value. While less than 10 percent of women and 9 percent of men in the sample are divorced, the numbers are higher among the subjectively and objectively attractive. Men especially are more likely to be divorced when both they and the interviewer perceive them as attractive. Self-image is key: 15 percent of women who think they're attractive

TABLE 6.2 Characteristics of Divorcees and Marrieds, 18- to 23-Year-Olds

	Divorced		Still Married	
	Percent of Women	Percent of Men	Percent of Women	Percent of Men
Very immature	10.1	8.9	6.1	5.7
Very attractive	24.4	50.3	14.9	27.8
Very self-centered	9.0	13.4	7.5	8.9
Very independent	69.8	61.3	49.1	62.2
Very distant from mother	61.8	60.2	58.0	69.5
Very distant from father	29.6	35.9	33.1	46.4
Five or more lifetime sex partners	56.1	72.7	34.7	41.0
Had premarital sex	82.3	86.8	88.1	86.5
Had sex before age 16	48.5	52.3	39.0	31.7
White	84.3	66.2	75.2	72.1
Black	3.2	12.0	8.9	10.4
Hispanic	7.6	19.6	13.8	14.2
Asian	4.0	2.2	1.6	1.8
Intact family of origin	36.2	46.6	53.1	53.9
Attended church weekly as adolescent	32.9	39.0	43.8	39.6
Political conservative	18.5	23.8	21.8	28.1
Political liberal	13.2	2.5	12.8	9.9
Lives in rural area	21.3	28.8	22.0	21.7
Lives in South	52.4	72.2	49.9	50.4

Source: Add Health

have divorced, even if the interviewer disagrees with them. Perceived unattractiveness, as the theory would suggest, is more closely associated with staying married.

Unfortunately, we can't determine for sure whether such self-assessments really contributed to the divorce, or whether divorcees consider themselves attractive or immature or self-centered or independent as a result of getting divorced. Misperceptions of unattractiveness among women may be the result of divorcing, not a contributor to it. Regardless of the causal direction, such traits understandably provide marital challenges.

While we can't assess exactly why the more sexually experienced emerging adults are divorcing at a rate well above their less-experienced

TABLE 6.3 Remarriage Market Perceptions: Dual Evaluations of
Attractiveness of Divorcees Ages 18–23

	Women	Men
Total	9.6	8.7
Perceived Self as Very Attractive, affirmed by Interviewer	14.4	19.1
Perceived Self as Very Attractive, contradicted by Interviewer	15.4	11.0
Perceived Self as Unattractive, affirmed by Interviewer	7.5	11.6
Perceived Self as Unattractive, contradicted by Interviewer	13.3	5.1

Source: Add Health

peers, two processes are potential suspects. First, it might be that memories of past sexual experiences intrude upon the sexual lives of the married partners. These memories could be good ones (which make their marital sex seem inferior in comparison) or bad ones (which could still color the marital sex in negative ways). Second, the repeated practice of sex without long-term commitment might make committed sex seem foreign or boring and make an exciting sex life difficult to integrate into a bonded, committed relationship. Settling down can be hard to do.

MOVING IN TOGETHER

For all the talk in this chapter about marriage, most emerging adults just aren't there yet. Many haven't thought much about the idea. Before that step—or instead of it—most emerging adults will cohabit. Some will do so for a relatively short period, others for years, and still others permanently. Between 50 and 70 percent of couples today are thought to be cohabiting before marrying.[46] Around 15 percent of all 18- to 23-year-olds in the Add Health study said they were *currently* cohabiting, and nearly 60 percent of the study's women had cohabited at least once before age 24. As a path to marriage, however, such arrangements are unreliable: about one in five actually results in a marriage.[47] Cohabitation does, however, serve to increase exposure to a stable partner, mimic aspects of marriage, and heighten opportunities for sex. And first-time cohabitors who are engaged to be married before moving in together display higher rates of making it to marriage than those who moved in first.

Sex is seldom the *primary* reason most emerging adults choose to cohabit. Some wish to spend more time together and perceive practical benefits to keeping just one address, since one place seems to be where they're always at anyway. Some fear the commitment of marriage or wish to test their compatibility first. Some fear divorce. Others are simply mimicking the patterns of their peers. Some cohabit as a political statement against marriage traditionalists or as an act of rebellion against their parents or home culture.

And yet the decision to cohabit is often a fairly passive one. The process has been dubbed by some researchers as "sliding" into cohabitation (rather than deciding to cohabit).[48] Most emerging adult couples who move in together have no explicit plans to marry someday, since marriage seems far in the future. And given that men tend to begin their first cohabitation experience just before turning 23, and women just over 21, marriage is—on average—still several years off.[49] Indeed, the rising age at first marriage is closely accompanied by the growing prevalence in cohabitation. This makes sense. Expectations of what ought to accompany a marriage are very high, as we noted earlier. Financial security—or at least some semblance of job stability—is a timeless priority, yet it has grown more difficult to accomplish to one's satisfaction.[50] As a result, the commitments of marriage that once were undertaken—as recently as 1970—at the average age of 20 for women and 23 for men—have been replaced by cohabitations that begin around those same ages. There is still a connection between cohabitation and marriage; emerging adults who cohabit are still more likely to move into marriage at younger ages than those who remain single. But the proportion of *all* cohabitations that are resulting in marriage is decreasing.[51]

Sociologist Monica Gaughan, whom we quoted earlier about sex and searching for a mate, describes cohabitation's twin primary functions:[52]

> Cohabitation reduces uncertainty about lifetime prospects with a particular partner by providing the opportunity to gather more information about that person while enjoying some of the benefits of marriage such as companionship [and] pooling resources.

In other words, cohabitation is thought to help you know a person better, save money, increase time spent together, and provide more frequent opportunities for sex. The key word in her quote, however, is "uncertainty." That is why most emerging adults cohabit. Ben (22, from Pennsylvania) echoes that reason: "I think if you do end up marrying that person, you can kind of understand their habits better. After living together you can be more sure." Carri, a 21-year-old single mother from rural Virginia, considers cohabitation a form of risk reduction, moral qualms about it aside:

> I always state my view that I think anybody that's going to get married should live together before they get married. And I know that sounds like a bad thing in certain people's opinions. But to me, you find out how that person really is, you learn how they live in their life, and you learn whether you really want to live the rest of your life with them.

Andrea, a 20-year-old from North Carolina, is similarly adamant when asked if she would consider cohabiting again, since she already had done so once:

> Absolutely. Absolutely. [*OK. Why?*] Because I think it's totally necessary. . . . You don't really see a person until you're in that kind of atmosphere with them. I mean, people will become totally different people when you're around them 24 hours a day, have to share things with them, and . . . it's not just you guys are doing fun things together. It's you guys have responsibility together.

For Andrea, cohabitation is about minimizing the risk of overlooking something problematic by jumping too quickly into marriage. Three years together is her ideal before marrying: "Time tells all. Time tells tempers. Time tells arguments." (She had to file a restraining order on her last boyfriend.)

Eric, a 20-year-old from Ohio, is more passive about it than Andrea or Carri, but he still approves of the idea: "I think if you're romantically involved with someone and you know them and can trust them pretty well, it's not a big deal to live with them, I guess. I just see [it] as more good, it seems [to be] what people do." It's what people do. He's right about that.

Not all cohabitations are the same, of course. How cohabiting couples conceive of their relationship matters for what happens next. In a study of the reasons people give for cohabiting, couples who cited intimacy-based reasons—like wishing to spend more time with each other—were among those most likely to stay together, followed by those who elected to cohabit for practical reasons like combining expenses. Couples who were out to "test" their relationship, however, failed far more often. They were more anxious and reported significantly more attachment concerns, which ultimately doomed the relationship they were testing.[53]

Predictably, couples who perceive cohabitation as a substitute for marriage are the least likely to be married five years later. (Indeed, to be married was never their intention.) Couples who consider it coresidential dating or a trial marriage are more likely to marry but still less likely than those who think of it as a move toward marriage. This last group—and they're the largest of the four—is the most likely to actually be married within the next five years. Both African Americans and Hispanics, however, who report marital intentions in their reason for cohabiting remain less likely than others to subsequently marry.[54] And it's not just race or ethnicity that differentiates here. The poorer are hit hardest of all: a report using data from the Fragile Families Study found that only 15 percent of unwed mothers married their cohabiting partners in the year following the birth of their child. The longer a cohabiting relationship continues, the less likely it is that the outcome is ever going to be marriage.

Despite its obvious growing popularity—76 percent of emerging adults think it's fine to cohabit—cohabiting before marrying is associated with elevated probability of divorce, especially if the cohabitation occurs prior to engagement. (Of course, cohabitation is no guarantee of relationship failure, just as marrying earlier than your peers is no guarantee of future divorce). In the NSFG, about 65 percent of first cohabitations transition to marriage within five years, while around 15 percent of them will still be cohabiting after five years.[55]

Cohabiting more than once is considerably more challenging. While serial monogamy is the norm among emerging adults, serial cohabitation currently isn't. For instance, divorce rates among female serial cohabiters—who later marry—are more than twice as high as for women who only cohabit with their eventual husband.[56] Serial cohabitation could indicate a persistent inability to form stable, committed relationships. Making an eventual marriage work isn't impossible for them, but it's less likely and probably more difficult.

Although research conclusions may seem hostile to cohabitation, there's nothing inherently political about the results. These are simply the empirical patterns from numerous studies conducted by many different researchers using a variety of datasets. And they generally point to more pessimistic conclusions about cohabitation. Sure, not every cohabiting experience will turn sour or nix someone's hopes of marrying a partner. In the world of sociological generalizations, there are always plenty of examples that don't fit the trend. But exceptions only prove what's possible, not what's probable.

Earlier in this chapter, we explored early marriage and how increasing numbers of emerging adults believe that marrying young is nearly a guaranteed failure, an act that raises their odds of divorce close to near certainty. And yet cohabitation's poorer odds are largely lost on emerging adults, many of whom see it in exactly the opposite way: as a key, rather than a barrier, to marital success.

The University of Michigan's *Monitoring the Future* study—an ongoing study of American high-school students and young adults—reveals a linear rise in the share of young Americans who think it's a good idea for a couple to live together before getting married in order to find out whether they really get along. When the study first began asking that question, in the late 1970s, agreement ran at about 45 percent among boys/young men and 32 percent among girls/young women. In 2000, 66 percent of the males and 59 percent of the females concurred. By 2010, such percentages most certainly have continued to rise. Statistics be damned, emerging adults are *convinced* that cohabitation is the shrewdest pathway to long-term relational happiness and success. It's not that they're opposed to marriage. No—they're opposed to divorce, and they want to protect themselves from it. (Who can blame them?) Thus marriage can wait, because it's too important to screw up. Underneath this belief lies the assumption that ending a long-term cohabitation is easier than ending a marriage. While we suspect that's true, few acknowledge the fact that the process looks similar: each involves moving out and locating a new place to live, severing ties, possible legal wrangling over shared debts and assets, and stress over how to handle mutual friends. Sociologist Christian Smith concurs. In his study of emerging adults, he concludes:

> A significant number of emerging adults appear to have suffered hurtful if not devastating breakups involving romantic partners with whom they thought they were very seriously involved, often, they assumed, on the road to marriage. Usually, but not always, the most damaged party is the woman involved, not the man.[57]

The pain of breaking up a brief marriage and a cohabiting relationship is probably distinguishable, but only by degree.

While cohabitation decisions seem to come naturally to many, even those who are aware of the odds against them forge ahead, convinced that they will thwart the pattern. Following the release of yet another study about the hazards of cohabitation, CNN anchor Wolf Blitzer interviewed a pair of cohabiting New Yorkers about their take on the findings. One responded in hope: "I think the message I would give to the viewers, especially on behalf of the people who are living together, is to have faith in each other, and not get distracted by all the statistical analysis that's going on."[58]

CONCLUSION

There can be no doubt that the "institution" of marriage is in the throes of deinstitutionalization.[59] Marriage won't disappear, but the norms that have long characterized the institution are weakening. Emerging adults are not only delaying marriage, but are also increasingly open to alternative family forms. Nonmarital childbearing has eroded norms about marriage being the only appropriate family form for raising children, and cohabitation has eroded norms about marital sex being the only form of legitimate sex. Additionally, changes in women's labor-force participation and household divisions of labor, the advent of no-fault divorce in 1970, and the prospect (and actualization, in some states) of gay marriage have further deinstitutionalized marriage as we know it. Stating all this implies nothing about the wisdom or politics of these tectonic shifts. Indeed, Americans have by-and-large wanted these changes and if given a voting chance would affirm most of them.

Most emerging adults still wish to marry, just not yet. The average age at marriage continues to climb as young Americans adhere to a variety of shared imperatives about the value of being independent. A minority of emerging adults, however, marry well before the median age. While marrying young poses several risks, some of those are overstated in common narratives. Since marrying naturally risks divorce, some do both, all before age 24. Divorcing is more common among emerging adults who perceive greater and continued marriage- and sex-market value for themselves. Cohabitation carries risks of its own, but it has nonetheless become a very popular alternative or intended precursor to marriage. It's believed to reduce uncertainty in potential spouses, but repeated use of this new "institution" undermines or perhaps indicates a lack of ability or interest in fashioning long-term relationships and successful marriages. In the end, it's not that Americans are giving up the pursuit of marriage. They're not. But the pathways to marriage have become more circuitous and lengthy. Some like it that way; others—more women than men—find this frustrating.

SEVEN

Red Sex, Blue Sex

Relationship Norms in a Divided America

WHEN THE *NEW Yorker*'s Margaret Talbot telephoned in Autumn 2009 to talk about the unplanned pregnancy of Governor Sarah Palin's teenage daughter, our conversation revolved around the question of what shapes the sexual decisions of conservative Christian adolescents. We chatted about some of the themes in *Forbidden Fruit*, about how Christian parents tend to talk to their teens less about the details of sex and pregnancy than about sexual morality—what they want, or rather, *don't* want their kids to do. But then our conversation wandered toward political culture in America and to this book and this particular chapter, which was just beginning to take shape. We were already planning to name it "Red Sex, Blue Sex," but we informed Talbot that she could use that title for her article if she wished. She did, and her November 2009 story about the prolific reproductive lives of conservative American teens struck a nerve. It is, after all, in red states that we see the greatest number of churches, the strongest preference for abstinence-based sex education, *and* the highest teen-pregnancy rates. Liberal readers relished the irony: those who most disparaged teen sex and promoted "family values" were forced to recognize their own children's precocious sexual behavior.

RED SEX

The *New Yorker* article made it clear that conservative Americans—whom we call reds, despite the historical irony of that term—are mistakenly thought of as sexually prudish. It's an honest mistake, though, since it's from their leadership that we hear the loudest complaints about the sexual state of things in America. And that much is true: Cultural conservatives are more outspoken on matters of sex and family, their own personal behavior sometimes notwithstanding. We're not talking here about the heart of conservative Christianity, but rather the more broadly conservative subculture of Americans. This subculture includes evangelicals but is not limited to them. At the University of Texas—despite popular opinions about how liberal an institution it is—there are lots of culturally conservative students, many of whom are very sexually active. *Equating* conservatism with Christianity in America must go. It's a correlation and little more than that. Liberals don't have the corner on sexual permissiveness and conservatives don't own religion.

Martin can testify to that. He was a 19-year-old from Virginia when our research team spoke with him for the second time. He had tried college but had dropped out after a year. It just wasn't for him. Instead, he settled comfortably back into his working-class roots, becoming an electrician: "We do everything from basic electrical to industrial, to commercial, to motor control, to power generation, security, to fire, cameras. We do a lot of stuff." By ignoring the popular narrative that said he needed a college education to successfully navigate life, Martin had found his niche. And a girlfriend. Not terribly religious and yet very culturally conservative, Martin is one face of "red" America.

Although sexually experienced with a previous girlfriend, Martin wasn't having sex at age 19 because he was dating Bethany, the 15-year-old daughter of a police officer. Indeed, sex with her would've been against the law, and he was well aware of that. But the two were hardly unsexual. Martin said they did "everything but," a common revelation. A vocal opponent of homosexual behavior, Martin is more conservative about others' sexual decisions than his own. Although he believes the Bible says that sex before marriage is wrong, he adds, "A lot of it, I think, has to do with society to a certain extent." While it's not exactly clear what he means by that, we suspect it's a way of claiming that sex is normal relationship behavior today, regardless of what might have been acceptable in the past. Like many conservatives, he offers a nod to the standard while excusing his diversion from it: "I'll tell you, I believe in it. But I'm not perfect. . . . I mean nobody is. But I'll be the first person to tell you I'm not."

While premarital sex has largely dropped off the map of salient issues among many conservatives, marriage has not. Marriage is a central institution in Martin's mind, not so much because it alone ought to contain sexual behavior, but because marriage is about children, and it's "what good people do." Martin sees himself as increasingly old-school, a hallmark of many reds and the plain definition of conservative: "I don't think you should have kids outside of marriage. . . . That's just somethin' I've never believed in." Sex—and even brief periods of cohabitation—are acceptable, but both must serve marriage, not subvert it. "I think marriage is, you know, that's an agreement. That's not something that should be broken up," he asserted.

Fast forward to age 22, and Martin is still seeing Bethany—she's now his fiancée. Three years older, he waxes nearly verbatim on the subjects of marriage and morality. Since she's no longer underage, the two are sexually active. He stays over at her house on weekends and sleeps in her bedroom. Her parents are fine with it.

Martin nevertheless asserts that the right thing to do would have been to wait, but that was unrealistic "in this day and age," and he never really gave it much thought. Instead, he too is living out the story of emerging adulthood, albeit more rapidly than many of his college peers, whose fun and "rebellion" against institutional expectations is delayed:

> I was raised . . . [like] what I've seen: You're born, you go through your teenage years, you have your fun, you settle down, you get married, you have your family, you raise the family, the cycle starts over. It's just, it's the way things go. And it's just the cycle of the world, I guess would be the best way to put it.

Martin hopes to marry Bethany in two years. Building some financial security before marriage and children is important to him—he currently lives at home for free—and Bethany will help. In fact, Martin is counting on her income not just now but far into the future. In that, he's like 74 percent of unmarried American young men who agree that "any woman you would consider marrying should be able to work steadily and contribute to the family's income."[1] Married women with children in red America value—or at least need—employment no less than those in blue America.

This is red sex, or at least one very common representation of it. It is the face of the rural and small-town South, Midwest, and West. It's romantic. It's fairly relational. It's quick to sex and nearly as quick to marry. It's mindful of and deferential toward organized Christianity. It bears children early and more often than does blue sex. It publicly balks at abortion yet experiences no shortage of them. It tolerates divorce—sometimes several of them—because a happy marriage is a key piece of the American good life.

Although Martin's story may look more like red*neck* sex than anything else, his is not the only form of red sex, as we will shortly reveal. But it's certainly one common pattern repeated regularly in our interviews with emerging adults. And although we will spend time here documenting the differences between red sex and blue sex, where reds and blues differ most profoundly is *not* in the sex itself or the sexual partners. Where they differ more obviously is in the place of sex in life, the relative importance and order of sex vis-à-vis marriage and family, and the appropriate ages for each stage. For conservatives— whether they're evangelical or Catholic or not very religious at all— sexual relationships are *meant* to foster or follow marriage, even if they don't. Their cohabitation patterns more closely predict subsequent marriage than do those of other American religious traditions.[2] And plenty of reds are cohabiting, especially the less religious among them.

While we have suggested elsewhere[3] that conservatives are uniquely subject to the cultural collision of old-world, family-focused values with the new world's sexualization of youth, there's another, simpler explanation to their sexual behavior that is often overlooked. *It's hard to be antisex when you're pro-marriage and pro-family*. American conservatives are a relational bunch. Whether they're religious or not—and there are plenty of both types—conservatives really like ideas and ideals like that of a man and a woman together, romance, home, togetherness, kids, and family—all of which imply sex. This is not to say that their relationships do not struggle and break apart. Many of them do. In that way they are vigorous supporters of the American narrative of serial monogamy. Reds value loyalty and dependability, even if— and perhaps because of—their experiences of veering off of those pathways. In fact, conservative Americans are now regularly reminded that their marital relationships are collapsing at a pace either comparable to or exceeding those of their more liberal and less religious cousins. This shouldn't surprise anybody, since one cannot get divorced if one is not married, and more liberal Americans are increasingly likely to delay or avoid marriage and cohabit instead. A mature sense of responsibility and marital realities is simply more scarce early in emerging adulthood, whether you're red or blue. And since a developed ethic of marital responsibility eludes many young married reds, plenty divorce. (But not so many as you might think, given the numbers outlined in the last chapter.) With less romanticized views, blues tend to anticipate these sorrows and marry later than reds, thus experiencing fewer divorces.

Many reds are even fine with homosexuality, although plenty profess to neither understand it nor wish to think about it too much. Most cultural conservatives are committed individualists rather than collectivists. As a result, they may think homosexuality as an idea is wrong or at least suboptimal but would never claim that people should always suppress their desires. In general, most reds want to be perceived as tolerant of other people's sexual relationships and choices. Lesbianism is arguably more palatable to them than relationships between men. Like many reds, Andy (20, from Nevada) is far more conservative on the subject of male homosexuality. He offers a porn-shaped dichotomy with which many men overtly or covertly agree:

> I said to this one girl, Pamela, I was like, "Yeah, lesbians are so cool." She's all, "Yeah, gay guys are cool." So I said, "Hell no. That's sick. That's wrong." She's all . . . "Well, what's the difference?" She always asks me that. So, I don't know. I don't know. [It's] because I'm a guy.

Red emerging-adult men know they shouldn't like pornography, but many do. Led by Utah, eight of the top 10 states in terms of online porn consumption voted Republican in the 2008 presidential election.[4] Blues don't offer an emphatic opinion about porn, while red women disparage it the most. When we interviewed Hannah, she was a 19-year-old from Alabama who had hooked up extensively for a short period of time in high school. She thought porn was the biggest social problem today:

> People just aren't paying enough attention to what their kids are doing. They're not paying attention to what they're watching. They're not paying attention to what they're doing on the computers. I'm extremely against any type of pornography but it's so overspread these days that you know, 8-, 9-, 10-, 11-year-olds are getting a hold of it.

Even if their men are quietly enjoying lesbianism online, reds are no fans of real lesbians marrying. Their opposition to gay marriage is not because they're inherently hostile to homosexual sex—some are, but most are not. Gay marriage is not subject to negotiation, however, because marriage as an idea cannot be for reds about anything besides a man and a woman. Civil unions? Fine. Legal rights for partners? Not a problem. But reds perceive that the battle over the definition of marriage is more than simply over legal standing. It's a symbolic lunge for their throat, a contest over their identity and the historic centrality of marriage in American and western civilization. Gay marriage is comparable in that way to concerns about gun control, contesting parental rights, demilitarization, and the notion that government can run things better than the people themselves can. It's a package deal for conservatives, who perceive blues as largely favoring all of those things.

BLUE SEX

Jeff is a freshman at a state university in Minnesota, a blue state. He's an overachiever, very future focused, and gifted. He has had little trouble steering clear of temptation. But he doesn't intend to *always* steer clear: "I'm not perfect, you know. I like to enjoy myself. I am at . . . the number-one party school, so I'm gonna have some fun." Jeff has not had sex yet, which is in consonance with his persona and academic orientation, and is typical of younger blues. He has no real qualms about losing his virginity, either—another blue trait. Unlike Martin, Jeff feels no need to make deferential remarks about marriage or morality. While he hopes to marry someday, he also considers the idea "kind of corny." He passively notes, "Hopefully I'll find someone that I'm in love with and happy with and all that garbage. I don't know."

Like many blues in college, Jeff is utilitarian about life and insists that relationships right now must take a back seat to grades, enjoying college, having some fun, and preparing for a career. Love and marriage can wait. The delay in pursuing sex so far is about his future focus; nothing is worth getting sidetracked in school. Indeed, relationships must play a secondary role in emerging adulthood—that's a basic rule among blues. When asked about the purpose of dating and relationships, Jeff's opinion became clear: "Have fun. Learn about someone else. I mean, not get too hardcore committed or anything like that."

Not all blues are in college, of course. Allison is 18 and dropped out of college after a year at a state university in Illinois. There are two men in her sexual history, one of whom is her current boyfriend, Brendan. Allison met him while she was with Jason, who was several years her senior. She had tired of Jason, and wanted a change and Brendan looked inviting: "I have a great body, so I'm going to show it off, and all these clothes I really shouldn't be wearing." It worked. Although unreligious, she nevertheless struggled over the morality of just dropping Jason:

> I thought I could probably marry Jason someday ... but then I met this new guy, and I like him. But I don't want to break up with Jason, because I do love him. I want to be with him, too. And, like, I don't want to hurt his feelings. And I'm young, and you know you only live once. Guys come and guys go. . . . I was just like, "You gotta look out for yourself sometimes," you know? Not just other people.

Allison is largely dissociated from her family and childhood friends: "I just hang out with [Brendan] all the time." She sleeps over at his house—and with him—frequently, and uses condoms "every single time. . . . I probably should get on birth control, but I never have the time to make appointments. I just always forget." Her daily routine is simple: "Work [as a waitress], boyfriend, work, boyfriend, work, boy-friend, work, boyfriend." She hopes to get back into college with Bren-dan and take classes with him, but is not actively working toward making that happen. What are the long term prospects with Brendan? "I'm just trying to play it as it goes. I don't want to be like, 'We're going to be together for a long time.' Or you know, whatever happens, happens." Her dialogue around sex and relationships is filled with common normative claims, and repeated one cliché after another. In a few short sentences, we detect several norms:

- If you don't follow your heart, you'll always wonder what might have been.
- Men tend to move on in relationships. If women don't, they'll eventually get hurt.
- What matters most is you. A relationship can only augment the self.
- Sexual relationships just happen, and they run their course in due time.
- Youth shouldn't be wasted. It's the best time to try on new experiences and relationships.

These norms are not the propriety of blues alone. Reds often believe them too, since they draw on what we call "romantic individualism," a powerful American narrative that knows no social-class boundaries. The generation of romantic love and excitement is popular among reds and blues, rich and poor. Dozens and dozens of films annually bring in untold billions of dollars in service to its themes: love, the pursuit of romance, sexual fulfillment, the quest for a soul mate.

Red and Blue Differences

In emerging adulthood, the point of sex for most blues is enjoyment. Reds like sex no less than blues, but they feel compelled to motivate sex for reasons beyond that. For reds, sex is supposed to serve some overarching relational purpose, as Hannah articulates (in hindsight):

> I don't see having sex as just getting into bed and doing the deed. I see it as, you know, just showing your affection and your love for somebody. It's an important thing in a relationship. It's making love. Not, you know, just humping somebody's leg or something crazy like that. . . . It's a very emotional connection between two people, not just a physical need."

So just how different are the sex lives of emerging-adult reds and blues? Table 7.1 displays Add Health sexual outcomes, sorted by gender, self-identified political orientation (a range from very conservative to very liberal), and current educational status.[5] As we've already noted in chapter 4, emerging adults who never went to college see a great deal more sexual action than those who have finished their schooling or are currently enrolled. Indeed, being red or blue pales in significance to pursuing or avoiding higher education. Other patterns emerge as well. First, conservative, educated, emerging-adult women are the most likely (by far) to remain virgins, are the least likely to report having had anal sex, are the most likely to have used contraception at last sex, report the fewest number of partners either in their lifetime or in the past year, and generally have the least amount of sex. In other words, red, educated women are the most sexually conservative and risk averse. That doesn't mean they don't have sex. The data suggest that most of them do, but they do in relational patterns that emphasize commitment. On the opposite end of the spectrum, blue men and women who didn't go to college at all are among the most sexually permissive emerging adults, by most of the indicators here. They have the most lifetime partners. Less educated red men, however, don't trail by much and display the highest number of recent partners (2.5 in the past year, on average). Reds aren't as positive about anal sex as blues, but all of the groups indicated that fewer than one in three have tried it.

	Percent virgin	Percent have had anal sex	Percent that used birth control at last sex[a]	Mean lifetime partners	Mean partners in last year	Mean frequency of sex in last year[a]
Men						
Liberal, not in college	12.9	29.6	75.6	7.9	2.2	65.2
Liberal, in college or college grad	23.2	16.5	82.5	4.3	1.4	62.0
Conservative, not in college	13.7	18.6	65.2	7.1	2.5	59.7
Conservative, in college or college grad	28.7	18.4	76.2	3.4	1.2	51.9
Women						
Liberal, not in college	6.5	32.9	60.6	8.6	1.8	61.0
Liberal, in college or college grad	16.1	20.8	82.8	4.5	1.5	66.3
Conservative, not in college	18.2	26.1	61.3	4.7	1.3	59.5
Conservative, in college or college grad	40.5	14.6	83.9	2.7	0.9	46.2

Source: Add Health
[a]*Among those who have had vaginal sex*

Despite the rhetoric about conservatives avoiding contraception, we see little difference in their usage patterns. Collegians are simply far more likely to use it, regardless of their political colors. Among college students and graduates, blues tend to report slightly higher numbers of both lifetime and recent sexual partners than reds do. Both reds and blues like sex, and—save for educated, conservative women—tend to have sex at comparable frequencies. None of the groups averaged below 52 times per year, or above 66 times.

Red and blue differences over sex, then, are less about sexual *practices* than *mentalities*. They're about ideals, attitudes, and stories—the ways people are "supposed to" think about sex. One example of this is in the evaluation of others' sexual choices. While reds no less than blues have been well educated into the American ethic of tolerance, blues are simply more accepting of others' sexual decisions than are reds. Plenty of blues with whom we spoke reject short-term sex for themselves, but they don't extend that judgment to the decisions of other people. If their friends want to hook up, they don't stand in the way. In fact, Dahlia and Natalie (below) have been far more conservative in their own sexual behavior than Martin and Hannah and many other reds. When our research team last spoke with Natalie, at age 22, there was only one person with whom she'd had sexual intercourse, and that just last year:

> He was the only one I felt comfortable enough with and wanted to [have sex] with. All the other guys that I dated, even though I did other things with them . . . I just didn't feel like they were the person to [have sex with]. I wasn't ready with them. I wasn't comfortable enough with them. So I knew that for myself, I didn't want to. And they were all really great, and they were all very okay with me not wanting to, so I think that I did choose the right guys, because nobody pressured me to do anything, so that was good. But I did do other things with them. You've gotta have a little fun.

Reds and blues both hook up, as Natalie implies, but reds are more apt to regard hookups as wrong or regrettable or to report ambivalence about them. Blues don't.

Blues are pragmatic about sex and marriage. Reds are idealistic about them. Thus for blues, cohabiting is fine. End of story. It's the default, expected option among the majority of them. Marriage will often follow, but pressure toward that end will most likely emerge slowly, over several years. For reds, cohabiting can be a long-term arrangement—especially among less-educated reds—but it continues to be imagined as a temporary fix, with traditional marriage understood as the preferred arrangement. Since blues are more likely than reds to pursue advanced education, they tend to be more strategic about their relationships, slower to sex, less likely to draw a strong link between sex and marriage, more supportive of abortion (but hardly flippant about actually getting one), and perceive fewer direct connections between their religious beliefs and their sexual decision-making. They're also far more paranoid about pregnancy than reds are. While they wouldn't judge someone for having a child outside of wedlock, they will for having a child so early in life. Natalie declares that it would be "a horrible thing" if she were to get pregnant right now: "I don't care what other people would think, but I just, I want certain things in my life, and a baby would just not be part of it right now. It would definitely not help my career." Children and family are important to blues and reds alike, but they're important at different times. For blues, it's later. For Dahlia, now 21, everything points to the essential norm of using birth control: "If they knew that I didn't [use contraception], I'm sure most people in my life would ask me *what* I was doing!"

REDS AND BLUES: SAME GOALS, DIFFERENT TIMETABLE?

As ought to be inferred by now, red and blue emerging adults aren't living on two different planets. They share much in common. Both drink from the same stream of modernity, whose tributaries—individualism and consumerism—reach every American community. Reds and blues often chase similar things: they both like sex, they're serial monogamists, and they esteem marriage. For both, sexual attraction and romantic love, once considered too fragile to sustain marriage, have instead become the primary criteria both for entering and exiting the institution. Some blues object to marriage and will intentionally form permanent cohabitation arrangements, while some reds will accidentally do the same (minus the ideological objection). Educated young reds see the realities of the marriage market and tend to commit comparatively early. Blues are more apt to ignore it or insist that it doesn't matter because they dislike key aspects of it: the double standard, the gendered fertility schedule, and the train of emotional sentiment in sexual relationships. Both still marry in comparable numbers—just at different ages—and both expect a great deal from marriage. Reds have more children, but not double the number blues do. And reds tend to have them earlier.[6] The evidence, then, suggests that blues and reds have plenty in common but place themselves on *different timetables*.

Sexual experimentation for reds is primarily reserved for the mid-to-late teenage years, and for blues, it is the decade of the 20s. Blues are more positive about the *idea* of sexual experimentation—including sex with different people and possibly members of the same sex (especially among women)—if not always the reality. Reds prefer to confine sexual experimentation to a more circumscribed set of contexts and period of time, and they are more apt to avoid same-sex sexual behavior as part of the experimental repertoire. Most reds believe they ought to be done with it by their early 20s, at which point it's time to settle down and assume adult roles and responsibilities. Hannah is one of these. As a 19-year-old, she was pleasant, attractive, and a self-professed redneck: her friends drove pickups, and she would see them at the community college, at work, at the "mud hole," or at Wal-Mart. Her parents were divorced, and her father had recently remarried—for the fourth time—and relocated to South Carolina. Her mother had fared similarly:

> I wouldn't call my mom promiscuous, but she hasn't exactly been with the same guy for years and years and years. So she didn't show a real value in staying with the same man. She seemed to be always looking for something better. I feel that she has the inability to actually settle down with what she's got.

Like her mother, Hannah too played the hopeless romantic. She had experienced a brief period of consecutive short-term sexual relationships, and was very fond of Kevin, her first fiancé. She was interested in "settling down" with him. As with Kevin, she had hoped that each of her earlier sexual relationships would turn into something stable and long-term. No luck, in keeping with the fruitless approach we noted in chapter 3.

Like plenty of reds, Hannah began having sex early. She took pride in what she believed to be delaying her first experience of intercourse: "I waited until such a late age of 17," she said, betraying a red culture in which early sex is common. Hannah is a clear cultural conservative, with a dash of occasional Christianity thrown in. Kevin's parents were high-school sweethearts, and in rural Alabama, Kevin too hoped to find his wife while still in high school.

Hannah was very positive about the idea of children in her future—indeed, she had her heart set on that role—and wasn't on the pill (but did use condoms, most of the time) with Kevin. Kevin, she dreamed, could be "the classic dad. I want him to throw the kids around and tickle them and have fun. I want him to help them out with their homework if he can, and if we have a son, teach him how to throw a baseball. If we have a little girl, preach to her about boys."

When Hannah was interviewed three years later, she was pregnant—by her husband, the tenth sexual partner of her life. And it wasn't Kevin. Hannah and Kevin didn't last, but Hannah and Ben, a sailor in the navy, have lasted about a year so far, save for a two-week separation following his stressful return from a long deployment. She speaks lovingly of Ben, as she did Kevin, and notes widespread social support for having wed:

> Everybody was ecstatic (when we announced our engagement). We probably didn't have a single negative opinion. Everybody's always seen that we've been really happy with each other, and I guess he's always, his family's always seen him as the type to just get married and start a family right away. My family's always seen me as the type to get married and start a family, and it just kinda fit.

Realistically, we're not optimistic about Hannah and Ben's chances. She lacks parents and peers capable of showing her how a marriage works through the universal challenges that assail it. Most of the social institutions that could help reinforce their marriage—religious community, close friends, and extended family—are largely absent from their lives. One—the military—remains. She and Ben are living near a naval base several states away from where they grew up. He's on a schedule that includes long deployments. They have few exemplars and few places to turn to when times get tough. They've dodged one bullet already. And she's only 22.

Kari, an 18-year-old from Texas, is a freshman in college. She grew up Catholic but isn't actively practicing. She is dating—and sexually active with—a 25-year-old colleague from work (she's a part-time restaurant hostess). Like Hannah, she too exhibited a brief period of sexual hookups for which she now feels profound regret. She thinks she was too young to have lost her virginity at 16 but nevertheless asserts that she was "with that person for a long time," a total of two years. For reds, duration matters. It makes sex more defensible, more moral. Blues, who arguably hook up less than reds, are more intellectually tolerant of relationshipless sex. Reds may do it, but they make apologies for it. Kari's hookups occurred mostly "on the rebound" from serious relationships, signifying that even such deviant sex (for her) is still connected to the centrality of committed, romantic relationships. Her hookups threaten not only her own self-image, but—more importantly for Kari—how others perceive her: "I don't want people to think of me in a way that I'm not." She is not what she did, she contends.

Kari is a traditionalist who definitely senses clear categories of right and wrong—and fully believes that she violated those. She regrets the months-long sequence of sexual partners that she experienced and vows to never do that again. She's familial, maternal, and marriage-minded, like Hannah. She doesn't think sexual faithfulness—a clear value—will be a problem for her anymore. She's comfortable in her current relationship, just like Hannah was. Unlike Hannah, however, Kari won't think of giving up work or education for marriage. She's come too far and worked too hard in high school to put so much stock in relationships to carry her through into the future.

Reds—even those that value and pursue higher education—seem to take on substantial relationship commitments more rapidly than blues. Table 7.2 displays the percent of *college graduates* in the Add Health dataset—up to age 27—who said they had ever gotten married or were currently cohabiting. The results are striking evidence of red-blue differences in relationship settings. Fully 39 percent of all college-educated, politically conservative women reported having already gotten married, but *only one percent* of them said they were currently cohabiting. For them, marriage is 30 times more preferable than cohabitation. Blue women who are college graduates, however, tip way in the other direction: 19 percent of them are currently cohabiting, while 12 percent report having married. Seldom do social scientists witness such stark contrasts as this one. Among men, the same pattern continues, although here again, the differences are not as striking as among women. Triple the share of red males are married, compared with cohabiting, and slightly more blue males are cohabiting than are married. Blue men seem in no hurry to marry, at seven percent.

Cultural conservatives are more likely to get married—and sooner—than are cultural liberals. And they link their personal happiness more

TABLE 7.2 Percent of College Graduates Ever Married or Currently Cohabiting, by Gender and Political Leaning

	Ever Married	Currently Cohabiting
Male, political conservative	21.7	6.9
Male, political liberal	6.9	10.2
Female, political conservative	38.9	1.3
Female, political liberal	11.6	19.1

Source: Add Health

closely to family and marriage than do cultural liberals. (But we suspect cultural liberals obsess about their romantic and sexual relationships no less than conservatives do.) In a country where well over 90 percent of married people have had sex before they say "I do," it's pretty clear that cultural differences don't influence how much Americans enjoy sex. Some may prefer to avoid it for a time and save it for a more committed relationship, but there's no evidence that blue Americans somehow like sex more than do reds, or that they have more sex, more orgasms, or a more satisfying sex life.

Other cultural differences do exist. Cultural conservatives tend to be more relational in their sexual attitudes and tend to stake boundaries about the moral legitimacy of sex within certain relationship forms. They may break their own rules and transgress their own boundaries—and we know they do—but they aren't interested in rewriting the rules or moving the boundaries, even if they can't articulate why those rules and boundaries are there in the first place.

One way in which reds and blues are quite distinguishable is in their marital-timing norms. For blues, it is *not* normative to marry before age 25, though some do. They aim first for other goals, such as completing college, securing a good job, or pursuing graduate education. For reds, marriage by 25 *is* more common, and failure to attract a spouse by then can be perceived as a modest risk (of having trouble finding a spouse). During early adulthood, then, these two moral claims—establishing an acceptable career trajectory and finding a spouse—often conflict with each other for reds, since getting married too young is viewed by many as an impediment to one's life chances. Red emerging adults must navigate this time of life by managing the competing demands of two different narratives with different conceptions of the ideal life trajectory.

GEOGRAPHIC MOBILITY AND THE "POLITICS" OF SEX

Since political education or perspective formation is hardly very deliberate among most emerging adults—most young Americans think like their parents think, or else slowly shift away during college—we suspect there's more to the story about red and blue sex than meets the eye. In other words, we're not so sure that red and blue sex differences are really about partisan politics, despite how we've dubbed them. It's far more likely that the measure of political orientation we use here is what social scientists call "endogenous." That is, one's political orientation is itself the product of other things, including region of residence, race, religious affiliation, their parents' political attitudes, etc. In other words, the influence of red and blue perspectives on shaping sexual decision-making is not simply testimony to the power of politics over the private sphere, but instead suggests the power of an overarching cultural orientation in people's lives.

For example, it's difficult to separate religion from political culture in the United States. Hannah can miss months of church on end and still feel like she retains and exhibits the values of Christianity. We can run statistical models—as we often do—to distinguish what social scientists call the "independent effects" of, say, living in the South. We would control for other factors like religious involvement, political affiliation, or evangelical Protestant congregational membership. But while statistical models can technically separate out such effects, human beings never experience such separation of important and compelling influences upon their lives. The factors are always bundled.

So what are we to make of Hannah and her brief experiment with multiple sexual partners and her relationship-go-round? Is this pattern the product of her parents' divorce that spurred her to seek out stability in romantic relationships? Is it her parents' visible sexual blunders? Did her modest religious socialization bring it about? Is it the Southern, conservative cultural valuing of marriage? Is it the Christianity in the air? In truth, for Hannah it's all of these, for she doesn't experience them independently. Nobody does.

Thus it's likely that the red and blue sexual-norm associations are in part the product of other things. One of those things, we believe, is *mobility*: an event—or series of events—that results in one or more location changes.[7] And it alters people more than we might think. Very many children, youth, and young adults change addresses—that is, they move around either within a state or between states, typically at the behest of a parent or parents. And when they do so—especially if repeatedly—something shifts in how they approach relationships, both with friends and romantic partners. They get used to breakups. And they get used to meeting new people. They become familiar with cultural change as well as exposure to different worlds. They become a bit more cosmopolitan, even flexible. All of these are associated with blueness. Among emerging-adult women, being politically conservative—and again we're convinced that this measure is at least as much about personal culture as it is partisan conviction—is significantly associated with *staying in one place*. For men, it's associated not only with fewer in-state moves, but fewer between-state moves as well.

The fewer times men and women reported having moved in the past six or seven years, the more likely they were to identify as political conservatives. The most conservative women occupied, on average, 1.8 addresses in seven years, compared with 2.7 addresses among the most liberal women. Moderates reported exactly two addresses. Women who moved across state lines more often are also more likely to say they're politically liberal: the bluest report 1.5 states of residence, compared to the reddest, at 1.1 states. The same goes for men: the most conservative report 1.6 addresses, moderates 2.1 addresses, and liberals 3.1 addresses.

Now for the leap to sex: We tested whether moving frequently when younger is associated with more sexual partners. Since people may move to live with sex partners, we restricted our analysis to respondents who were no older than 21 (the age after which cohabitation patterns seem to swell). Table 7.3 displays the association between sex partners and youthful relocations. Women who still live in their hometown report an average of just under four lifetime sexual partners, while women who've moved three or four times report five partners, and those who've moved seven or more times report just over seven lifetime sexual partners. For men, a more pronounced pattern emerges: the least mobile men report just over four partners, and the most mobile men over 12 partners. The same association

TABLE 7.3 Mean Number of Sex Partners among Never-Marrieds, Lifetime and in the Last Year, by Geographic Mobility since June 1995, Age 21 and Under

	Men		Women	
	Lifetime	Last year	Lifetime	Last year
Number of Addresses				
Lived at 1 address	4.3	1.6	3.7	1.3
Lived at 2 addresses	5.2	1.8	4.7	1.5
Lived at 3–4 addresses	6.4	2.0	5.0	1.5
Lived at 5–6 addresses	7.9	2.1	5.4	1.6
Lived at 7–10 addresses	12.2	3.2	7.1	2.1

Source: Add Health

works whether we evaluate lifetime sexual partners or more recent ones.

Perhaps we should still be more skeptical about respondents' possibly moving in order to cohabit. Moreover, a skeptic might presume that the pattern is a simple age function: the older you are, the more likely it is that you've moved. In more advanced statistical models (shown in Table A7.1, in appendix A, p. 263), we tested whether mobility either *within* or *between* states is significantly associated with having more sexual partners. Even after controlling for age, race/ethnicity, education, region of residence, and whether one comes from a two-parent, intact family, the association remains statistically significant. In other words, it's not simply explicable by age, social class, or parental divorce. Mobility, it seems, not only expands one's cultural— and as a result, political—horizons, it also helps fashion *mentalities* about relationships that are more inclined to their cessation and generation than to their continuity.

The *reason* for the mobility, of course, matters. Some mobility is the result of parental divorce, in which case the cessation of friendships and relationships by moving may pale in significance to the cessation of the nuclear family form.[8] (But the association of number of sex partners with mobility remains significant in spite of that).

Indeed, the biologically intact two-parent family of origin emerges as a very important influence on emerging adults' lives and decisions. The act of divorce deconstructs ideas about the stability of romantic and sexual relationships and contributes to the powerful narrative that proclaims that all significant relationships come to a natural end. Even blue, irreligious respondents who've had the security of an intact family seem to fare much better in their relationships. They delay first sex longer, and they choose partners and a mate more wisely than do emerging adults who've experienced breakdown within their nuclear family unit. The interviews replay this theme powerfully, even though most of the emerging adults with whom we spoke weren't conscious of the connection.

Thus just as people *learn* sexual behavior, they also learn lots of other things. And when they move from place to place with increasing frequency, they increasingly learn that relationships are tenuous. Their own sexual histories reflect it. Of course moving frequently doesn't guarantee such a mentality or history. But mobility in general—for whatever reason—makes the mentality more possible, plausible, and understandable.

THE BIG DIFFERENCE FOR REDS: COLLEGE AND RELIGIOSITY

Andy is a 20-year-old high school dropout who lives in rural Nevada. He is red like Martin, but with more pronounced problems. Like a misfit, hapless character out of a dark version of *Napoleon Dynamite*, Andy lives with his mother and stepfather, despite his *own* paternal status. His mother met and married his stepfather in Las Vegas, where—according to Andy—he had worked as a motivational speaker. His siblings' lives are in various states of disarray, with one just out of jail. Andy has trouble keeping a job, and he is the father of a three-month-old girl, the product of a year-and-a-half-long sexual relationship with Brenda, his on-again, off-again girlfriend. He doesn't live with her; she lives with her parents. He tried living there but got in a fight with Brenda's father, who threw him out. He helps out financially with formula and diaper expenses, and he keeps his daughter on weekends. He genuinely loves the child: "Everybody says she looks like me, the poor thing." Yet on two occasions during the interview, he remarked that he was "stupid" for not wearing a condom that time. Although he has had sex with several different women, he claims he's been faithful to Brenda since the two started seeing each other. The aversion to consistent contraception among the least-educated emerging adults fits Andy's story well.

The birth of Andy and Brenda's daughter evoked mixed emotions from their families. Andy's dad, who lives in Wisconsin, didn't know "whether to say congratulations or sorry," Andy said:

> And I was like, "Oh, I don't know. I guess 'congratulations' kind of would . . . make me feel kind of better." And he's all, "Okay, well, congratulations, son." And then he's like, "Well, did you tell your mom?" And I was like, "Hell, no!" And he's all, "Oh geez." He's all, "Well, I ain't telling her." [*So what did she say when you told her?*] She shit a brick. . . . I don't even remember what she said to me, but it wasn't nice. It wasn't pretty.

Brenda's family reacted about as well: "Her dad told me . . . 'You're a dumb ass' [laughs]. . . . He just laughed at me. But her mom is like, 'Time to get a job, mother-fucker,' because I hadn't had a job for like the last month."

The presence of Andy's daughter within his life provides practical motivation for improving his own behavior and character. Andy is thinking, for instance, about the example he sets of substance use. The harder drugs he reported a few years before are behind him now: "I don't want my daughter to grow up watching me smoke pot [and] say, 'That's cool. I'm gonna try that shit.'" Andy also claims that he's in the process of "getting right with God," a common red mantra. He was baptized recently in his mother's Methodist church and says he is now trying "to obey the Lord." What exactly he means by that is unclear to us and perhaps to him as well. While he now regularly attends the church with his mother, he just doesn't seem to catch what's going on there. Together with many reds, he values religion. But he isn't sure what it really entails or about his own future stake in it:

> I don't even, you know, read the Bible. I mean, I do, but not as much as I should. I don't, you know, I don't pay as much attention at services as I should. So I'm thinking I might just, you know, just go to work and just totally forget about it.

What the future holds for Andy is about as clear as his past has been stable. He seems to have trouble anticipating consequences from his sexual decisions, though he does his best to handle the consequences as they arise. Despite his lack of job prowess, his poor relationship skills, and his modest interest in religion, abortion was never a valid option for this red:

> It's up to God to take lives, you know. If God didn't think we were ready to have a kid, then He would have, you know, not necessarily killed the baby but I mean, not let it live, you know. So I just said, "We'll just let it go through and see what the Lord has to say, you know, see what the Lord does. . . . [But Brenda said,] "The hell with that. . . . I think it's murder." She just thinks straight out that [abortion] is murder: "I ain't doing that." So, we're both on the same page. And her mom is like, "You guys are dumber than shit."

When we had spoken with Andy two years prior—before Brenda and before their daughter arrived—he had stated plainly that when pregnancies occur, babies are born and somehow supported: "That would be messed up not to, you know?" So his thinking on the subject has not changed.

Despite the morality Andy confers upon abortion and homosexuality, he doesn't really consider his own sexual behavior as a moral issue, or at least not one that he gives much thought to. Andy displays what we call *selective permissiveness*, a hallmark of some cultural conservatives, first noted in chapter 2. This perspective holds the general population to traditional gender roles and restrictive sexual and relationship standards while exempting themselves from adherence to those standards. In fact, Andy doesn't express regret about any of his sexual decisions, only about practical matters like contraception. He also illustrates a compelling example of what social psychologist Jonathan Haidt calls *confabulation*, the human tendency to more easily fashion a strong moral judgment than the ability to rationally defend it.[9] As we noted earlier in the chapter, Andy thinks gays are sick and lesbians are cool. He doesn't really know exactly *why* that's the case, but the feeling is unmistakable. He knows it in his gut, and no argument will change his mind.

While Andy and Martin display a common face of emerging-adult conservatism, other reds look dramatically different. They are more optimistic, more ambitious, and slower to have sex, in fact. The experience of college and the commitments of Christian faith tend to make a monumental difference in the lives of reds. Some semblance of Christian morality may have prompted Andy and his girlfriend to keep their baby rather than elect abortion, but beyond that, the evidence of religious influence on his sexual decision-making is slim.

Table 7.4 reveals a stark contrast in the sex lives of two types of white, conservative American. Andy's type—male, white, conservative, only modestly religious and not currently pursuing a college degree— is among the most sexually active of emerging adults: They've had (on

TABLE 7.4 Sexual Activity among White, Conservative, Never-Married 18- to 23-Year-Olds

	Men			Women		
	Mean lifetime partners	Percent virgins	Sex in past year[a]	Mean lifetime partners	Percent virgins	Sex in past year[a]
Modestly religious, not four-year college student or graduate	7.5	14.7	83	4.8	16.6	69
Religious, four-year college student or graduate	0.9	52.4	35	1.4	63.0	29
All others	5.9	15.4	59	5.0	14.5	59

Source: Add Health
[a]*Among nonvirgins*

average) between seven and eight sexual partners already, and they report a frequency of sex that averages just under once every four days, a rate not far below married young adults. Women who fit this profile similarly distinguish themselves from their fellow white conservatives—women who are more religious and more educated—by averaging over three more sexual partners, fewer than one-third the number of virgins, and more than double the frequency of sexual intercourse. Moreover, this less-educated, less-religious type of conservative is also among the most likely to get married, have children, and get divorced—*all by age 23*.

It's important for social observers, then, to distinguish among the conservative masses. Most of them are not terribly religious during young adulthood. Age 22 is the least religious year of the entire life course, on average. Many of our survey respondents and interviewees, blue and red, are currently religiously unplugged.[10] But among those who do display religiosity, it's quite clear that faith plays a role in shaping their sexual decision-making. It doesn't mean that our religious interviewees were ubiquitously virgins; they weren't. But it does mean that their sexual behavior tends to be less prolific. More devoutly religious emerging adults tend to exhibit fewer partners and less sex, as Table 7.4 suggests. The association between religiosity and sexual conservatism here does not hold for blues, however (results not shown). It only appears among reds. In other words, political conservatism and religiosity seem to coalesce and reinforce each other in shaping sexual decisions. Where only the latter exists, its influence is weaker.

Dalton is a 20-year-old evangelical from Texas and a junior at a Christian university. Likable and confident, he has not had sexual intercourse yet. He even displays the abstinence pledge ring he wore to our first interview. Unlike many other young men, though, Dalton thinks he's not as sexually driven as some of his peers. He has had two relatively long-term girlfriends, but has always stopped before going "too far." For him, the line is intensive kissing, and no further, though he notes that the topic of what *is* too far is a perennially popular one among fellow Christian students. The damage he anticipates that sex would cause his self-image (via guilt) is reason enough to stop well short of intercourse. In fact, he drew the line with a previous girlfriend out of a sense of both maintaining his own personal code and "protecting her character." Dalton is both very religious—a devout evangelical Christian—and very culturally conservative, having been raised in an Air Force family that stressed obedience and the importance of family and honor. He told us he would never consider cohabiting with a woman before marriage. Not only would it be immoral, "my grandma just would go nuts." In fact, he thinks of girls in terms of how his family would receive them. Certain girls are "ho bags" and off limits, while others are just the type to "take home to Mom." And dating ought to have a clear end in mind:

> I've always been taught that dating is a precursor to getting married, and you can't treat it . . . like off and on and off and on. So you need to take it serious with the people that you're dating. I know people that are like boyfriend and girlfriend that have no plans on getting married whatsoever. And I think that's completely pointless.

A former short-term missionary, 19-year-old Danielle just started her freshman year at a state university in the mid-South. She plans to be active in campus ministry and to date only Christians. She's also a virgin and intends to remain that way until she marries. She went to a True Love Waits rally in high school, which she describes as "awesome." Her parents told her that they waited for marriage, and she feels enabled to do so as well.[11] Unlike some women who are holding out (but aren't very marketable to begin with), Danielle has no trouble attracting men: she's had two long-term boyfriends, including one who's now 23 and just out of the navy. She's also begun taking birth control pills to relieve a recurrent problem with cysts. While all of these indicate elevated sexual opportunity, Danielle seems firm in her commitment. It helps that her boyfriend attends another college. Boyfriends elsewhere can be a convenient excuse for women to pay little attention to the local sexual marketplace.

She articulates just how sexualized American culture has become: "I just think we keep compromising." Sex "just adds more drama to life and more confusion. And it's just sad." Drama is right, if chapter 5 is any indicator. If she could change one thing about today's society, it would be "how guys and girls view themselves and . . . [how they] treat each other and their bodies. . . . It's like, so sad that girls think that they have to like, parade around just to make someone like, fall in love with them." She has no false expectations about the challenges facing her virginity, however: "It just seems so impossible sometimes." Indeed, religious tension over sexual decisions seems more evident among women than men. Journalist Paula Kamen remarks about her interviewees: "When discussing sexual issues, the women I met brought up no other topic more often than religion. They mentioned religion as a factor in how they were dealing with almost every sexual issue, such as homosexuality, premarital sex, abortion, openness when discussing sex, the family, and especially sexual pleasure and guilt."[12]

Many Christian emerging adults openly admit that they push the boundaries of their community's sexual morality. Kaci, a 19-year-old evangelical college freshman from Texas, confesses her criteria are probably indefensible religiously; she just elects not to think about it. She describes the rules in her relationship with her boyfriend, a youth pastor in training: no vaginal intercourse, no mouth on anyone's genitals. But hand jobs and fingering are fine. And "both of our clothes are never off at the same time." Recall that in chapter 2, we pointed out that "technical virginity" *becomes* a religious thing over time. In high school, it was the domain of the most ambitious teens—the ones who wanted to have sexual experiences but feared pregnancy and its life-wrecking capacity. In college, the technical virgins are devout Christians who dread the guilt of trespassing across that final boundary.

While Christian emerging adults draw the line over what's moral and what's not in different places, most of them recognize that even a generous reading of relevant biblical texts won't favor the morality of having a series of nonmarital sexual partners. Thus their sex is far more likely to be relational than associational and to develop less rapidly and after greater displays of commitment. Like other young Americans, they too are living out the powerful story of serial monogamy. They just try to keep the serial part short.

"Morals"

Kendra is a sophomore at a university in California, but she commutes from home, which limits her interaction with campus culture. Kendra is a virgin, pretty confident about it, and very comfortable with it. She intends to abstain from sex until she's married. And she's a very planful person, a trait that is consistently associated with delaying sex among teenagers: "I tend to overanalyze things in life instead of just living in the moment or living for the day." She wants to make a career out of planning other people's weddings—perhaps the perfect job for a conservative, domestic, planful idealist. Like Dalton, Kendra seems disinterested in sex. What has not been introduced into her plan yet, however, is a boyfriend. That may change everything, as it has for so many emerging-adult women.

Kendra attends a nondenominational evangelical church, but ironically doesn't exude religiosity and isn't involved apart from attending church on Sundays (which of course is far more than most collegians do). In listening to her, it becomes clear that her sexual conservatism is more cultural and familial in its sources than religious. This can be detected in part by her use of terminology that has little to do with distinctively religious motivation:

> I don't tend to hang out with people who have different morals than I do. It just, I think that would be a very difficult situation. But the people that I am friends with, they have the same beliefs, the same morals, so . . . we keep each other in check.

Like many reds, Kendra is big into terms like "core beliefs," "morals," and "values." They are religious *derivatives* that serve as indicators of cultural conservativeness. Like the evolution of those now-infamous mortgage-backed derivatives (in the Great Recession), religious derivatives emerged from traditional religious ideas but are no longer obviously religious in nature. All people have core beliefs and values, but reds are more apt to speak of them, label them, and identify them with *morals*. They are personal principles which can be transgressed but never denied. As such they provide a window into red perspectives on relationships, sexuality, and responsibility. What exactly they mean is not always clear, but morals as a class emphasize traditional themes, including monogamy, fidelity, loyalty, and family.

WHY RED AND BLUE MATTERS: SEX, MARRIAGE, AND THE SECOND DEMOGRAPHIC TRANSITION

Talk of red and blue sex has import beyond the lives of the particular emerging adults who illustrate their themes. Red and blue values form the locus of institutional struggle over what the United States will become. Western societies' lengthy economic prosperity—all recessions aside—is believed to have brought about a scenario in which men and women alike are losing traditional motivations to marry. Marriage no longer anchors the adult life course in several European countries, and some demographers are now projecting that the United States is on track for the same destination, albeit more slowly. In other words, they think America is turning blue. Marriage is no longer perceived as the economic asset (or cultural requirement) it once was, especially to women. In step with later and fewer marriages, fertility declines as well.[13]

Nonmarital births, however, are on the rise, climbing from 4 percent of all births in 1940 to 40 percent in 2009. In the early 1960s, *over half* of all first births were to married couples who had conceived the child before they were married (in, most likely, a "shotgun" wedding).

By 1990, that number had dipped down to 27 percent. It wasn't that far more babies were being conceived within marriage but that far fewer first births were occurring there.[14] The age groups of 20–24 and 25–29 are driving this trend, moreover, something heretofore unprecedented. (By contrast, teenagers previously characterized most nonmarital births.) Additionally, an increasing share of nonmarital childbearing is to intentionally cohabiting partners—forerunners perhaps of more permanent cohabitation arrangements in which fathers are believed to be present at rates exceeding temporary cohabitations.[15]

Meanwhile, the financial risks of divorce loom large among young men who operate—in their minds—with a "50 percent chance of success" mentality about marriage.[16] Imbalanced sex ratios in colleges, congregations, and some workplaces continue to undermine women's chances of finding the sort of ideal mate they'd prefer. And yet expectations for how a marriage *ought* to look and feel remain very high.[17] No one wishes to settle. Indeed, we shouldn't be surprised that expectations about marriage are so high, since women and men no longer have to enter it to live a fulfilling life. Since most can make it economically on their own, fewer elect to "settle" than ever before.

Demographers identify these as symptoms of the *second demographic transition* (SDT).[18] The first demographic transition occurred in the West well over 100 years ago when the death rate began to drop, mirroring an earlier decline in the birth rate. Those two declines are thought to be central to the economic development of nations.

Before the Industrial Revolution, families needed children not simply because parents loved kids but because they needed help around the house and farm. Children were necessary for household production. Today, however, children are objects of consumption, not production. When children are no longer economic assets, the optimal economic behavior of women changes. In other words, it becomes more economically efficient for women to earn money to buy things than to produce those things themselves (or with help from their children).

While the last stage in the demographic transition is believed to be one of stability—where both birth and death rates are low and population size remains relatively stable—some scholars sense more change afoot for postindustrial economies. Birthrates have fallen so dramatically that, were it not for immigration, they would eventually lead to population decline and an imbalanced age structure in which the relatively few young would soon bear a significant financial burden in caring and providing for the comparatively many aged. A variety of countries in Asia and Europe are in this state already, experiencing what's called the "low fertility trap," the point at which expectations of low fertility become so entrenched in the social system that they become self-perpetuating and very difficult to emerge from.[19] That trap is believed to spring when a country's total fertility rate (TFR) falls to 1.3.[20]

The Czech Republic, Poland, Ukraine, South Korea, Hong Kong, Japan, Hungary, and Singapore are in the trap already, while several large powers—like Russia, Germany, Italy, and Spain—teeter just above it, with a TFR of around 1.4. The United States' TFR of 2.05 is now above that of Iran, Chile, and Thailand—countries most of us perceive of as much less-developed—and not far below such countries as Mexico, Vietnam, Turkey, Brazil, and Argentina. The globe's average woman has 2.55 children, a figure far lower than most of us have been taught to presume.

Even if the worst projections about population decline don't come true and the trap fails to spring as advertised, the imbalanced age structure of many Western countries will remain pronounced, prompting tough calls to either increase the tax burden on the young or cut benefits to the aging. (The Greek austerity measures of 2010 come to mind.) Demography really is destiny, but it's hardly ever recognized as such, because demographic challenges—in this case, fertility reductions—are slow to develop, difficult to alter, and are the unintended byproducts of often rational and optimal decisions by regular people to have fewer children and a life richer in economic success and personal experiences.

Moral Hazard and the SDT

Low fertility is a good example of a *moral hazard*, an unintended situation that occurs when people are insulated from risk—in the American case, by the actions of the federal government to provide Social Security, unemployment benefits, and Medicare. Such hazards arise when individuals (or institutions) don't bear the full consequences of their actions and as a result, tend to act differently than they otherwise would. In this case, since we're confident that the federal government has our back should we fall on hard times, we're less likely to have larger families (in order to spread the cost of our own care among our more numerous children). Instead, we rely on the government to bear some responsibility for our care. This is truer in most European countries than in the United States, where social welfare benefits are far more modest. We're not making a moral or political claim here about the wisdom of larger or smaller families or of federal provision of social security and health insurance to the aged. It's simply an observation that when an institution ensures the public's future well-being, their fertility behavior will change toward a greater and increasing reliance on that institution and a lesser reliance on children for elder care.

All of this points to the fact that getting worked up about lower-than-replacement-level fertility is very, very hard. Too many of us have enjoyed its fruits: greater career success, fewer limitations, higher income, mobility, freedom. Those are worth a great deal. Any potential penalties or unintended consequences seem just too far down the road—and with too many possible alterations along the way—for the average person to care about. And since any individual's personal fertility contribution is but a drop in the bucket, the rational actor continues to pursue the path of maximal freedom and options, in consonance with the most compelling scripts about the ideal emerging-adult life.

Regional Variations in the SDT

Although we're familiar with entire states being tinted red or blue while watching presidential election coverage, the second demographic transition is far more subtle in its coloration of America. Blue states—or more accurately blue regions, cities, and metropolitan areas—typically display more traits associated with the SDT. They have higher rates of cohabitation, higher average ages at first marriage, lower and later fertility rates, lower divorce rates, and higher abortion rates.[21] Red locales typically have lower rates of cohabitation, lower average ages at first marriage, higher fertility rates, and lower abortion rates. SDT indicators, however, cut through states as well: there are SDT regions and metropolitan areas within traditionally red states as well as communities that resist the SDT within blue states. Indeed, America continues to witness an increasing geographic clustering of social values concerning marriage, fertility, politics, and religion.[22] Overlay five different county-level maps portraying (1) support for marriage, (2) actual fertility, (3) cohabitation rates, (4) political affiliation, and (5) religious adherence, and you will quickly realize that you're looking at five very similar maps.

But not all SDT indicators cluster together—another indication that the SDT will look different in the United States than in Europe. Economists Ron Lesthaeghe and Lisa Neidert point out that there are states and counties that appear red by SDT indicators yet display comparatively low levels of teen pregnancy and nonmarital childbearing. The Dakotas, Iowa, Nebraska, Kansas, Wyoming, Idaho, and Utah exemplify this tendency. Nevada, Florida, Delaware, and California, however, display the reverse pattern: though blue by SDT indicators, each displays an elevated teen pregnancy and nonmarital childbearing rate, both classic red traits.

The second demographic transition is related to our sex lives, because our sexual relationship patterns do more than simply reflect existing interests in smaller families. They structurally help cause declining fertility. Prevailing contemporary norms about serial monogamy, the normalization of pre-premarital sex, and widespread contraceptive use are consonant with the SDT, such that some analysts are tempted to conclude that any larger ideological conflict about sex, marriage, and family is over.[23] Not so fast, we say. We're not so sure that the United States' marital and family future is tracking unequivocally toward that of Europe's. It very well may be, but a handful of variables could delay or even alter its eastward drift. One way in which the United States does not mimic Europe and the SDT is in its persistent *prioritization of marriage*, albeit at different preferred ages. Americans enter marriage, exit, and then repeat the process.[24] And yet the vast majority of emerging adults in America still wish to marry and most of those will. Indeed, few among them display what demographers would label as a key indicator of the SDT in Europe: the tolerance of *permanent* cohabitation arrangements. Such permanent arrangements remain comparatively rare in the United States, although our relationship patterns are slowly trending in that direction.

IS THE UNITED STATES BECOMING BLUER OR REDDER?

The question of whether the United States is turning colors is like that posed by economists Pippa Norris and Ronald Inglehart in their study of data from the omnibus World Values Survey.[25] They asked whether the world was becoming more or less secular. And the answer they offer is "yes." More people are becoming secular than ever before; religious-service attendance in the West continues to decline. Yet Norris and Inglehart also confidently stated that the world is becoming a more religious place, because the religious citizens of the world are more interested in reproduction than are the secular.

The same concept holds true with our question. More and more Americans are turning blue in how they understand the morality of sex—dominated by the idea of serial monogamy and the importance of cohabiting before marrying and having children. Reds think comparably about sex but cohabit less and for shorter durations, and they marry earlier and have more children. Blues grow more swiftly by conversion, often in the form of higher education and social class mobility. Reds tend to grow by reproduction.

Take no strong cues about a blue or red future from elections, since those primarily reflect economic questions (especially the perennial "Am I better off than I was four years ago?"). Nor should you read too much into policies and decisions about abortion or gay marriage, perennial culture-war subjects. Take your cues about our blue or red future instead from data on sexual-partnership patterns, cohabitation rates, and trends in age at marriage and fertility. *Those* will shape the future of the United States and will determine whether we will look more like Europe in 30 years, or not. Our bet is that our nation will slowly continue to grow bluer yet will display even more distinctive regional colors than it does today. Our confidence in this projection is modest, however: too many variables could likewise propel us in a redder direction. And no prediction can account for the powerful redirections that could accompany global events or catastrophes.

CONCLUSION

One way in which we map how culture shapes emerging adults' sexual decision-making is in their political culture. Reds and blues exhibit distinctive mentalities about sex and relationships. Blues hold fewer strong attitudes about sex and relationships and are less quick to evaluate the decisions of others. They are more pragmatic about sex and relationships, recognizing that their highest calling at present is to pursue the development of the self, preferably in the form of higher education and a career. Along the way, relationships are meant to augment that journey, not supplant it. Reds, on the other hand, struggle more over the ranking of these priorities. Politically, culturally, and often religiously conservative, reds tend to be more idealist than realist. Christian faith is supposed to be paramount—or at least respected— and yet it often competes with sexual and material desires. Some pursue higher education; others don't. They romanticize relationships and marriage, and often experience more of them—and at earlier ages—than blues do.

Reds and blues share much in common, including their commitment to serial monogamy and romantic individualism, two ubiquitous narratives among emerging adults. While reds and blues both hook up, reds feel guiltier about it and tend to explain the events as aberrations.

While the red sex–blue sex dichotomy can be a helpful binary tool, more significant sources of influence are found in emerging adults' decisions about higher education, religiosity, family structure changes that they've endured, and even such experiences as mobility during adolescence.

At a higher level of observation, many demographers suspect that the United States is beginning to look more like Europe in its relationship and fertility patterns. And yet the development of this second demographic transition here may continue to look different than on the Continent, primarily because we remain a "marrying" country. Even blues like the idea and tend to marry, albeit later than reds and typically following at least one stint of cohabitation. Americans also tend to have more children than do most Europeans, where abortion and contraception are more readily available and affordable. Whether America will look redder or bluer in the future is the subject of educated guesses that balance projections (based on fertility rates and immigration patterns) with the diffusive power of widely shared mentalities about the place of sex and relationships in the pursuit of the good life. We will just have to wait and find out when we get there.

EIGHT

The Power of Stories and Ten Myths about Sex in Emerging Adulthood

I don't know how to take responsibility for myself, OK. . . . I don't know what to do. I'm an idiot. Tell me what to do.

—Ben Stone in Knocked Up

W HILE RED AND blue America may enact their sexual values differently or at different times, sexual values themselves do not simply evolve. Instead, sexual values and other ways of relating are taught and learned. They reflect the grand narratives that animate our lives and our shared cultures, as well as our economic realities.

A narrative, or story, is "a form of communication that arranges human actions and events into organized wholes in a way that bestows meaning on the actions and events by specifying their interactive or cause-and-effect relations to the whole."[1] Stories are more than just chronicles or histories. They have sets of characters, plots, points, scripts. As sociologist Christian Smith notes in his book *Moral, Believing Animals*, we can't live without stories that tell us what is real and significant, to know who we are, what we should do, and why. Most of us don't relate to our own stories as evaluative critics of them. Instead, we are the actors who are swept up in them.

When we asked Kate, a 20-year-old sexually experienced interviewee, how she came to think about sex in the way that she does, she responded by simply noting the scripts surrounding her: "I just think that it's a mixture of everything that I've heard you're supposed to do." When a woman perceives pressure to sleep with her boyfriend because they've been going out for four months already—even if he hasn't verbalized it—she's listening to a story that says that that is what good girlfriends are supposed to do at this point in a romantic relationship. Her friends may tell her outright, but it's far more likely that she's catching cues from them and their relationships, from media, from conversations, and from her own observations and guesswork that yes, this is "what I'm supposed to do next." When a young man cycles through online porn, he wonders whether he too can ever have sex like that. The people in the photos and videos are. He thinks it would be unbelievable to experience what he's seeing. Some of his friends report (and perhaps distort) amazing encounters with women who've said yes, with no strings attached. He hopes he'll get the chance and that it'll unfold like that. This, too, is a story about sex.

All the statistical analyses in the world can fail to uncover the role of stories in shaping how people make decisions about sex. The same is true about pursuing career goals, getting married, getting divorced, and numerous other important decisions in life. People don't do things because they're a collection of variables. People don't act in certain ways simply because they're male or female, or because they're 20 years old, or because they're white or because their parents got a divorce. Nor do they meticulously weigh the costs and benefits of different action strategies before moving forward. Rather, people pay attention to—and live out—compelling and attractive stories. Marketing experts figured this out long ago; it's taking social scientists a bit longer.

Stories tend to issue in sets of particular scripts. We have referred regularly in this book to the idea of *scripts*, starting in chapter 1. Sexual scripts specify not only appropriate sexual goals—what we ought to want—they also provide plans for particular types of behavior and ways to achieve those sexual goals: the right thing to say at the right time, what not to do, who leads, how to hook up, where they should go, who should bring the condom, what's too much to ask of someone, etc.

One of the reasons many people find the sex articles in *The Onion* so humorous is because unlike any other published source, *The Onion*'s so-called "articles" often detail the distinctly unspoken, unwritten norms about sexual conduct. There really are an unbelievable number of subtle social norms in the sphere of sex, from how to figure out what sounds are appropriate or necessary to make while having sex, to how men want women to look in order to be sexually desirable to them (not overweight, but not too skinny either), to the strange norms of faceless, online romance. It's remarkable, too, how rapidly new social scripts for appropriate sexual goals and behavior must and do develop. Who knew as recently as 1995 how to act in pursuing romance via online dating sites? And yet today, there are strong norms about how to conduct oneself online, what's too forthright, what works, what doesn't, what can be shared, and what you ought to refrain from saying.

One of our interviewees was convinced that men with larger penises were "better in bed," even though she'd had limited sexual experience herself. How did she know this? From a popular story about it that continues to circulate widely. We're not suggesting it's either true or false; that's not the point. The point is that it's a story that shapes even the thoughts, motives, and decisions of the inexperienced. Stories are why sex advice columns are so appealing. They satisfy the thirst for information about what sexual scripts "other people" are following. (Never mind that a columnist will only respond with their own preferred script).

People are also subject to intensive competition between sexual scripts. While almost everyone knows that a condom affords adequate protection against sexually transmitted infections when used correctly, lots of other scripts interrupt this public health effort—including the script that asserts that condoms reduce pleasure, the script that says it's too awkward to actually talk about condoms (or anything, for that matter) during sexual interactions, and the script that suggests a woman doesn't trust her partner if she asks him to use a condom.

While there is great variety among sexual scripts, some scripts about sex are available—or at least widely affirmed—and some are not. What scripts people can access depends on lots of things, like where they live, what their friends are doing, what their parents think, what opportunities they have, and what attractions they offer, among other things. Emerging adults in Manhattan can more readily say yes to some sexual scripts that emerging adults in Lubbock, Texas, could not. And the Texans have access to socially shared scripts that are all but dismissed by their New York peers. The two sets of scripts rest upon different master narratives about the nature of the good life, what's desirable and smart and true (and what's not), as well as the meaning of sex and the purpose of relationships.

So what happens when someone lacks access to alternative stories about sex? Simple: they don't easily envision alternatives to what they know. This is why intellectual history is so important. So much about our lives could be *different*. There isn't a natural progression of values and norms toward some obvious, universal end.

TRANSMITTING SCRIPTS

So who transmits scripts, and how do they do it? Friends and peers are the top transmitters, by far. Parents are a close second, though their sway tends to decline with age. Institutionally, popular sexual scripts are powerfully distributed by video and audio media (in other words, movies, songs, and television shows). Beyond them, corporations use sexual scripts to sell their products, as we noted in chapter 4. Religious leaders attempt to press their adherents to neglect popular sexual scripts in favor of more circumscribed, conservative or marriage-oriented ones. Sex and sexual health educators often have an altogether different script than the media and religious leaders. And with an ear and eye to what competing institutions and organizations are purveying, each tweaks its message with a good deal of regularity.

It wouldn't be fair to suggest that media ideas about sex are simply internalized in the minds of American youth. Not everyone sees or hears the same thing when they're watching or listening to sexualized content. One person's yum is another's yuck. And—recalling our own adolescence—plenty of sexualized content just doesn't even register. So people vary widely in what sexual scripts and ideals they uptake from mass media. But what registers matters. Jane Brown, professor of journalism and an expert on mass media influence, asserts without doubt that the sexual content of media shapes our sexual decision-making. It comes down to stories, she reasons: "People use stories they see . . . as reference points about what's important . . . and what is considered appropriate and inappropriate behavior."[2] The media, Brown claims, keeps sex on our agendas, reinforces a narrow and consistent set of sexual norms, and rarely exposes us to responsible sexual actors. That is how it affects sexual decision-making: by limiting access to alternative scripts. Psychologist Monique Ward's experimental research project supports Brown's claims: she found that duration of exposure to television content expressing four common norms—that men are sex-driven, that women are sex objects, that appearance is paramount in dating, and that dating is a game—corresponded to heightened endorsement of those norms when compared with viewers who were not exposed to the same content.[3] Moreover, the association is strongest in women, suggesting that women more than men are shaped by media stories about sex. But men consistently endorsed those norms at higher levels than women; they just didn't exhibit a "treatment" effect like women did. (Yet more support for sexual economics claims and the persistence of the double standard.) Perhaps this is why during our interviews more women than men made reference to sex in their media diet. We often asked where they get the ideas they have about sex, and after the standard parents-and-friends line, we heard about films and television shows, especially *Sex and the City*: "Yeah, we are pretty open to talking about (sex). I think the *Sex and the City* revolution opened up the door, you know, for people to be able to communicate openly about those sorts of things." "Actually I have learned from TV that sex is kind of, like, just not a big deal," another admits.

Emerging adults really are just looking around trying to figure out from each other what they ought to want and do, and when. They can convince each other of all sorts of things. If the advice in *Cosmopolitan* articles suddenly turned sexually conservative—which of course won't happen—we're convinced that millions would begin to give such ideas new consideration.

INSTITUTIONALIZING SEXUAL SCRIPTS

That scenario is unlikely because scripts become institutionalized. Most of us feel sexual desire for lots of different people with a great deal of regularity, but knowing when, how, and why to channel that desire in the ways we do is the result of social norms that emerge from common stories about what sex ought to be like and with whom it should and shouldn't be experienced (and where, and when, and how, etc.). Yet when the majority of people choose very similar paths, it points out just how structured or institutionalized those paths really are.

Institutionalization refers to predefined patterns of conduct that channel action in one direction as against the many other directions that would theoretically be possible. To say that a segment of human activity has been institutionalized is to say that it has been subsumed under social control (that is, people will police each other's behavior). What does this have to do with sex? An example will help here. Danielle is a 19-year-old college student in Texas. During our interview we discussed fraternity and sorority life on campus. She spoke of an annual Fall football weekend during which it is customary for fraternity members to invite "dates" to spend the weekend with them in Dallas. For couples who are already in a sexual relationship, it's obvious both whom to invite and what to do after an evening of barhopping. For fraternity brothers who aren't in such a relationship, the answer to both questions isn't so apparent. But whoever they invite is expected to spend the night with them in a hotel room with another comparable couple, one pair in each bed. Danielle went, and got drunk along with the man who invited her. Too drunk for sex, in fact. She didn't really have to make a decision about whether to "sleep with him," since both were too busy actually sleeping.

The point here is not to answer a question about "did they" or "didn't they." Rather, it's about the institutionalization of a historically awkward arrangement as both normal and subsumed under social control. Why don't women and men who aren't already sexually active with each other sleep in separate hotel rooms for the weekend? Because the housing arrangement has come to be socially policed in one direction. The question "Why are we doing it this way?" becomes answered as "This is the way it's done." To contest it is to invite the social sanction or rejection of (desirable) men. The script about the weekend is structured to "override" anyone's own personal feelings or desires to the contrary. Fraternities are particularly skilled at this: they've structured ways of operating that maximize the likelihood that the brothers will access sex. It's not accidental. It's institutional. Popular sexual scripts—together with the constraints of sexual economics and market realities—have combined to generate a set of structured pathways that characterize the way forward for most emerging adults.

Parents who might question such an arrangement feel powerless to do so, or else themselves now regard the football weekend as "the way it's done." It's attained a firmness in consciousness. It's become real in a way that it can no longer be changed or challenged so readily by parent or child. It becomes the world they know. Since they had no part in shaping it, it confronts them as a given reality. Institutions appear in this same way—as given, unalterable and self-evident. Moreover, humans tend toward conformity, in part because we are social beings, constituted by our relationships. While we have the ability to reflect upon and react to the expectations (and scripts) of others, we don't often do that. To attempt to thwart even bad ideas or suboptimal scripts runs the risk of social sanction—rejection. While we spoke with many interviewees—both women and men—who aren't fond of the sexual scripts to which they have access, most feel powerless to stop the train or even complain about the train's destination or their fellow passengers' behavior. It's the world they know. It could be different. But it's not.

Instead, we have the world we have described herein. It's a world that's hard on relationships and soft on loyalty and commitment. It's a world that values sexual experimentation, options, and variety. It's a world that, frankly, seems more appealing to men than women. While women have fought a long and noble fight to enjoy greater equality with men, we're not sure that the struggle has paid off in the domain of sex as it has in education or the workplace. Women are now freer to have sex like men, but most—if they're honest with themselves—don't wish to.

To conclude this book, then, we list and describe ten myths that have emerged from common sexual and relationship scripts. (We are not, however, *personally* contesting or endorsing these myths). We call them myths not so much because they're categorically untrue. We call them myths because the empirical data from surveys and interviews suggests they aren't true *most of the time*. In other words, these ten myths may be believed by many emerging-adult men and women, but the evidence supporting them just isn't there.

First, long-term exclusivity is a fiction.

We have no doubt that what constitutes a relationship has become less serious and of shorter duration than in previous generations and that long-term exclusivity is less common.

Indeed, many emerging adults consider it foolish and unhealthy *not* to explore different sexual relationships. At the same time, many express that they desire the feelings of security and acceptance that come from long-term exclusivity.

Sexual experimentation is valued, but cheating on a monogamous partner is clearly not. So emerging adults don't know what to do with their own and others' sexual history; a partner's past actions signal their personal priorities and how they *might* act in the future. Many choose either to ignore sexual histories or to cover them up. And for good reason: as we noted in chapter 3, women especially are sanctioned for their sexual past.

Long-term exclusivity is not a daydream, however. It remains eminently possible. When we ask our students in class how long half of all marriages last, they fumble around for a response, guessing five years, or seven, or 10 tops. Their minds, of course, are focused on the average time-until-divorce. But the answer, which never occurs to them, is *a lifetime*. The GSS, administered to a nationally representative sample of American adults every two years, always finds that extramarital affairs are true only of a minority: about 12–13 percent report it. And there has been no trend either upward or downward on this count since 1991.[4]

Second, the introduction of sex is necessary in order to sustain a fledging or struggling relationship.

We understand the logic behind this myth, as well as its believability. Still, it's just not true scientifically. *Most* relationships fail, and the sooner relationships become sexual, the greater their odds of failure. This is not to suggest that all such relationships *will* fail—just that they're more apt to. Relationships started with sex are even more tenuous (see Table 3.3, in chapter 3, p. 73). No shortage of emerging adults, however, think the data must somehow be wrong. Hence, they act like it's not true, only to become part of the same data pattern themselves.

No doubt in some relationships a partner may insist on sex relatively early in a relationship. In that sense, many would assert that indeed such a relationship will fail without sex. It's probably true. We, however, would assert that such a relationship is largely doomed to failure even if sex is provided.

The shrewd emerging adult will remember the claims of sexual economics about the value of sex *to men* but also that imbalanced gender ratios in communities and colleges continue to give men more power over the direction of their relationships, since they're the rarer sex. Some women, like Cami—whom we met at the beginning of chapter 2—fight back. For her, waiting on sex is a formula for relationship success, not defeat: "For me personally, I think if you wait, it would probably be a really good way to know that you were in love and the guy thought you were valuable enough to wait for." She is an idealist, no doubt, but what she wants is what many wish to witness for themselves: commitment, love, and sacrifice. Sexual economics theory—as well as the data analyses herein—suggests that if she remembers that sex has considerable exchange value for an attractive woman like herself, she's more apt to get what she wants. It won't be easy, of course, since many men would simply move on in search of lower-cost sex. But some won't. They'll pursue.

Third, the sexual double standard is inherently wrong and must be resisted by any means.

To call the sexual double standard wrong is a little like asserting that rainy days are wrong. We may not like them, but they're not going away. The double standard in sex is real and quite durable, and there's only one effective way to resist it—and that is for women to attempt to feel and think and pursue sex like men. Plenty attempt this, but only a minority can *sustain* it—we saw how that typically turns out (in chapter 5). Women may enjoy sex as much as men do, but on average they don't pursue it as often or for the same reasons.

To erase the double standard, we would have to alter the deep-rooted psychology of *most* men and women as well as the structured ways in which they relate—not simply the social scripts accessible to them. Scripts change; altering psychology and the baseline economics of relationships is not so easy. So much about sexual attraction, desire, behavior, and response exhibits robust gender differences. Yet the way the term "double standard" is popularly used implies that men occupy the optimal position; as in, "Why should women be held to a higher standard than men?" On the contrary, perhaps it ought to be lauded that women generally *do* set higher standards for their relationships.

Unfortunately, many well-meaning adults and educators want so badly to dismantle the double standard that they work to normalize any and all consensual sexual relationships, rather than considering whether common experiences of sexual regret are in fact telling us something.

Fourth, boys will be boys. That is, men can't be expected to abide by the sexual terms that women may wish to set.

Since the double standard is real, then "boys will be boys," right? That is, they'll want to maximize orgasms while minimizing commitments, and they'll prefer no strings attached. The reality, however, is that this scenario is *not* fixed. Men live up to—or down to—the expectations placed upon them. Yes, boys will be boys if nothing different is expected of them in the domain of sex; that is, if the price of sex remains persistently low. But it has not always been as low as it is now, nor will it necessarily remain low. It will *likely* remain low for the foreseeable future, though, due to several market forces—including imbalanced gender ratios in major American institutions like higher education and religious congregations (two places in which historically, many have located partners), easy access to high-quality porn (since masturbation now mimics real sex better than ever before), the near-complete collapse of female collusion to restrict either access to sex or the timing of its introduction in relationships, and how few constraints there are on the freedom of sexual relationships (including marriage) either to begin or end.[5] So if sexual economics theory holds true—and our results generally confirm its premises—boys will be boys whenever market forces allow it, as they currently do. One former (male) college student articulated how he learned what was expected of him in conducting modern sexual relationships: "I, perhaps unconsciously, observe women to try and determine how they want to be treated. When I see girls at a party who seemingly have no self-control, I'll admit that it's really tough to visualize them as" anything but sexual objects.[6] If the average price of sex should rise, however, men's sexual behavior could become subject to more constraints. In such a scenario, men would pay the more expensive price for sex—whatever that price should happen to be. In other words, men will work for sex. But they won't if they don't have to.

Fifth, it doesn't matter what other people do sexually; you make your own decisions.

Other people's sexual choices matter. Collectively they function as a powerful constraint on our own behavior. As the norm of serial monogamy becomes a more robust characteristic of the wider sexual market, the mantra of letting everyone choose what they want to do becomes moot. This is because free choice *disappears* when the majority of men and women become constrained by the structured expectations of fairly prompt sex within romantic relationships, fewer expectations for commitment and permanence, etc. In other words, if a critical mass of men and women enjoy an extended series of sexual relationships and expect sex fairly promptly within them, it becomes quite difficult for a minority to do otherwise.

As relationships become *expected* to end, the minority who wishes for more commitment or permanence ends up searching for these things in a pool of partners characterized by a distinct lack of interest in—or expectations of—the same. While we're not suggesting that serial monogamy *ruins* anyone, years-long serial monogamy as a structured trait of the sexual market doesn't make rational sense for the pursuit of the average woman's goal of finding a man who will stick around. Commitment-minded men, too, discover that structured expectations about them can affect women's willingness to trust them. Indeed, a minority of young adults have no interest in the norms of emerging adulthood: they want to date, they want to keep sex within relationships, they want to keep partners to a minimum, they want to eventually marry and have a family. And yet there's a big difference between wanting to avoid emerging-adult sexual norms and actually skirting them. Few manage to do that, because sociologically, what other people do does matter.

Sixth, porn won't affect your relationships.

Wrong. Porn now affects virtually everyone's relationships, even if neither partner actively spends time with it. How so? Back to the sexual market and its power to set sexual standards in the community: if a critical mass of emerging adult men consume porn regularly—by most estimates we're there now—it cannot but shape sexual market dynamics. If porn-and-masturbation increasingly satisfies some of the male demand for intercourse, it *reduces the value of intercourse*, access to which women control. "It ain't sex, but it ain't bad," many men would confess. Since high-speed digital porn gives men additional attractive sexual options—more supply for his demand—it by definition takes some measure of price control away from women. As a result, the cost of real sex can only go down. Porn becomes easier, and so must women (on average).

Talk of the "false" or "unrealistic" expectations that porn can generate will eventually diminish, not because the reality of real sex will set in for the porn-inspired men but because the reality of pornified sex will settle in for women. They will increasingly accommodate their sex lives to it. A recent conversation brought this home to us. An acquaintance of ours who was about to get married asked her evangelical Christian girlfriends what she ought to do to spice up her honeymoon. Among their suggestions was to get a Brazilian wax job. Why? Because, her friends claimed, their own spouses wished for it. Such wishes don't come from nowhere. While this one may seem like a minor request, such male-centered sexual norms remind us that the terms of sexual contracts continue to favor men and *what they want* in relationships, even while *what they offer* in relationships seems to be diminishing. While couples—and certainly religious organizations—have and will continue to debate the morality of personal porn use, porn's effects on the wider sexual market and its norms affect most Americans under 50, whether they're married or not.

This is new, too. Online porn is a uniquely modern problem in that it—like hooking up—thrives in part because of its speed and because it encourages men (and some women) to compartmentalize sex as a consumer product to be regularly and briefly consumed. Unlike relationships, it doesn't require work. And our lives, after all, are very busy. Sex has to fit in somehow (since sex is also increasingly considered a need rather than a desire). Thus porn is increasingly fitting into modern relationships—including marriages—just as hooking up is among single emerging adults.

Seventh, everyone else is having more sex than you are.

Although this could be true—especially if you've never engaged in any sort of sexual activity or haven't done so in years—in most cases, it's probably not. Even though the majority of emerging adults are either having sex or have had sex in the fairly recent past, most still overestimate how much sex is actually going on around them. As we explored in chapter 4, this common phenomenon is called "pluralistic ignorance," and it happens when individuals within a group begin to believe that their own *private* attitudes, beliefs, or judgments are more conservative and rare than the *public* norms they see displayed by others. This is especially easy to do on college campuses, where a sexual elite—by definition a minority—still seems to garner the greatest attention and appears as the face of campus life. Again, sexual activity in emerging adulthood is certainly commonplace, but the data from chapters 2, 3, and 4 suggest that the average numbers of sexual partners emerging adults have are not as high as many imagine.

Eighth, sex need not mean anything.

This myth might not be a myth for you if you own a set of XY chromosomes. But if you're an XX, the odds are simply against it. It's not impossible, of course: you may be among those women who tolerate casual sex better than your peers. You might even like it. But if you don't already know the answer, we wouldn't bet on it. Chapter 5 elaborated on the emotional challenges to women of both casual sex and the end of committed sexual relationships. For some, concluding a relationship is better than remaining in it. But that doesn't mean all endings are happy ones. Moreover, the use of social-networking sites allows people to stay in touch with previous sexual partners. For men in particular, this inspires a sort of bizarre quest to sustain the modern-day equivalent of a harem, further obfuscating women's subsequent relationship decisions, as their past breakups aren't now as clean as they could be.

Many women eventually come to sense that the set of sexual scripts available to them—as well as the state of the sexual market, to the extent that they can understand it—do not serve their interests very well. But as noted above, the norms have become institutionalized and difficult to alter. Most don't know how to work around them, or they fear that in doing so, they will be ignored by men. So plenty acquiesce and find themselves hurt in the process. At the same time, many women defend the modern way of conducting relationships, since older models are perceived to have suffered from reduced options and greater constraints.

The sexual revolution, then, bore mixed fruit. While some women cherish its triumphs, others—like Becky, a 23-year-old graduate student at NYU—think the sexual revolution was really about men and ruined family life.[7] It was, she felt, about men's wishes to have sex with more women. What resulted, she claims, is that women lost the right to say "no" as the price of sex went into freefall. Yet women like Becky often sense that, instead of finding fault with substandard men, their most vocal opponents are *other women* who have either come to prefer the new arrangement or see the old system as too traditional. Such contests among women are getting increasing press, as journalists begin to document the attractions and repulsions of—and disputes over—discounted sex among women.[8] In the end, a sorority sister from Texas may have put it best: "men make the rules and women enforce them."

Ninth, marriage can always wait.

According to most surveys and the vast majority of our interviews, emerging adults still want to get married. The most popular script about marriage, however, is that you should wait quite some time before entering it. Marital partner-seeking in college has diminished considerably, especially in secular colleges and universities and outside the American South. Marriage now serves emerging adults' other interests and plans, rather than the other way around. It is clearly no longer the principal institution of adult life, as families are considered additions (even accessories) to the unrivaled, unfettered individual. It's hard to even imagine it differently.

Many emerging adults wait years to marry, even though they may not want to, because of a powerful story that defines a married couple as financially stable, independent, and finished (or nearly finished) with their education. As a result, marriage rates in the working class are falling even faster than among the middle and upper-middle classes.

Emerging adults are also finding marriage partners in new and creative ways—ways which don't necessarily work as well as they are hoping. Years removed from the natural interaction patterns of college life, adults increasingly turn to science for assistance. Online dating algorithms and personality tests maximize their exposure to different potential partners, in the hope that this will somehow ensure a good (eventual) fit. Many lose sight of the fact—or more commonly, realize it too late—that there is a marriage market out there, just like there's a sexual market. It's a pool that does *not* grow deeper and more impressive with age. Just like the NBA draft, optimal candidates tend to get selected earlier rather than later. For women, age is at least partly a debit in the marriage market; it decreases fertility and for some, their attractiveness to interested men. (On the other hand, in an era when men's economic productivity is declining, women's income is becoming an increasing attraction.) For men, age tends to be a credit, increasing their access to resources and improving their maturity and self-confidence, thus making them more attractive to women.

This is *not*, however a clarion call to marry before one is prepared to, educated about it, thinking realistically about it, is in love, etc. We have no interest in dragging immature men and women into marriages for which they are unprepared. (Although, to be fair, not all such marriages turn out bad. Most married adults can look back and honestly admit they were not entirely prepared for marriage, but learned how to navigate and thrive within it.) Our point is more modest than that: it's to remind emerging adults who wish eventually to marry that there is a real marriage market out there and that sexual economics affects it, too. All talk of commitment-phobic men, or angst about settling for men who are "good enough," is linked to the trends we've described herein. Therefore, we simply wish to encourage men and women who've met someone who is "marriage material" to think twice before rejecting the notion that they're just not ready yet. Life plans seldom develop exactly as adults anticipate and on the schedule they wish for.

Tenth, moving in together is definitely a step toward marriage.

Moving in together might come as a reassuring thrill to many emerging adults, but in the majority of cases, it doesn't achieve permanence. And yet most emerging adults will cohabit. First experiences with cohabitation have the best shot at ending in marriage, but it's hardly a certainty. Getting engaged first boosts the odds, of course. Subsequent cohabitations are less successful.

For many of them—especially the younger among them—marriage is not a stated goal. It's not even on their radar screen. For most, cohabitation is inviting because it mimics some of the more attractive aspects of marriage. (Otherwise, who would do it?) But like so many aspects of contemporary relationships, cohabitation is easier on men, and its popularity is a reflection of their strength in the sexual marketplace (as opposed to the economic marketplace, where their position continues to weaken). Cohabitation is a win-win situation for men: more stable access to sex, without the expectations or commitments of marital responsibilities. The more difficult relationship problems don't even have to be solved. (You're not *married*, after all.) The impulse to spend more time with each other and to become more intimately familiar with each other is understandable. But cohabitation is still about uncertainty and risk management for both men and women. It's holding back to see how things go. It certainly feels logical when evaluated against the backdrop of serial monogamy and family experiences with divorce. But since few like to dwell for long in uncertainty, cohabitation is inherently unstable. It overwhelmingly leads to either marriage or breakup within a few short years. Those that conclude with marriage lend credibility to the popular narrative about its wisdom, while those that simply end become ignored or forgotten. (But they are data, too.)

In conclusion, we hope it's become obvious that sexual decision-making does not occur in "a simple arena of conscious choice."[9] Far from it. Numerous contingent circumstances, market dynamics, and competing desires, motivations, and wishes all intersect to either enable emerging adults to accomplish their goals or stifle their efforts to achieve what they're seeking. In other words, sex is complicated. This is why we've employed a dual focus in this book on the theories of sexual *economics* and sexual *scripting*. Some would assert that they're contradictory and can't both be true, but we couldn't disagree more. Sexual economics and scripting theories are not contradictory.[10] The former describes how things are—the relatively stable traits of the playing field itself. It focuses on macro characteristics like the sexual market and its long-term stability and pricing structure. While sexual scripts are often structured, their focus tends to be more microinteractional—the norms by which individuals attempt to make things happen sexually. Sometimes the two forces—the micro and the macro, the scripts and the economics of relationships—harmonize. More often than not, however, they seem to collide within emerging adults' lives, generating all sorts of data for books like this one.

APPENDIX A

Regression Models

REGRESSION ANALYSIS IS a statistician's way of performing a controlled experiment. In order to isolate the effects of one variable on another, we must account for, or hold constant, other factors that might confound the association. Regression allows us to do this by simultaneously evaluating the independent effect of each variable on the outcome of interest. When coefficients are presented, a number greater than zero means that an increase in that variable has a *positive* association with the dependent variable (outcome) under examination. If the coefficient is less than zero, then an increase in that variable has a *negative* association with the outcome. When odds ratios are presented, a value greater than one indicates an *increase* in the odds of a higher level of the dependent variable, while values less than one are indicative of a reduction in the odds of a higher level of the outcome.

These tables also bring up the question of statistical significance. Because the surveys we use are samples of the American emerging adult population, there remains the possibility that findings are a result of chance due to sampling error. That is, results may vary slightly because different samples of the population would yield slightly different results. Because of the large number of respondents in the datasets we've used, however, we can be confident that the results are similar to what would be obtained from analyses of the population of American emerging adults. Furthermore, we have performed tests of statistical significance that determine the actual likelihood that our findings are due to chance, or sampling error. A coefficient or odds ratio with a (+) next to it suggests that there is less than ten percent chance that the difference is due to sampling and is not a "real difference." One star (*) means there is less than a five percent chance, two stars (**) indicates less than a one percent chance, and three stars (***) signifies that there is less than a one-tenth of one percent chance that the finding is due to sampling error. If nothing appears next to a coefficient or odds ratio, it is implied that there is no statistically significant effect of that variable on the outcome.

Performing multivariate analyses like these boosts confidence that the associations between the variables in question are actually not the result of some other confounding variable.

TABLE A2.1 Estimated Odds Ratios from Logit Regression Models Predicting Never Having Had Sex, Never-Married Respondents, 18- to 23-Year-Olds.

	Men (N = 3,820)			Women (N = 4,117)		
	Model 1	Model 2	Model 3	Model 1	Model 2	Model 3
Demographics						
Age	.80***	.80***	.81***	.81**	.82**	.82**
Black	.65	.74	.54+	.54*	.73	.52*
Hispanic	1.12	1.11	.92	1.46+	1.51*	1.19
Asian	2.53***	2.19**	1.65*	1.24	1.35	1.00
Lives in the South	1.01	.96	0.97	1.09	1.06	1.01
Educational Attainment						
Attended college, no degree	1.27	1.36	1.38	1.27	1.31	1.29
Two-year college student	1.72*	1.77*	1.87**	1.56*	1.53*	1.50*
Four-year college student	2.09***	2.16***	2.44***	2.49***	2.28***	2.43***
Earned an associate's degree	1.62	1.66	1.78	1.71	1.60	1.36
Earned a bachelor's degree	2.79***	2.77***	2.93***	3.49***	3.27***	3.42***
Political Views						
More conservative	1.05	1.07	.99	1.44***	1.43***	1.34**
Democrat	1.10	1.12	1.16	.96	1.04	1.06
Republican	1.37+	1.41+	1.50*	1.45*	1.47*	1.55**
Other party	1.83	1.91	1.91	1.55	1.58	1.49
Religious Characteristics						
Evangelical Protestant	1.06	1.00	.85	.84	.84	.80
Black Protestant	.85	.75	.68	.80	.78	.73
Catholic	.68*	.63*	.65*	1.10	1.06	1.13
Mormon	3.01*	2.52+	1.80	2.59+	2.90*	2.51+

	Men (N = 3,820)			Women (N = 4,117)		
	Model 1	Model 2	Model 3	Model 1	Model 2	Model 3
Jewish	.90	.92	.94	1.43	1.33	1.39
Other religion	1.38	1.28	1.15	1.75*	1.69*	1.50
No religion	3.46**	3.32**	2.60*	1.45	1.28	1.16
Religious service attendance	1.23**	1.22**	1.21**	1.06	1.04	1.06
Importance of religion	1.61***	1.65***	1.57**	1.37**	1.32*	1.29*
Personality and Family Structure						
Planful		1.04*	1.03		.97	.96
Likes taking risks		.85*	.91		.88*	.94
Thinks of self as popular		.60***	.65***		.60***	.66***
Intact family		.92	.98		1.35	1.45
Mother-child relationship quality		1.17*	1.14+		1.16+	1.15
Father-child relationship quality		.94	.92		1.14*	1.13+
No mother figure		2.14	1.66		2.32	2.12
No father figure		.49	.10		1.59	1.47
Behavioral Factors						
Frequency of drunkenness			.68***			.62***
Sexually abused by sixth grade grade			.82			.82
−2 log likelihood	3005.1	2899.9	2762.3	3264.0	3129.4	2987.8

Source: Add Health

*+ p < .10 * p < .05 ** p < .01 *** p < .001*

Notes: Reference groups are white, did not go to college, does not identify with a political party, and mainline Protestant.

TABLE A2.2 Estimated Coefficients from Negative Binomial Regression Models Predicting Number of Lifetime Sex Partners, 18- to 23-Year-Olds

	Men (N = 3,431)			Women (N =4,222)		
	Model 1	Model 2	Model 3	Model 1	Model 2	Model 3
Demographics						
Age	.16***	.15***	.15***	.13***	.12***	.14***
Black	.41**	.33*	.33*	.11	.00	.08
Hispanic	–.02	–.03	–.01	–.26**	–.29**	–.25**
Asian	–.56***	–.46**	–.39**	–.32**	–.27*	–.18
Lives in the South	.00	.04	.02	.08	.10	.10*
Ever married	–.28**	–.23**	–.24**	–.24***	–.24***	–.20***
Educational Attainment						
Attended college, no degree	.09	.06	.08	.01	.03	.10
Two-year college student	–.26**	–.25**	–.21**	–.04	–.04	.02
Four-year college student	–.32***	–.32***	–.24***	–.43***	–.37***	–.27***
Earned an associate's degree	–.53***	–.55***	–.52***	–.08	–.08	.00
Earned a bachelor's degree	–.62***	–.55***	–.35**	–.49***	–.39***	–.25***
Political Views						
More conservative	–.02	–.03	.00	–.17***	–.16***	–.12***
Democrat	.05	.01	–.01	.07	.07	.01
Republican	–.07	–.08	–.08	–.05	–.02	–.02
Other party	.04	–.04	–.02	–.02	–.06	.21
Religious Characteristics						
Evangelical Protestant	.27*	.24*	.14	.06	.06	.08
Black Protestant	–.04	.03	–.06	.01	.08	.14
Catholic	–.02	.00	–.08	–.01	.01	.01
Mormon	–.42	–.31	–.13	.08	.08	.43*
Jewish	–.09	–.16	–.03	–.25	–.20	–.20

	Men (N = 3,431)			Women (N =4,222)		
	Model 1	Model 2	Model 3	Model 1	Model 2	Model 3
Other religion	–.19+	–.19+	–.18*	.00	.03	.06
No religion	–.35**	–.31*	–.24*	–.20+	–.07	.03
Religious service attendance	–.11**	–.10**	–.07*	–.08**	–.07*	–.06**
Importance of religion	–.08+	–.08+	–.04	–.11**	–.06+	–.04
Personality and Family Structure						
Planful		–.01	–.02+		–.03***	–.02***
Likes taking risks		.14***	.08**		.09***	.07***
Thinks of self as popular		.25***	.17***		.08*	.01
Intact family		–.09	–.16+		–.12*	–.08
Mother-child relationship quality		–.01	–.01		–.03	–.01
Father-child relationship quality		–.04+	.00		–.09***	–.07**
No mother figure		.15	.03		.04	.05
No father figure		–.37+	–.16		–.56***	–.42**
Behavioral Factors						
Frequency of drunkenness			.10***			.14***
Had sex before age 16			.83***			.67***
(Partner) Ever had an abortion			.49***			.42***
Sexually abused by sixth grade			.16			.17*
Constant	1.92***	1.96***	1.56***	1.80***	1.95***	1.47***
–2 log likelihood	20591.4	20371.7	19702.5	21256.9	21047.7	20210.3

Source: Add Health
*+ p < .10 * p < .05 ** p < .01 *** p < .001*
Notes: Reference groups are white, did not go to college, does not identify with a political party, and mainline Protestant.

TABLE A2.3 Estimated Coefficients from Negative Binomial Regression Models Predicting Number of Sex Partners in the Last Year, Never-Married Respondents, 18- to 23-Year-Olds

	Men (N = 3,011)			Women (N =3,378)		
	Model 1	Model 2	Model 3	Model 1	Model 2	Model 3
Demographics						
Age	.01	.02	.01	−.02	−.02	−.02
Black	.37*	.29*	.30*	.17	.13	.24*
Hispanic	−.06	−.06	−.01	−.19+	−.20*	−.13
Asian	−.34+	−.26	−.18	−.23+	−.25+	−.14
Lives in the South	−.01	.03	.02	−.05	−.03	.00
Educational Attainment						
Attended college, no degree	.10	.08	.08	.18	.18	.21+
Two-year college student	−.17*	−.17+	−.16+	.04	.04	.07
Four-year college student	−.15*	−.15*	−.11+	−.17*	−.14*	−.09
Earned an associate's degree	−.30*	−.32*	−.26*	−.22+	−.20	−.13
Earned a bachelor's degree	−.30**	−.26*	−.15	−.18*	−.11	−.03
Political Views						
More conservative	.03	.03	.04	−.11**	−10**	−.05+
Democrat	.03	.01	−.04	.08	.10	.05
Republican	−.03	−.05	−.05	−.05	−.05	−.08
Other party	−.13	−.13	−.06	.28	.25	.30
Religious Characteristics						
Evangelical Protestant	.18+	.18+	.14	.17*	.18*	.18*
Black Protestant	.12	.18	.16	.06	.09	.14
Catholic	.10	.12	.05	.06	.09	.08
Mormon	−.42	−.36	−.23	.34	.32	.50*
Jewish	.09	.04	.13	−.11	−.08	−.07

TABLE A2.3 (continued)

	Men (N = 3,011)			Women (N =3,378)		
	Model 1	Model 2	Model 3	Model 1	Model 2	Model 3
Other religion	−.07	−.04	−.03	.08	.11	.16
No religion	−.17	−.16	−.09	−.18	−.10	−.05
Religious service attendance	−.04	−.04	−.02	−.03	−.03	−.04
Importance of religion	−.07	−.08+	−.04	−.08*	−.04	−.02
Personality and Family Structure						
Planful		−.01	−.01		−.02	−.02
Likes taking risks		.13***	.07*		.08**	.06*
Thinks of self as popular		.19***	.13**		.06+	.00
Intact family		−.09	−.14+		−.10	−.07
Mother-child relationship quality		−.01	.00		−.06*	−.05*
Father-child relationship quality		.01	.03		−.03	−.01
No mother figure		−.13	−.08		−.44*	−.44*
No father figure		.11	.17		−.25	−.12
Behavioral Factors						
Frequency of drunkenness			.12***			.15***
Had sex before age 16			.36***			.29***
(Partner) Ever had an abortion abortion			.56***			.30**
Sexually abused by sixth grade grade			.51***			.12
Constant	.59***	.52***	.28**	.39***	.49***	.22**
−2 log likelihood	11455.0	11316.6	10981.0	10148.4	10073.6	9769.5

Source: Add Health.

*+p < .10 *p < .05 **p < .01 ***p < .001*

Notes: Reference groups are white, did not go to college, does not identify with a political party, and mainline Protestant.

TABLE A2.4 Estimated Odds Ratios from Logit Regression Models Predicting Ever Having Had Oral Sex and Anal Sex, Never-Married Respondents, 18- to 23-Year-Olds

	Men (N = 1,024; 1,026)		Women (N = 1,162; 1,166)	
	Has had oral sex	Has had anal sex	Has had oral sex	Has had anal sex
Demographics				
Age	1.08	1.09	1.20**	1.20**
Black	.46	.50*	1.08	.88
Hispanic	.53*	.98	.39**	.57*
Other race	.49	1.03	.21***	.38*
Lives in suburbs	1.01	1.16	.74	.94
Lives in rural area	.71	1.20	.69	1.32
Intact family of origin	.56*	.84	1.13	.92
Lives with parents	.74	.71	.53*	.93
Educational Attainment				
No high school degree	.46*	.91	.54+	1.37
Attended college, no degree	3.86*	1.24	.50+	1.08
College student	1.23	.54*	.96	1.03
Earned an associate's degree	.84	2.07+	1.30	.91
Earned a bachelor's degree	1.11	1.09	1.01	.58
Religious Characteristics				
Religious service attendance	.74**	.77**	.77**	.75**
Importance of religion	.78	1.02	.48**	1.02
Evangelical Protestant	1.26	2.69*	.82	.81
Black Protestant	2.06	5.29**	.54	.65
Catholic	1.13	1.69	.78	1.17
Other religion	1.00	1.70	.65	.74
No religion	.64	2.01	.33+	.74
–2 log likelihood	963.6	1020.5	1045.4	1246.1

Source: NSFG

*+p < .10 * p < .05 ** p < .01 *** p < .001*

Note: Reference groups are white, lives in urban area, high school grad but no college, and mainline Protestant.

TABLE A5.1 Coefficients from Ordinary Least-Squares (OLS) Regression Models Predicting CESD Score at Wave 3 and Odds Ratios from Order Logit Regression Models Predicting Frequency of Crying at Wave 3, 18- to 23-Year-Old Women

	CESD Score (N = 2,908)			Frequency of Crying (N = 2,914)		
	Model 1	Model 2	Model 3	Model 1	Model 2	Model 3
Number of lifetime sex partners	.09***	.04*	.03	1.03***	1.02*	1.02+
Number of sex partners in last year	.08	.07	.04	.97	.96	.95
Frequency of sex in last year	−.09	−.14*	−.09	1.05	1.04	1.04
Age	−.27***	−.24**	−.32***	.87***	.87***	.86**
Frequency of drinking, Wave 3		.03	.21**		1.12**	1.12**
Ever had an abortion		1.41**	1.15**		1.18	1.22
Sexually abused by sixth grade		1.49**	1.08*		1.25	1.22
Ever attracted to another female		1.80***	1.43***		1.77***	1.58**
Had sex before age 16		.38	.05		1.08	1.02
CESD score, Wave 1			.22***			
Frequency of crying, Wave 1						1.63***
Body mass index, Wave 3			.03+			1.01
Thinks of self as intelligent, Wave 3			−.50**			.93
Thinks of self as popular, Wave 3			−.37*			.84*

	CESD Score (N = 2,908)			Frequency of Crying (N = 2,914)		
	Model 1	Model 2	Model 3	Model 1	Model 2	Model 3
Physical attractiveness, Wave 3			–.15			1.00
Thinks of self as self-centered, Wave 3			.31*			1.00
Likes taking risks, Wave 3			–.04			.92
Constant	9.98***	9.09***	11.38***			
R-squared	.03	.07	.16			
–2 log likelihood				5001.9	4947.5	4807.0

Source: Add Health

$+ p < .10 \ * p < .05 \ ** p < .01 \ *** p < .001$

Note: Models 3 include, but do not display, controls for race, parents' education, region of residence, family structure, and educational attainment.

TABLE A5.2 Odds Ratios from Ordered Logit Regression Models Predicting Life Satisfaction at Wave 3 and Odds Ratios from Logit Regression Models Predicting Depression Diagnosis by Wave 3, 18- to 23-Year-Old Women

	Life Satisfaction (N = 2,914)			Ever Had Depression Diagnosis (N = 2,912)		
	Model 1	Model 2	Model 3	Model 1	Model 2	Model 3
Number of lifetime sex partners	.96***	.98	.99	1.05***	1.02**	1.02+
Number of sex partners in last year	.92**	.91**	.92*	.96	.95	.96
Frequency of sex in last year	1.02	1.05*	1.05+	1.09+	1.06	1.07
Age	1.03	1.02	1.08+	.92+	.93	.91

	Life Satisfaction (N = 2,914)			Ever Had Depression Diagnosis (N = 2,912)		
	Model 1	Model 2	Model 3	Model 1	Model 2	Model 3
Frequency of drinking, Wave 3		.98	.86***		1.13**	1.10+
Ever had an abortion		.68*	.75+		.69	.78
Sexually abused by sixth grade		.45**	.52**		1.95**	2.07**
Ever attracted to another female		.45***	.47***		2.44***	1.98***
Had sex before age 16		.69**	.80*		1.43*	1.45*
CESD score, Wave 1			.95***			1.07***
Body mass index, Wave 3			.98*			1.02
Thinks of self as intelligent, Wave 3			1.36***			1.05
Thinks of self as popular, Wave 3			1.44***			.74**
Physical attractiveness, Wave 3			1.09			1.03
Thinks of self as self-centered, Wave 3			.99			.96
Likes taking risks, Wave 3			1.16**			1.05
–2 log likelihood	6163.8	6047.6	5751.6	2568.1	2472.5	2336.5

Source: Add Health.

$+ p < .10 * p < .05 ** p < .01 *** p < .001$

Note: Models 3 include, but do not display, controls for race, parents' education, region of residence, family structure, and educational attainment.

TABLE A5.3 Odds Ratios from Logit Regression Models Predicting Having Taken Prescription Medicine for Depression or Stress in Last Year at Wave 3, 18- to 23-Year-Old Women

	Model 1	Model 2	Model 3
Number of lifetime sex partners	1.03*	1.01	1.01
Number of sex partners in last year	1.06	1.05	1.06
Frequency of sex in last year	1.11	1.08	1.08
Age	.93	.93	.90
Frequency of drinking, Wave 3		1.16**	1.11
Ever had an abortion		1.20	1.46
Sexually abused by sixth grade		1.72+	1.85+
Ever attracted to another female		2.38***	1.99**
Had sex before age 16		1.03	1.10
CESD score, Wave 1			1.05*
Body mass index, Wave 3			1.00
Thinks of self as intelligent, Wave 3			.98
Thinks of self as popular, Wave 3			.79+
Physical attractiveness, Wave 3			.84+
Thinks of self as self-centered, Wave 3			.94
Likes taking risks, Wave 3			.86
−2 log likelihood	1653.5	1603.9	1499.6

Source: Add Health.

$+ p < .10 * p < .05 ** p < .01 *** p < .001$

Note: Models 3 include, but do not display, controls for race, parents' education, region of residence, family structure, and educational attainment. N = 2,915.

TABLE A7.1 Coefficients from Negative Binomial Regression Models Predicting
Number of Sex Partners

	Men (N = 4,174; 4,184)		Women (N = 4,457; 4,478)	
	Lifetime sex partners	Sex partners in last year	Lifetime sex partners	Sex partners in last year
Number of addresses since June 1995	.09***	.04*	.08***	.06***
Number of states lived in since June 1995	.10*	.10*	−.02	−.03
Political conservatism	−.05	−.01	−.21***	−.14***
Age	.15***	.01	.12***	−.01
−2 log likelihood	24742.4	15936.7	21713.7	12870.3

Source: Add Health

*+ p < .10 * p < .05 ** p < .01 *** p < .001*

Note: Models include, but do not display, controls for educational attainment, race, region, and family structure.

Original Research Interview Methods

I<small>N THIS BOOK</small>, we report data from approximately in-depth interviews drawn from two sources: the National Study of Youth and Religion (whose interview schedule is available from its organizers upon request) and with 40 undergraduate students attending the University of Texas at Austin (UT-Austin). The student interviews were conducted between 2007 and 2009. A list of potential interviewees was generated from an approved sample of students provided by the UT-Austin College of Liberal Arts. Below is the approved interview questionnaire used for these semistructured interviews.

UT-AUSTIN INTERVIEW QUESTIONNAIRE

- Thanks for agreeing to do this interview and taking the time to talk with me.
- We use these interviews to really hear from your perspective, and in your own words, how college life is experienced, how you think about romantic relationships, and your opinions and beliefs about them.
- Some of what we may talk about today is pretty personal, but we're trying to get a sense of how college students think about and experience their relationships. Together with others' accounts, this will help tell us a lot about what it's like being a young adult today.
- I really want you to just feel at ease to talk freely and honestly with me. This is a chance for you to talk openly about whatever you want to say, to express whatever ideas or feelings you have, to talk about things that might be too uncomfortable to tell other people.

- There are no right or wrong answers, I just want to know whatever you honestly think or feel. If you do not understand a question, just tell me that you don't know the answer.
- **You may decline to answer any questions you don't want to talk about. That is fine. Just let me know.** But please try to be honest in all of the answers that you *do* give.

* I want to talk some about your thoughts about physical involvements and sexual activity, like: what kinds of physical intimacy or sexual activities are good or bad, safe and unsafe, right or wrong for people your age to do.

* When or under what conditions do you think it is appropriate and not appropriate for people your age to be sexually involved with each other? Why?

- **[If they say "always" or "almost always" appropriate]** Is it ever NOT okay to enter a sexual relationship?
- Does this depend on different kinds or levels of physical intimacy? What things do you think are okay and what things, if any, are not? Why?
- Is it okay if the two people think they're emotionally ready for sex? What does that mean?
- Do kinds of relationships or stages in a relationship change the rules on this?
- IF <u>NOT</u> NECESSARY TO WAIT: Does a person need to be in a relationship with someone to have sex with them? For how long?
- Do your religious beliefs affect your attitudes toward sex or behaviors? How so?

* **[If some relationships aren't appropriate]** Do you think people should wait to have sexual intercourse until they are married or not? Why?

* Are your friends having sex?

- What do you think motivates people to have sex (physical pleasure? desire for social acceptance? social status? pressure? feeling grown up? or what?)?
- Have you yourself ever had sex?
- **[if yes]** You mean intercourse, or oral sex, or . . .?
- **[if yes]** What were the circumstances of the first time you had sex?
  - About how old were you?
  - How do you feel about that? Positive experience? Negative?
  - Did you feel like you had really thought your decision to have sex through, or did it just sort of happen?
  - Did/do you know the person well? Were/are you in a relationship?
- IF NO: Have you decided to wait until you are married, or a later age, or have you just not had the opportunity yet?
- IF WAITING UNTIL MARRIED: Have you made an actual pledge to abstain from sex until marriage? IF YES: What are your reasons for doing this?
  - Did you come up with the idea on your own, or is it through a school or church group that you decided to do this?

○ How hard is it to keep your pledge? How hard will it be in the next couple of years?

*[If yes] Previously, had you <u>ever</u> taken a pledge to abstain from sex until marriage?

- How do you feel about that now?
  ○ Do you have any regrets? Do you feel guilty for breaking the pledge?

*What do you think of other people that make that kind of pledge?

- Is it possible to keep? Do you think most people will keep it? Why or why not?

*How has your thinking about physical involvements and sex changed over the past couple of years?

- Do you still pretty much see things the same way, or have you changed? How? In what ways?
  ○ Why do you think you've changed in how you think about [-----]?

* [If have had sex already] About how often do you have sex?

- Do you have different kinds of sex or primarily intercourse? Who decides?
- Would you say that you are happy with your sexual life, or not that happy about it?
- Ever feel guilty about having sex?
  ○ [If yes] Can you describe a time when you felt guilty? Why do you think you felt guilty?
  ○ Do feel guilt about sex fairly often, or rarely?
- Do your parents know? How would (or do) they feel about that if they knew?

* [If have had sex already] About how many people have you had sex with?

  ○ Do you have sex fairly regularly? (About how often?)
  ○ How many people have you ever had sex with? (An estimate is fine)
  ○ Were you in relationships with all these people when having sex with them?
    ■ IF NOT: Where did you meet them? How did you end up having sex?
  ○ Do your [parents] know you['ve had/ are having] sex?
    ■ How (do/would) they feel about it?
  ○ Do your friends know you['ve had/ are having] sex?
    ■ How (do/would) they feel about it?
  ○ If you are in a relationship with someone, are you faithful to them always?
    ■ Have you ever cheated on someone? How so? What happened?
    ■ Have you ever been cheated on? How so? What happened?

* Are you familiar with the term "hooking up"? What does it mean?

- [If yes] Can you tell me what an average "hook up" looks like?

- About how many "hook ups" have you experienced?
- Of those, how many involved intercourse?
- If a college student wanted to "hook up" with someone, how would they go about doing that?

* About what percent of UT students do you think have already had sex?

- About what percent do you think have had sex in the past month?
- About what percent do you think have had more four or more sexual partners in their lifetime?
- About what percent do you think are planning to wait until they're married to have sex?

*Now I want to ask you a few questions about your thoughts on birth control or protection against sexually transmitted diseases.

- How do you feel about people using birth control or contraceptives? Should they, shouldn't they? Why or why not?
- Do you feel like you know much about birth control or contraceptives?
  - Where have you learned what you know?
  - Do you wish you knew more or not? IF YES: About what? From where?

IF THE RESPONDENT <u>HAS</u> HAD SEX (IF HAS <u>NOT</u> HAD SEX, SKIP TO NEXT SECTION):
*Do you yourself use birth control or contraceptives?

- IF YES: What kind or kinds? (Condoms, pills, Depo, patch, ring, Norplant, withdrawal, etc?)
  - When did you first start using something?
  - Did you initiate it on your own or did someone else? Who?
- Do you typically use protection or birth control every time you have sex, most of the time, or once in awhile?
  - IF NO: What keeps you from using protection or birth control?
- Where do you get the birth control/contraceptives you use?
  - Do you usually take the initiative yourself, or do you mostly rely on your partner?
  - Do you ever feel pressure or anxiety about trying to obtain birth control? How so?

*How much do you worry about getting (someone) pregnant?
*Have you ever gotten (someone) pregnant or had any scares?

- IF YES: Can you tell me a little about the circumstances and what happened?
  - When did this happen? Who was involved? How did you feel?
    - How did the pregnancy end? Miscarriage, abortion, birth?
    - How do you feel about that?
- IF NO: What would happen if you did? What would you do?

*How much do you worry about getting a sexually transmitted infection or disease?

- Have you had any experiences with this?
  - Can you tell me a little about the circumstances and what happened?
- Has anyone you know had a sexually transmitted infection or disease?
  - Can you tell me a little about the circumstances and what happened?

* Have you ever had a negative sexual experience?

- [if yes] Is that something you would be willing to talk about?
- [if yes] What were the circumstances? Why was it negative for you?
- How did you deal with it? How do you think it has affected you? [be prepared here to provide help information to respondents in need]
- Have you ever been asked to perform a sexual act that you yourself would have preferred not to do?

* Pornography is more prevalent in American society than it used to be. What are your thoughts about pornography?

- Do you ever look at pornography? Why (or why not)?
- Do you think pornography is a bad thing, a good thing, or makes no difference?
- Do you think porn changes how people think about sex?
- Is porn good for learning about sex? [If yes] How you have learned from it?

*Are there any things you wish you would have known earlier about sex?

- Are there any things you would have done differently if you had known more, earlier?
  - What? Why?

*Do you have any particular regrets about your sexual history?

Notes

Chapter 1

1. Lawrence Finer, "Trends in Premarital Sex in the United States, 1954–2003," *Public Health Reports* 122 (2007): 73–78.

2. Some criticize the Guttmacher study's conclusions. Are their analyses correct? Yes, though some context is helpful: the 95 percent figure they cite is based on an event-history analysis of data from the National Study of Family Growth (NSFG). By age 44, 95 percent of respondents reported having had premarital sex. This figure includes married *and* unmarried respondents. However, if we took a cross-section of only married adults and looked retrospectively at their premarital sexual behavior, we'd arrive at a figure of 85 percent for women and 90 percent for men. The 95 percent figure noted in the media includes people who were not married and may never do so. Their sexual activity has been entirely nonmarital and may remain so—their future is not known. So of all the married adults in the NSFG, 85 percent of women and 90 percent of men reported having experienced intercourse before they got married.

3. Sociologists John Gagnon and William Simon were among the first to write about this distinction, drawing a line between sex that's actually pre-premarital—since most contemporary adolescent sexual partnerships are not comprised of eventual spouses—and the sex that occurs with an eventual spouse. See, for example, John H. Gagnon and William Simon, "The Sexual Scripting of Oral Genital Contacts," *Archives of Sexual Behavior* 16 (1987): 1–25.

4. A team of researchers identify scripts as part of what they call *internal sexual culture*, which refers to "the set of scripts that inform and guide sexual behaviors, preferences, and identities within a given market." Such scripts provide information, suggest sexual roles, assign value to potential partners, and detail behavioral expectations concerning sex. Internal sexual culture is distinct from what the same group labels *external sexual culture*, or "the sets of meanings that help individuals organize sexual markets," thought of as cultural scenarios, or widely held and shared ideas about "appropriate sexual objects, aims, and activities," often conveyed through popular media such as music videos, lyrics, films, and magazines. See Stephen Ellingson, Edward O. Laumann, Anthony Paik, and Jenna Mahay, "The Theory of Sex Markets," in *The Sexual Organization of the City*, eds. Edward O. Laumann, Stephen Ellingson, Jenna Mahay, Anthony Paik, and Yoosik Youm (Chicago: University of Chicago Press, 2004), 3–38. The quotes above are from pages 22–23.

5. Michael W. Wiederman, "The Gendered Nature of Sexual Scripts," *The Family Journal* 13 (2005): 496–502.

6. The term *emerging adulthood* can be attributed to Jeffrey Jensen Arnett and his work on this age of people, though the idea of it has been revealing itself to social scientists since the mid-to-late 1990s. See Arnett's book *Emerging Adulthood: The Winding Road from the Late Teens through the Twenties* (New York: Oxford University Press, 2004).

7. Frank F. Furstenberg, Jr., Sheela Kennedy, Vonnie C. McLoyd, Ruben G. Rumbaut, and Richard A. Settersten, Jr., "Growing Up Is Harder to Do," *Contexts* 3 (2004): 33–41.

8. David Brooks, "The New Lone Rangers," paragraphs 10–11, *New York Times* (online), July 10, 2007. Available at http://select.nytimes.com/2007/07/10/opinion/10brooks.html (accessed July 14, 2007).

9. Amy Schalet, "Must We Fear Adolescent Sexuality?" *Medscape General Medicine* 6 (2004): 1–22.

10. Furstenberg et al., "Growing Up Is Harder to Do."

11. See, for example, the following: Dan Black, Gary Gates, Seth Sanders, and Lowell Taylor, "Demographics of the Gay and Lesbian Population in the United States: Evidence from Available Systematic Data Sources," *Demography* 37 (2000), 139–54; Christopher Carpenter and Gary J. Gates, "Gay and Lesbian Partnership: Evidence from California," *Demography* 45 (2008), 573–590; Lisa M. Diamond, *Sexual Fluidity: Understanding Women's Love and Desire* (Cambridge, MA: Harvard University Press, 2008); Lisa M. Diamond, "Was It a Phase? Young Women's Relinquishment of Lesbian/Bisexual Identities over a 5-Year Period," *Journal of Personality and Social Psychology* 84 (2003), 352–64.

12. Add Health is a program project directed by Kathleen Mullan Harris and designed by J. Richard Udry, Peter S. Bearman, and Kathleen Mullan Harris at the University of North Carolina at Chapel Hill, and funded by grant P01-HD31921 from the Eunice Kennedy Shriver National Institute of Child Health and Human Development, with cooperative funding from 23 other federal agencies and foundations. Special acknowledgment is due Ronald R. Rindfuss and Barbara Entwisle for assistance in the original design. The Add Health study design and survey questionnaires, as well as information about how to obtain the Add Health data files, is available on the Add Health website (http://www.cpc.unc.edu/addhealth). No direct support was received from grant P01-HD31921 for this analysis.

13. A description of the 2002 NSFG research design is available online at www.cdc.gov/nchs/data/series/sr_01/sr01_042.pdf. Survey questionnaires for this study are also available at www.cdc.gov/nchs/data/nsfg/nsfg_2002_questionnaires.htm.

14. For more information on the College Women's Survey, see Norval Glenn and Elizabeth Marquardt, *Hooking Up, Hanging Out, and Hoping for Mr. Right: College Women on Dating and Mating Today* (New York: Institute for American Values, 2001).

15. Information about the CSLS research design can be found in Paula England, Emily Fitzgibbons Shafer, and Alison C. K. Fogarty, "Hooking Up and Forming Romantic Relationships on Today's College Campuses," in *The Gendered Society Reader*, ed. Michael Kimmel and Amy Aronson (New York: Oxford University Press, 2007). An online codebook is also available at www.stanford.edu/~rjthomas/survey/onlinecodebook9-2.xls.

16. Although the NSYR was developed to track the religious beliefs and behaviors of young Americans, religion comprises only one component of their interviews. There are extensive sections on relationships, sexuality, family, education, future goals, moral decision-making, and friendships, making it a remarkably apt data source for use here. Since the NSYR wave-3 interviews became available late in our analyses, we draw upon a sample of 75 interviews from the total pool of 230.

17. A description of the NSYR Wave 2 in-depth interview methods can be found at www.youthandreligion.org/research/docs/w2_iv_guide.pdf. The Wave 3 methodological information is available at www.youthandreligion.org/research/docs/wave3methods_11_5_08_FINAL_with_iv_guide.pdf./

Chapter 2

1. Specifically, 66 percent of adult women ages 18–23 in the Add Health study reported—at the time of the interview—that they were in a romantic relationship (either cohabiting, dating someone exclusively, dating regularly, or dating once in awhile) and that they had been having some form of sex—oral sex, intercourse, or something else—with that dating or cohabiting partner. The "under 6 percent" figure is derived by dividing the percent of women who are dating but not having sex by the total percentage of all young women who are in a romantic relationship of any sort.

2. Kathleen Bogle, *Hooking Up: Sex, Dating, and Relationships on Campus* (New York: NYU Press, 2008).

3. Judith Treas, "How Cohorts, Education, and Ideology Shaped a New Sexual Revolution on American Attitudes toward Nonmarital Sex, 1972–1998," *Sociological Perspectives* 45 (2002): 267–83.

4. Jane D. Woody, Robin Russel, Henry J. D'Souza, and Jennifer K. Woody, "Adolescent Non-Coital Sexual Activity: Comparisons of Virgins and Non-Virgins," *Journal of Sex Education and Therapy* 25 (2000): 261–68.

5. Albert D. Klassen, Colin J. Williams, Eugene E. Levitt, Laura Rudkin-Miniot, Heather G. Miller, and Sushama Gunjal, "Trends in Premarital Sexual Behavior," in *AIDS: Sexual Behaviors and Intravenous Drug Use*, ed. Charles F. Turner, Heather G. Miller, and Lincoln E. Moses (Washington, DC: National Academy Press, 1989). Recall, as well as virginity loss itself, may be subject to more social desirability bias among older than younger generations. In other words, while simply generating this statistic is an accomplishment in itself, it may still be an underestimate.

6. Mark Regnerus, *Forbidden Fruit: Sex and Religion in the Lives of American Teenagers* (New York: Oxford University Press, 2007). In another study—the 1992 National Health and Social Life Survey—42 percent of men and 19 percent of women who were born between 1933 and 1942 reported having had sex before age 18; that wasn't substantially different from people born 10 years later, but it certainly was from those in the 1953–1962 birth cohort, in which 53 percent of men and 41 percent of women said they'd had sex before age 18. And among individuals born between 1968 and 1973—those roughly between ages 37 and 42 in the year 2010—fewer than half were virgins when they were 18. For NHSLS data on sex, see Edward O. Laumann, John H. Gagnon, Robert T. Michael, and Stuart Michaels, *The Social Organization of Sexuality: Sexual Practices in the United States* (Chicago: University of Chicago Press, 1994).

7. *Centers for Disease Control and Prevention* (online), June 4, 2008. Available at http://www.cdc.gov/media/pressrel/2008/r080604.htm?s_cid=mediarel_r080604 (accessed May 4, 2009).

8. We explored the effects on virginity loss of the timing of puberty and menarche. In analyses of the Add Health data, the only thing puberty matters for long-term is for boys' virginity status: the more developed they were earlier, the less likely they were to be a virgin at Wave 3. Pubertal timing and early menarche played no role in predicting subsequent number of sexual partners, or for the sexual behavior of women.

9. Bliss Kaneshiro, Jeffrey T. Jensen, Nichole E. Carlson, S. Marie Harvey, Mark D. Nichols, and Alison B. Edelman, "Body Mass Index and Sexual Behavior," *Obstetrics and Gynecology* 112 (2008): 586–92.

10. Carolyn Tucker Halpern, Martha W. Waller, Aubrey Spriggs, and Denise Dion Hallfors, "Adolescent Predictors of Emerging Adult Sexual Patterns," *Journal of Adolescent Health* 39 (2006): 926.e1–926.e10; Caitlin S. McLaughlin, Chuansheng Chen, Ellen Greenberger, and Cornelia Biermeier, "Family, Peer, and Individual Correlates of Sexual Experience among Caucasian and Asian American Late Adolescents," *Journal of Research on Adolescence* 7 (1997): 33–53; Elizabeth L. Paul, Brian McManus, and Allison Hayes, "'Hookups': Characteristics and Correlates of College Students' Spontaneous and Anonymous Sexual Experiences," *The Journal of Sex Research* 37 (2000): 76–88.

11. Jeffrey Jensen Arnett, *Emerging Adulthood: The Winding Road from the Late Teens through the Twenties* (New York: Oxford University Press, 2004).

12. Ibid., 89.

13. Regnerus, *Forbidden Fruit*.

14. Denise Donnelly, Elisabeth Burgess, Sally Anderson, Regina Davis, and Joy Dillard, "Involuntary Celibacy: A Life Course Analysis," *The Journal of Sex Research* 38 (2001): 159–69.

15. See, for example, Laura Carpenter, *Virginity Lost: An Intimate Portrait of First Sexual Experiences* (New York: New York University Press, 2005).

16. Miller McPherson, Lynn Smith-Lovin, and Matthew E. Brashears, "Social Isolation in America: Changes in Core Discussion Networks over Two Decades," *American Sociological Review* 71 (2006): 353–75.

17. Andrew J. Cherlin, *The Marriage Go-Round: The State of Marriage and the Family in America Today* (New York: Knopf, 2009).

18. Laura Sessions Stepp, *Unhooked: How Young Women Pursue Sex, Delay Love, and Lose at Both* (New York: Riverhead, 2007).

19. Even marriage doesn't make this go away: 17 percent of all married respondents below age 25 agreed that they often think there's someone better for them out there, a figure more than double that of any other age category. Data come from the Texas Healthy Marriage Initiative Baseline Survey, a telephone survey of 2,001 Texas adults conducted by the Office of Survey Research at the University of Texas at Austin in 2006–2007.

20. Philip Weiss, "The Affairs of Men: The Trouble with Sex and Marriage," *New York Magazine* (online), May 18, 2008. Available at http://nymag.com/relationships/sex/47055 (accessed December 23, 2008).

21. Klassen et al., "Trends in Premarital Sexual Behavior."

22. Keep in mind that on average, the sexual history of a 23-year-old began about six or seven years ago, considerably longer than for an 18-year-old. For the sake of brevity, however, they're all combined here.

23. Laumann et al., *Social Organization of Sexuality*.

24. In other cases the direction of influence seems clear: having more partners cannot change your race, cannot make you avoid going to college (at least not directly), and cannot alter more stable traits like risk proclivity and planfulness.

25. Gina Kolata, "The Myth, the Math, the Sex," *New York Times* (online), August 12, 2007. Available at http://www.nytimes.com/2007/08/12/weekinreview/12kolata.html (accessed September 20, 2007).

26. Norman R. Brown and Robert C. Sinclair, "Estimating Number of Lifetime Sexual Partners: Men and Women Do It Differently," *The Journal of Sex Research* 36 (1999): 292–97.

27. Joyce C. Abma, Anjani Chandra, William D. Mosher, Linda S. Peterson, and Linda J. Piccinino, "Fertility, Family Planning, and Women's Health: New Data from the 1995 National Survey of Family Growth," *National Center for Health Statistics Vital Health Statistics* 23 (1997). Whereas about twice as many 15- to 24-year-olds reported on paper they'd had four or more sexual partners in the last 12 months (when compared with being asked by another person), three times as many 25- to 44-year-olds reported the same.

28. Paula Kamen, *Her Way: Young Women Remake the Sexual Revolution*. (New York: New York University Press, 2000).

29. Why more than five? There's no particular reason for this number. We evaluated the same statistics for more than two partners and at least ten partners, and none of the patterns changed notably, so we settled on a middle-range number like five. It's not that this exercise helps us distinguish what matters from what doesn't. Rather, it helps readers to envision a particular type of person with a set of traits, behaviors, experiences, or family backgrounds.

30. Laumann et al., *Social Organization of Sexuality*, 112.

31. Kamen, *Her Way*.

32. The NSFG, however, asked questions about oral sex in a very straightforward fashion: (On giving oral sex): "Have you ever put your mouth on a [female's vagina/man's penis] (also known as oral sex or [cunnilingus/fellatio])?" (On receiving oral sex): "Has a [female/male] ever put [her/his] mouth on your [penis/vagina] (also known as oral sex or [fellatio/cunnilingus])?"

33. One way young adults address this is by using slang terms, like "eat out" or "give head," which are gender differentiated. But slang terms can be as vague to the uninformed as the medically accurate terms.

34. F. Scott Christopher, *To Dance the Dance: A Symbolic Interactional Exploration of Premarital Sexuality* (Mahwah, NJ: Lawrence Erlbaum Associates, 2001).

35. Jenna Mahay, Edward O. Laumann, and Stuart Michaels, "Race, Gender, and Class in Sexual Scripts," in *Sex, Love, and Health in America*, ed. Edward O. Laumann and Robert T. Michael (Chicago: University of Chicago Press, 2004), 220.

36. Laumann et al., *Social Organization of Sexuality*.

37. Janice I. Baldwin and John D. Baldwin, "Heterosexual Anal Intercourse: An Understudied, High-Risk Sexual Behavior," *Archives of Sexual Behavior* 29 (2000): 357–373; Diana Flannery, Lyndall Ellingson, Karen S. Votaw, and Elizabeth Ann Schaefer, "Anal Intercourse and Sexual Risk Factors among College Women, 1993–2000," *American Journal of Health Behavior* 27 (2003): 228–34; Sara B. Oswalt, Kenzie A. Cameron, and Jeffrey J. Koob, "Sexual Regret in College Students," *Archives of Sexual Behavior* 34 (2005): 663–69.

38. Since anal sex is much less common than oral sex, lumping them both into an "ever done it" regression analysis is perhaps nonsensical. Unfortunately, measuring and analyzing the frequency of oral sex has been uncommon in survey research.

39. Baldwin and Baldwin, "Heterosexual Anal Intercourse," 358.

40. Sandra L. Faulkner, "Good Girl or Flirt Girl: Latinas' Definitions of Sex and Sexual Relationships," *Hispanic Journal of Behavioral Sciences* 25 (2003): 174–200. Faulkner reports strong reticence to even discuss the subject in her interview project with Latina women: "An anal sex taboo was clearly present for the women. They would not readily volunteer anal intercourse when defining sex. Only 16 percent (n=5) of women indicated that they had experienced anal sex, although they reported engaging in it rarely to occasionally. Two participants provided no answer to the question. Many did consider anal intercourse to be sex but made sure to say they personally found it repulsive. Some of these feelings had to do with the association with homosexuality" (184).

41. Ane Bonnerup Jaeger, Anne Gramkow, Per Sorensen, Mads Melbye, Hans-Olov Adami, Bengt Glimelius, and Morten Frisch, "Correlates of Heterosexual Behavior among 23–87 Year Olds in Denmark and Sweden, 1992–1998," *Archives of Sexual Behavior* 29 (2000): 91–106; Anne M. Johnson, Catherine H. Mercer, Bob Erens, Andrew J. Copas, Sally McManus, Kaye Wellings, Kevin A. Fenton, Christos Korovessis, Wendy Macdowall, Kiran Nanchahal, Susan Purdon, and Julia Field, "Sexual Behaviors in Britain: Partnerships, Practices, and HIV Risk Behaviours," *The Lancet* 358 (2001): 1835–42; Claes Herlitz and Kristina Ramstedt, "Assessment of Sexual Behavior, Sexual Attitudes, and Sexual Risk in Sweden (1989–2003)," *Archives of Sexual Behavior* 34 (2005): 219–29.

42. *Centers for Disease Control and Prevention* (online), March 11, 2008. Available at http://www.cdc.gov/STDConference/2008/media/release-11march2008.htm (accessed December 26, 2008).

43. Adina Nack, *Damaged Goods: Women Living with Incurable Sexually Transmitted Diseases* (Philadelphia: Temple University Press, 2008).

44. Centers for Disease Control and Prevention, "Racial/Ethnic Disparities in Diagnoses of HIV/AIDS—33 States, 2001–2004," *Morbidity and Mortality Weekly Report* 55 (2006): 121–25.

45. Condom failure rate debates also make assumptions about the frequency of sexual activity that are often out of step with emerging adults' own sexual habits. The majority do not have sex multiple times each week.

46. For a very illuminating treatment of how STIs create stigma among women, see Adina Nack, "Bad Girls and Fallen Women: Chronic STD Diagnoses as Gateways to Tribal Stigma," *Symbolic Interaction* 25 (2002): 463–85.

47. Anne Esacove and Kimberly R. Andringa, "The Process of Preventing Childbearing: Women's Experiences and Emergency Contraceptive Use," *Qualitative Health Research* 12 (2002): 1235–47.

48. Esacove and Andringa, "The Process of Preventing Childbearing."

49. William D. Mosher, Gladys M. Martinez, Anjani Chandra, Joyce C. Abma, and Stephanie J. Willson, "Use of Contraception and Use of Family Planning Services in the United States, 1982–2002," *Advance Data from Vital and Health Statistics, No 350* (Hyattsville, Maryland: National Center for Health Statistics, 2004).

50. Kathryn Kost, Susheela Singh, Barbara Vaughan, James Trussell, and Akinrinola Bankole, "Estimates of Contraceptive Failure from the 2002 National Survey of Family Growth," *Contraception* 77 (2008): 10–21. See also Rachel K. Jones, Julie Fennell, Jenny Higgins, and Kelly Blanchard, "Better than Nothing or Savvy Risk-Reduction Practice? The Importance of Withdrawal," Paper presented at the 2009 annual meeting of the Population Association of America, Detroit, Michigan.

51. Data from the Spring 2007 American College Health Association (ACHA) National College Health Assessment Reference Group Data Report reveals an even higher estimate: 22 percent of students reported using withdrawal as a means of contraception at their last experience of intercourse.

52. The Deficit Reduction Act of 2005 made it more expensive for drug makers to recoup Medicaid-related rebates for campus clinic sales of birth control pills, prompting them to raise prices from as low as $3 to $10 per month up to current levels. See Katie Rooney, "The High Price of Campus Birth Control," *Time Magazine* (online), August 7, 2007. Available at http://www.time.com/time/specials/2007/article/0,28804,1651473_1651472_1650461,00.html (accessed December 26, 2008).

Chapter 3

1. Not a great deal has been documented about the nature and course of Americans' sexual relationships, in part because most survey data is collected from individuals. Gratefully, and at considerable cost, the Add Health study collected information about relationships.

2. Roy Baumeister and Kathleen Vohs, "Sexual Economics: Sex as Female Resource for Social Exchange in Heterosexual Interactions," *Personality and Social Psychology Review* 8 (2004): 339–63. These concepts better explain unmarried sexual behavior than married sexual behavior, although the theory holds import for the conduct of marital sexual relationships as well. For another helpful discussion of the economics of sex, see also Edward O. Laumann, Anthony Paik, and Jenna Mahay, "The Theory of Sex Markets," in *The Sexual Organization of the City*, ed. Edward O. Laumann, Stephen Ellingson, Jenna Mahay, Anthony Paik, and Yoosik Youm (Chicago: University of Chicago Press, 2004), 3–38.

3. Sexual markets should not be confused with sexual marketplaces, which are specific locations in which people tend to meet potential partners.

4. Roy F. Baumeister, Kathleen R. Catanese, and Kathleen D. Vohs, "Is There a Gender Difference in Strength of Sex Drive? Theoretical Views, Conceptual Distinctions, and a Review of Relevant Evidence," *Personality and Social Psychology Review* 5 (2001): 242–73; E. Sandra Byers and Adrienne Wang, "Understanding Sexuality in Close Relationships from the Social Exchange Perspective," in *The Handbook of Sexuality in Close Relationships*, ed. John H. Harvey, Amy Wenzel, and Susan Sprecher (Mahwah, NJ: Lawrence Erlbaum Associates, 2004), 203–34; Ilsa Lottes, "Nontraditional Gender Roles and the Sexual Experiences of Heterosexual College Students," *Sex Roles: A Journal of Research* 29 (1993): 645–71; Letitia Anne Peplau, "Human Sexuality: How do Men and Women Differ?" *Current Directions in Psychological Science* 12 (2003):

37–40; Pamela C. Regan and Leah Atkins, "Sex Differences and Similarities in Frequency and Intensity of Sexual Desire," *Social Behavior and Personality: An International Journal* 34 (2006): 95–102; Pamela C. Regan and Carla S. Dreyer, "Lust? Love? Status? Young Adults' Motives for Engaging in Casual Sex," *Journal of Psychology & Human Sexuality* 11 (1999): 1–24.

5. Steven E. Rhoads, *Taking Sex Differences Seriously* (San Francisco: Encounter Books, 2004), 115.

6. Cindy M. Meston and David M. Buss, "Why Humans Have Sex," *Archives of Sexual Behavior* 36 (2007): 477–507.

7. Daniel J. Kruger, "Young Adults Attempt Exchanges in Reproductively Relevant Currencies," *Evolutionary Psychology* 6 (2008): 204–12.

8. Laura Carpenter, *Virginity Lost: An Intimate Portrait of First Sexual Experiences* (New York: New York University Press, 2005).

9. Russell D. Clark and Elaine Hatfield, "Gender Differences in Receptivity to Sexual Offers," *Journal of Psychology & Human Sexuality* 2 (1989): 39–55.

10. Laurie L. Cohen and R. Lance Shotland, "Timing of First Sexual Intercourse in a Relationship: Expectations, Experiences, and Perceptions of Others," *The Journal of Sex Research* 33 (1996): 291–99.

11. Bing Hsu, Arthur Kling, Christopher Kessler, Kory Knapke, Pamela Diefenbach, and James E. Elias, "Gender Differences in Sexual Fantasy and Behavior in a College Population: A Ten-Year Replication," *Journal of Sex and Marital Therapy* 20 (1994): 103–18.

12. Kathleen D. Vohs, Kathleen R. Catanese, and Roy F. Baumeister, "Sex in 'His' Versus 'Her' Relationships," in *The Handbook of Sexuality in Close Relationships*, ed. John H. Harvey, Amy Wenzel, and Susan Sprecher (Mahwah, NJ: Lawrence Erlbaum Associates, 2004), 455–74. See also Peplau, "Human Sexuality."

13. Of course this claim does *not* include acts of sexual violence or coercion, but rather of consensual sex. What exactly constitutes consent is certainly debatable, especially in relationships that involve unequal power and where one partner values the relationship more than the other. But the point remains valid for the vast majority of relationships in which partners describe sex as consensual.

14. Kathleen Bogle, *Hooking Up: Sex, Dating, and Relationships on Campus* (New York: NYU Press, 2008).

15. Cohen and Shotland, "Timing of First Sexual Intercourse."

16. Lawrence Finer, "Trends in Premarital Sex in the United States, 1954–2003," *Public Health Reports* 122 (2007): 73–78.

17. Not to belabor the economic theory, but note the common difference in language: men "score" and women "give it up." Men are almost never perceived as "giving it up." Emerging adults' conversations suggest women have something of exchange value that men want.

18. Martie G. Haselton and David M. Buss, "The Affective Shift Hypothesis: The Functions of Emotional Changes Following Sexual Intercourse," *Personal Relationships* 8 (2005): 357–69.

19. Regan and Dreyer, "Lust? Love? Status? Young Adults' Motives," 14.

20. Baumeister and Vohs, "Sexual Economics."

21. Paula England, Emily Fitzgibbons Shafer, and Alison C. K. Fogarty, "Hooking Up and Forming Romantic Relationships on Today's College Campuses," in *The Gendered Society Reader*, ed. Michael Kimmel and Amy Aronson (New York: Oxford University Press, 2007).

22. Anne Grunseit, Juliet Richters, June Crawford, Angela Song, and Susan Kippax, "Stability and Change in Sexual Practices among First-Year Australian University Students (1990–1999)," *Archives of Sexual Behavior* 34 (2005): 557–68; Laura Hamilton and Elizabeth A. Armstrong, "Gendered Sexuality in Young Adulthood: Double Binds and Flawed Options," *Gender & Society* 23 (2009): 589–616; Ira Robinson, Ken Ziss, Bill Ganza, Stuart Katz, and Edward Robinson, "Twenty Years of the Sexual Revolution, 1965–1985: An Update," *Journal of Marriage and the Family* 53 (1991): 216–20.

23. Lucia O'Sullivan and E. Sandra Byers, "College Students' Incorporation of Initiator and Restrictor Roles in Sexual Dating Interactions," *Journal of Sex Research* 29 (1992): 435–46.

24. Carey Benedict, "Friends with Benefits, and Stress too," *New York Times* (online), October 2, 2007. Available at http://www.nytimes.com/2007/10/02/health/02sex.html (accessed October 3, 2007); Melissa A. Bisson and Timothy R. Levine, "Negotiating a Friends with Benefits Relationship," *Archives of Sexual Behavior* 38 (2009): 66–73.

25. Catherine M. Grello, Deborah P. Welsh, and Melinda S. Harper, "No Strings Attached: The Nature of Casual Sex in College Students," *The Journal of Sex Research* 43 (2006): 255–267; Hamilton and Armstrong, "Gendered Sexuality in Young Adulthood."

26. "One in 100: Behind Bars in America 2008," *Pew Center on the States* (online), February 28, 2008. Available at http://www.pewcenteronthestates.org/uploadedFiles/One%20in%20100. pdf (accessed December 29, 2008).

27. Paula Kamen, *Her Way: Young Women Remake the Sexual Revolution.* (New York: New York University Press, 2000).

28. Naomi Wolf, "The Porn Myth: In the End, Porn Doesn't Whet Men's Appetites—It Turns Them off the Real Thing," paragraphs 20–22, *New York Magazine* (online), October 20, 2003. Available at http://nymag.com/nymetro/news/trends/n_9437 (accessed June 11, 2009).

29. Jeffrey Jensen Arnett, *Emerging Adulthood: The Winding Road from the Late Teens through the Twenties* (New York: Oxford University Press, 2004), 92.

30. Bisson and Levine, "Negotiating a Friends with Benefits Relationship."

31. Mary Eberstadt, "Is Food the New Sex?" *Policy Review* 153 (online), February/March 2009. Available at http://www.hoover.org/publications/policyreview/38245724.html (accessed June 19, 2009).

32. Christian Smith, with Patricia Snell, *Souls in Transition: The Religious and Spiritual Lives of Young Adults* (New York: Oxford University Press, 2009).

33. The "cougar" phenomenon, which concerns women (typically older than emerging adults) who pursue younger men for sex, is thought to be increasingly popular as divorce rates rise in the United States. Whether true or false—and we lack the data to suggest an answer in either direction—the presence of cougars does not present a serious challenge to sexual economics theory, except to remind us that not all women seek resources in exchange for sex and that women—especially attractive ones—can easily attract men of any age if their primary intention is sex. It's when they require more than sex that the process becomes more challenging. Indeed, the presence of cougars confirms that men have fewer barriers to sex than women and typically must weigh benefits (the sex) with costs (what resources are expected of them).

34. See David P. Schmitt, "Short- and Long-Term Mating Strategies: Additional Evolutionary Systems Relevant to Adolescent Sexuality," in *Romance and Sex in Adolescence and Emerging Adulthood: Risks and Opportunities*, ed. Ann C. Crouter and Alan Booth (Mahwah, NJ: Lawrence Erlbaum Associates, 2006), 41–47.

35. The ideas discussed here reflect those found in Christian Smith's book *Moral, Believing Animals: Human Personhood and Culture* (New York: Oxford University Press, 2003).

36. Dietrich Klusmann, "Sexual Motivation and the Duration of Partnership" *Archives of Sexual Behavior* 31 (2002): 275–87.

37. Helen Fisher, "Broken Hearts: The Nature and Risks of Romantic Rejection," in *Romance and Sex in Adolescence and Emerging Adulthood: Risks and Opportunities*, eds. Ann C. Crouter and Alan Booth (Mahwah, NJ: Lawrence Erlbaum Associates, 2006), 3–28.

38. Edward O. Laumann, John H. Gagnon, Robert T. Michael, and Stuart Michaels, *The Social Organization of Sexuality: Sexual Practices in the United States* (Chicago: University of Chicago Press, 1994).

39. Laramie Taylor, "All for Him: Articles about Sex in American Lad Magazines," *Sex Roles* 52 (2005): 153–63.

40. For a fuller treatment and analysis of this, see Christine Elizabeth Kaestle, "Sexual Insistence and Disliked Sexual Activities in Young Adulthood: Differences by Gender and

Relationship Characteristics," *Perspectives on Sexual and Reproductive Health* 41 (2009): 33–39.

41. Lucia F. O'Sullivan and Elizabeth Rice Allgeier, "Feigning Sexual Desire: Consenting to Unwanted Sexual Activity in Heterosexual Dating Relationships," *Journal of Sex Research* 35 (1998): 234–43.

42. Emily A. Impett and Letitia A. Peplau, "Sexual Compliance: Gender, Motivational, and Relationship Perspectives," *Journal of Sex Research* 40 (2003): 87–100.

43. Kaestle, "Sexual Insistence." Kaestle finds that not only are women far more likely to repeat undesirable activities, but married women are more likely to do so than unmarried women, suggesting that in the context of relationship security men may be more apt to generate repeated requests that might otherwise be left unspoken or only attempted once.

44. Charles H. Cooley, *Human Nature and the Social Order* (New York: Scribner's, 1902).

45. Cindy Struckman-Johnson, David Struckman-Johnson, and Peter B. Anderson, "Tactics of Sexual Coercion: When Men and Women Won't Take No for an Answer," *Journal of Sex Research* 40 (2003): 76–86.

46. Denise A. Hines and Kimberly J. Saudino, "Gender Differences in Psychological, Physical, and Sexual Aggression among College Students Using the Revised Conflict Tactics Scales," *Violence and Victims* 18 (2003): 197–217; Matthew Hogben and Caroline K. Waterman, "Patterns of Conflict Resolution within Relationships and Coercive Sexual Behavior of Men and Women," *Sex Roles* 43 (2000): 341–57; Struckman-Johnson, Struckman-Johnson, and Anderson, "Tactics of Sexual Coercion"; Lisa K. Waldner-Haugrud and Brian Magruder, "Male and Female Sexual Victimization in Dating Relationships: Gender Differences in Coercion Techniques and Outcomes," *Violence and Victims* 10 (1995): 203–15.

47. Dolf Zillmann, "Influence of Unrestrained Access to Erotica on Adolescents' and Young Adults' Dispositions toward Sexuality," *Journal of Adolescent Health* 27S (2000): 41–44.

48. Timothy Buzzell, "The Effects of Sophistication, Access, and Monitoring on Use of Pornography in Three Technological Contexts," *Deviant Behavior* 26 (2005): 109–32.

49. Jason S. Carroll, Laura M. Padilla-Walker, Larry J. Nelson, Chad D. Olson, Carolyn McNamara Barry, and Stephanie D. Madsen, "Generation XXX: Pornography Acceptance and Use among Emerging Adults," *Journal of Adolescent Research* 23 (2008): 6–30.

50. For men, religiosity is a strong predictor of less frequent reports of both porn acceptance and usage.

51. Jane D. Brown, "Mass Media Influences on Sexuality," *The Journal of Sex Research* 39 (2002): 42–45.

52. Gail Dines and Robert Jensen, "Pornography and Media: Toward a More Critical Analysis," in *Sexualities: Identities, Behaviors, and Society*, ed. Michael S. Kimmel and Rebecca F. Plante (New York: Oxford University Press, 2004), 369–80.

53. Carroll et al., "Generation XXX."

54. For an account of this, see Baumeister and Vohs, "Sexual Economics." See also Shane W. Kraus and Brenda Russell, "Early Sexual Experiences: The Role of Internet Access and Sexually Explicit Material," *CyberPsychology & Behavior* 11 (2008): 162–68.

55. Y. Yamamoto, N. Sofikitis, Y. Mio, and I. Miyagawa, "Influence of Sexual Stimulation on Sperm Parameters in Semen Samples Collected via Masturbation from Normozoospermic Men or Cryptozoospermic Men Participating in an Assisted Reproduction Programme," *Andrologia* 32 (2009): 131–38.

56. Wolf, "The Porn Myth," paragraphs 7–8.

Chapter 4

1. Satoshi Kanazawa and Mary C. Still, "Teaching May Be Hazardous to Your Marriage," *Evolution and Human Behavior* 21 (2000): 185–90.

2. Just under 9 percent of college men said they were dating someone but not having sex, while about 5 percent of women said the same thing. These numbers are up from 5 and 4 percent, respectively, in the population at large and certainly higher than the 2.5 and 2.3 percent among those who aren't enrolled in any college.

3. Randy M. Page, Jon J. Hammermeister, and Andria Scanlan,"Everybody's Not Doing It: Misperceptions of College Students' Sexual Activity," *American Journal of Health Behavior* 24 (2000): 387–94.

4. See, as examples, Laura Sessions Stepp, *Unhooked: How Young Women Pursue Sex, Delay Love, and Lose at Both* (New York: Riverhead, 2007); Anonymous, MD, *Unprotected: A Campus Psychiatrist Reveals How Political Correctness in Her Profession Endangers Every Student* (New York: Sentinel, 2006); Donna Freitas, *Sex and the Soul: Juggling Sexuality, Spirituality, Romance, and Religion on America's College Campuses* (New York: Oxford University Press, 2008).

5. At present, Kathleen Bogle provides the most careful exploration and analysis of hooking up among college students. See Kathleen Bogle, *Hooking Up: Sex, Dating, and Relationships on Campus* (New York: NYU Press, 2008).

6. Paula England, Emily Fitzgibbons Shafer, and Alison C. K. Fogarty, "Hooking Up and Forming Romantic Relationships on Today's College Campuses," in *The Gendered Society Reader*, ed. Michael Kimmel and Amy Aronson (New York: Oxford University Press, 2007); Sessions Stepp, *Unhooked*.

7. Janet Reitman, "Sex and Scandal at Duke," paragraph 22, *Rolling Stone* (online), June 1, 2006. Available at http://www.rollingstone.com/news/story/10464110/sex__scandal_at_duke (accessed December 20, 2008). The Duke University lacrosse scandal began in March 2006 when a student from a nearby university—who worked as an exotic dancer—accused three members of the Duke men's lacrosse team of raping her at a party. Although charges were later dropped, the larger scandal nevertheless painted a suboptimal portrait of the sexualization of men's college athletic culture.

8. The survey question was asked as follows: "How many dates have you had since coming to college, and by a date I mean when the guy asked you, picked you up, and paid for the date. Would you say no dates, one or two, three to six, or more than six?"

9. While England's study is impressive and helpful, we should note its sample is not a probability sample from any of the participating colleges, undermining its ability to generate statistics that can be said to be representative of American college students. It's also an ongoing data collection project; the numbers reported here may change over time with additional data.

10. England, Shafer, and Fogarty, "Hooking Up and Forming Romantic Relationships."

11. But drinking does have a strong, linear, and enduring connection to the formation of casual sexual relationships: the more alcohol, the greater likelihood of sex. See Catherine M. Grello, Deborah P. Welsh, and Melinda S. Harper, "No Strings Attached: The Nature of Casual Sex in College Students," *The Journal of Sex Research* 43 (2006): 255–67; Barbara Leigh and John C. Schafer, "Heavy Drinking Occasions and the Occurrence of Sexual Activity," *Psychology of Addictive Behaviors* 7 (1993): 197–200.

12. Laura Hamilton and Elizabeth A. Armstrong, "Gendered Sexuality in Young Adulthood: Double Binds and Flawed Options," *Gender & Society* 23 (2009): 589–616.

13. This was especially true for African American women: if they wanted any sort of sexual relationship with an African American man on campus, he called the shots.

14. Elizabeth L. Paul and Kristen A. Hayes, "The Casualties of 'Casual' Sex: A Qualitative Exploration of the Phenomenology of College Students' Hookups," *Journal of Social and Personal Relationships* 19, no. 5 (2002): 639–61.

15. Ibid., 657–58.

16. Michael W. Wiederman, "The Gendered Nature of Sexual Scripts," *The Family Journal* 13 (2005): 496–502, quote from p. 497.

17. Lucia F. O'Sullivan and Michelle E. Gaines, "Decision-Making in College Students' Heterosexual Dating Relationships: Ambivalence about Engaging in Sexual Activity," *Journal of Social and Personal Relationships* 15 (1998): 347–63.

18. England, Shafer, and Fogarty, "Hooking Up and Forming Romantic Relationships."

19. Norval Glenn and Elizabeth Marquardt, *Hooking Up, Hanging Out, and Hoping for Mr. Right: College Women on Dating and Mating Today* (New York: Institute for American Values, 2001). The women in the CWS are less sexually experienced than those in England's CSLS survey and Hamilton and Armstrong's ethnographic study of a residence hall. In the CWS, 42 percent of the respondents had never had sex, 36 percent reported having had sex in the past month, and only 39 percent reported having ever hooked up.

20. Christian Smith and Patricia Snell, "The Darker Side of Sexual Liberation," Unpublished manuscript, 2009.

21. Tom Wolfe, *I Am Charlotte Simmons* (New York: Farrar, Straus and Giroux, 2004).

22. As Table 3.6 points out, alcohol use has a long and strong connection to hooking up in college. College students, who by self-selection tend to be more risk-aversive than young adults who never went to college, nevertheless drink more than their less-educated counterparts, according to the Add Health data: 27 percent of the latter drink at least once a week, while 36 percent of college students report the same. Among those who aren't in college, 22 percent say they drink five or more drinks in a row—which gets most people drunk—at least two or three times a month, compared with 29 percent of college students.

23. *Duke Women's Initiative* (online), 2003. Available at http://web.duke.edu/womens_initiative/docs/Womens_Initiative_Report.pdf (accessed July 26, 2009).

24. Carolyn Tucker Halpern, Martha W. Waller, Aubrey Spriggs, and Denise Dion Hallfors, "Adolescent Predictors of Emerging Adult Sexual Patterns," *Journal of Adolescent Health* 39 (2006): 926.e1–926.e10.

25. Susan Sprecher and Pamela C. Regan, "College Virgins: How Men and Women Perceive Their Sexual Status," *The Journal of Sex Research* 33 (1996): 3–15.

26. Paula Kamen also found this to be true of her interviewees. See Paula Kamen, *Her Way: Young Women Remake the Sexual Revolution.* (New York: New York University Press, 2000).

27. Overestimates of others' sexual behavior are found in Bogle, *Hooking Up*; Tracy A. Lambert, Arnold S. Kahn, and Kevin J. Apple, "Pluralistic Ignorance and Hooking Up," *The Journal of Sex Research* 40 (2003): 129–33; Page, Hammermeister, and Scanlan, "Everybody's Not Doing It"; Paul and Hayes, "The Casualties of 'Casual' Sex"; and Pamela C. Regan and Carla S. Dreyer, "Lust? Love? Status? Young Adults' Motives for Engaging in Casual Sex," *Journal of Psychology & Human Sexuality* 11 (1999): 1–24.

28. Page, Hammermeister, and Scanlan, "Everybody's Not Doing It."

29. Lambert, Kahn, and Apple, "Pluralistic Ignorance."

30. Ibid., 129.

31. Ibid., 129.

32. Page, Hammermeister, and Scanlan, "Everybody's Not Doing It."

33. National Center for Education Statistics, *Digest of Education Statistics: March 2009* (Alexandria, Virginia: U.S. Department of Education, 2009–020).

34. Marcia Guttentag and Paul F. Secord, *Too Many Women? The Sex Ratio Question* (Beverly Hills, CA: Sage, 1983); Frank A. Pedersen, "Secular Trends in Human Sex Ratios: Their Influence on Individual and Family Behavior," *Human Nature* 2 (1991): 271–91.

35. David P. Schmitt, "Short- and Long-term Mating Strategies: Additional Evolutionary Systems Relevant to Adolescent Sexuality," in *Romance and Sex in Adolescence and Emerging Adulthood: Risks and Opportunities*, ed. Ann C. Crouter and Alan Booth (Mahwah, NJ: Lawrence Erlbaum, 2006), 41–47. See also David P. Schmitt, "Sociosexuality from Argentina to Zimbabwe: A 48–Nation Study of Sex, Culture, and Strategies of Human Mating," *Behavioral and Brain Sciences* 28 (2005): 247–311.

36. For a more extensive discussion of the hypothesis and its intellectual sources, see Jeremy E. Uecker and Mark D. Regnerus, "Bare Market: Campus Sex Ratios, Romantic Relationships, and Sexual Behavior," *The Sociological Quarterly* 51 (2010): 408–35.

37. Guttentag and Secord, *Too Many Women*, 23. In American society at large, however, there remains a relative gender balance. So what difference does it make whether particular campuses have lots more women than others, if the population of young adults as a whole remains balanced? Quite a bit of a difference, since campuses themselves are communities that display distinctive cultures.

38. Nigel Barber, "On the Relationship between Country Sex Ratios and Teen Pregnancy Rates: A Replication," *Cross-Cultural Research* 34 (2000): 26–37; Scott J. South and Katherine Trent, "Sex Ratios and Women's Roles: A Cross-National Analysis," *American Journal of Sociology* 93 (1988): 1096–1115.

39. The campus-level data for this analysis comes from the *Four-Year College Admissions Data Handbook, 2001–2002* (Itasca, IL: Wintergreen/Orchard House, 2001). Information on the number of male and female students was missing from this source for two of the campuses, so these data were obtained from Peterson's, *4 Year Colleges 2002* (Lawrenceville, NJ: Peterson's, 2001) and from College Division of Barron's Educational Series, *Profiles of American Colleges 2001* (Hauppauge, NY: Barron's Educational Series, 2000).

40. Data analyses appear in Uecker and Regnerus, "Bare Market."

41. We should qualify that the predicted probabilities assume the effect of sex ratio is consistent across all levels, but this may not be the case. Conceptually, we suspect there are both low-end and high-end thresholds beyond which increasing imbalance doesn't matter as much.

42. We should note that these results do not imply any statement of ours about the wisdom of college admissions committees. Rather, as sociologists, we are revealing evidence of an unintended consequence to a social structural phenomenon occurring around us.

43. Marguerite Fields, "Want to Be My Boyfriend? Please Define," paragraphs 12 and 35, *New York Times* (online), May 4, 2008. Available at http://www.nytimes.com/2008/05/04/fashion/04love.html (accessed May 11, 2008).

44. Alexandra Jacobs, "Campus Exposure," paragraph 13, *New York Times Magazine* (online), March, 4, 2007. Available at http://www.nytimes.com/2007/03/04/magazine/04sexmagazines.t.html (accessed July 29, 2007).

45. Sandra L. Faulkner, "Good Girl or Flirt Girl: Latinas' Definitions of Sex and Sexual Relationships," *Hispanic Journal of Behavioral Sciences* 25 (2003): 174–200.

46. Page 321 from J. Sean McCleneghan, "Selling Sex to College Females: Their Attitudes about *Cosmopolitan* and *Glamour* Magazines," *The Social Science Journal* 40 (2003): 317–25.

47. Kamen, *Her Way*.

48. Jacobs, "Campus Exposure."

49. Tom Reichert, "The Prevalence of Sexual Imagery in Ads Targeted to Young Adults," *The Journal of Consumer Affairs* 37 (2003): 403–12.

50. Ibid.

51. Naomi Wolf laments such overt and constant arousal, convinced that "the power and charge of sex are maintained when there is some sacredness to it, when it is not on tap all the time."

52. Charles Horton Cooley, *Human Nature and the Social Order* (New York: Scribner's, 1902).

Chapter 5

1. Catherine M. Grello, Deborah P. Welsh, and Melinda S. Harper, "No Strings Attached: The Nature of Casual Sex in College Students," *The Journal of Sex Research* 43 (2006): 255–67; Craig A. Hill, "Gender, Relationship Stage, and Sexual Behavior: The Importance of

Partner Emotional Investment within Specific Situations," *The Journal of Sex Research* 39 (2002): 228–40; Emily A. Impett and Letitia A. Peplau, "Sexual Compliance: Gender, Motivational, and Relationship Perspectives," *Journal of Sex Research* 40 (2003): 87–100; Roy F. Baumeister, Kathleen R. Catanese, and Kathleen D. Vohs, "Is There a Gender Difference in Strength of Sex Drive? Theoretical Views, Conceptual Distinctions, and a Review of Relevant Evidence," *Personality and Social Psychology Review* 5 (2001): 242–73; Letitia Anne Peplau, "Human Sexuality: How Do Men and Women Differ?" *Current Directions in Psychological Science* 12 (2003): 37–40; Pamela C. Regan and Ellen Berscheid, *Lust: What We Know about Human Sexual Desire* (Thousand Oaks, CA: Sage, 1999).

2. Kara Joyner and J. Richard Udry, "You Don't Bring Me Anything but Down: Adolescent Romance and Depression," *Journal of Health and Social Behavior* 41 (2000): 369–91.

3. Christian Smith and Patricia Snell, "The Darker Side of Sexual Liberation," Unpublished manuscript, 2009.

4. Page 658 in Elizabeth L. Paul and Kristen A. Hayes, "The Casualties of 'Casual' Sex: A Qualitative Exploration of the Phenomenology of College Students' Hookups," *Journal of Social and Personal Relationships* 19, no. 5 (2002): 639–61.

5. Sara B. Oswalt, Kenzie A. Cameron, and Jeffrey J. Koob, "Sexual Regret in College Students," *Archives of Sexual Behavior* 34 (2005): 663–69.

6. National Center for Health Statistics, *Health, United States, 2006: With Chartbook on Trends in the Health of Americans* (Hyattsville, MD: National Center for Health Statistics, 2006).

7. Frances M. Culbertson, "Depression and Gender: An International Review," *American Psychologist* 52 (1997): 25–31.

8. Betsey Stevenson and Justin Wolfers, "The Paradox of Declining Female Happiness," *National Bureau of Economic Research Working Paper Series 14969* (online) May 2009. Available at http://www.nber.org/papers/w14969 (accessed November 4, 2009).

9. Paula Kamen, *Her Way: Young Women Remake the Sexual Revolution* (New York: New York University Press, 2000).

10. Selecting the appropriate modeling strategy here is a challenge, especially because of timing issues, directional likelihoods, and brevity. In the end, we settled on beginning with a simple assessment of the proximate sexual context, then add earlier sexual context, experience of trauma, drinking behavior, and same-sex attraction. Finally, we added self-assessments, demographic and family variables, and—where possible—a previous measure or indicator of the dependent variable in order to both map change and assess the continuity of emotional health patterns.

11. Other studies (including Grello, Welsh, and Harper, "No Strings Attached") note a more linear effect of recent partners on women's depression. But after accounting for lifetime partners and sexual frequency, we didn't see this result.

12. Since we stated at the outset that this is a study of heterosexual behavior, we are electing to simply note this same-sex attraction pattern of effect but won't delve into understanding its magnitude or interpreting its sources. Given the statistical rigor of the model, however, they are robust coefficients.

13. Erica L. Weiss, James G. Longhurst, and Carolyn M. Mazure, "Childhood Sexual Abuse as a Risk Factor for Depression in Women: Psychosocial and Neurobiological Correlates," *American Journal of Psychiatry* 156 (1999): 816–28.

14. Grello, Welsh, and Harper, "No Strings Attached"; Baumeister, Catanese, and Vohs, "Is There a Gender Difference in Strength of Sex Drive"; Peplau, "Human Sexuality."

15. Elizabeth L. Paul, Brian McManus, and Allison Hayes, "'Hookups': Characteristics and Correlates of College Students' Spontaneous and Anonymous Sexual Experiences," *The Journal of Sex Research* 37 (2000): 76–88.

16. Martie G. Haselton and David M. Buss, "The Affective Shift Hypothesis: The Functions of Emotional Changes following Sexual Intercourse," *Personal Relationships* 8 (2001): 357–69. Their study notes that significantly more men than women agree with the statement

that the first time having sex with someone is the best. Men were also more likely to say they tend to lose interest in a partner after having regular sex for a few months. This pattern is most poignant among men who've had numerous partners in the past. It's not limited to men, however. Tara, the 20-year-old from Louisiana first quoted in chapter 2, agrees, and commented on how the sex was better in her relationship when it was teetering on the brink. She, too, fits this study's conclusion, since she reported more sexual partners than any other interviewee (including men).

17. Jonathan Zimmerman, "Hooking Up's Gender Gap: Men Make the Rules on Sex Today," paragraph 7 *Chicago Tribune* (online), November 29, 2009. Available at http://archives. chicagotribune.com/2009/nov/29/opinion/chi-oped1129hookupnov29 (accessed November 29, 2009).

18. Janet Reitman, "Sex and Scandal at Duke," paragraphs 24 and 26, *Rolling Stone* (online), June 1, 2006. Available at http://www.rollingstone.com/news/story/10464110/sex__scandal_at_ duke (accessed December 20, 2008).

19. Kamen, *Her Way*, 96–97.

20. Anne Campbell, "The Morning After the Night Before: Affective Reactions to One-Night Stands among Mated and Unmated Women and Men," *Human Nature* 19 (2008): 157–73.

21. In her recent Add Health–based study of first sex and mental health among American teenagers, sociologist Ann Meier documents how teenage girls who experience first sex early (relative to their peers) exhibit heightened subsequent depression, but that the association varies considerably by the nature of their sexual relationship (romantic or otherwise), the emotional commitment within the relationship, whether it lasted or was terminated, and their social proximity to their "ex." See Ann Meier, "Adolescent First Sex and Subsequent Mental Health," *American Journal of Sociology* 112 (2007): 1811–47.

22. Smith and Snell, "The Darker Side of Sexual Liberation."

23. Gordon G. Gallup Jr., Rebecca L. Burch, and Steven M. Platek, "Does Semen Have Antidepressant Properties?" *Archives of Sexual Behavior* 31 (2002): 289–93. A more scientific treatment of the subject appeared 15 years before that, with the publication of P. G. Ney, "The Intravaginal Absorption of Male Generated Hormones and Their Possible Effect on Female Behavior," *Medical Hypotheses* 20 (1986): 221–31.

24. Pages 11–12 from Helen Fisher, "Broken Hearts: The Nature and Risks of Romantic Rejection," in *Romance and Sex in Adolescence and Emerging Adulthood: Risks and Opportunities*, ed. Ann C. Crouter and Alan Booth (Mahwah, NJ: Lawrence Erlbaum Associates, 2006), 3–28.

25. Deborah P. Welsh, Catherine M. Grello, and Melinda S. Harper, "When Love Hurts: Depression and Adolescent Romantic Relationships," in *Adolescent Romantic Relations and Sexual Behavior: Theory, Research, and Practical Implications*, ed. Paul Florsheim (Mahwah, NJ: Lawrence Erlbaum Associates, 2003), 185–212.

26. Grello, Welsh, and Harper, "No Strings Attached."

27. Blogger Lena Chen, made famous by her racy description of sex at Harvard (in the blog *Sex and the Ivy*), once posted: "My advice is to maximize orgasms while minimizing pain. I suggest dating as many people as possible at the same time so any single man's attention is irrelevant since you are too busy anyway. Basically, don't get invested. Men are shit. Let's not forget that just because one of us is operating under some sort of romantic delusion at the moment." Besides sex and sexual encounters, she blogs about her struggle with depression. We're not surprised. See Lena Chen, comment on "The Mating Game," paragraph 3, *Sex and the Ivy Blog* (online), posted August 5, 2008. Available at http://sexandtheivy.com/2008/08/ (accessed October 21, 2008).

28. Stuart Brody and Tillmann H. C. Krüger, "The Post-Orgasmic Prolactin Increase Following Intercourse Is Greater Than Following Masturbation and Suggests Greater Satiety," *Biological Psychology* 71 (2006): 312–15.

29. See Emily Bazalon, "Is There a Post-Abortion Syndrome?" *New York Times* (online), January 21, 2007. Available at http://www.nytimes.com/2007/01/21/magazine/21abortion.t.html (accessed August 12, 2009).

30. Grello, Welsh, and Harper, "No Strings Attached."

31. Catherine M. Grello, Deborah P. Welsh, Melinda S. Harper, and J. W. Dickson, "Dating and Sexual Relationship Trajectories and Adolescent Functioning," *Adolescent and Family Health* 3 (2003): 103–12.

32. Denise D. Hallfors, Martha W. Waller, Daniel Bauer, Carol A. Ford, and Carolyn T. Halpern, "Which Comes First in Adolescence—Sex and Drugs or Depression?" *American Journal of Preventive Medicine* 29 (2005): 163–70.

33. Penny Frolich and Cindy Meston, "Sexual Functioning and Self-Reported Depressive Symptoms among College Women," *The Journal of Sex Research* 39 (2002): 321–25.

34. Grello, Welsh, and Harper, "No Strings Attached."

35. David M. Buss and David P. Schmitt, "Sexual Strategies Theory: An Evolutionary Perspective on Human Mating," *Psychological Review* 100 (1993): 204–32.

36. Michaela Hynie, John E. Lydon, Sylvana Cote, and Seth Weiner, "Relational Sexual Scripts and Women's Condom Use: The Importance of Internalized Norms," *The Journal of Sex Research* 35 (1998): 370–80.

37. Anne Campbell, "The Morning After the Night Before"; Mary E. Larimer, Amy R. Lydum, Britt K. Anderson, and Aaron P. Turner, "Male and Female Recipients of Unwanted Sexual Contact in a College Student Sample: Prevalence Rates, Alcohol Use, and Depression Symptoms," *Sex Roles* 40 (1999): 295–308; Lucia F. O'Sullivan and Michelle E. Gaines, "Decision-Making in College Students' Heterosexual Dating Relationships: Ambivalence about Engaging in Sexual Activity," *Journal of Social and Personal Relationships* 15 (1998): 347–63.

38. Pamela C. Regan and Carla S. Dreyer, "Lust? Love? Status? Young Adults' Motives for Engaging in Casual Sex," *Journal of Psychology & Human Sexuality* 11 (1999), 15.

39. Campbell, "The Morning After the Night Before," 157.

40. Oswalt, Cameron, and Koob, 668.

Chapter 6

1. Laura Sessions Stepp, *Unhooked: How Young Women Pursue Sex, Delay Love, and Lose at Both* (New York: Riverhead, 2007).

2. Laurna Rubinson and Lisa DeRubertis, "Trends in Sexual Attitudes and Behaviors of a College Population over a 15-Year Period," *Journal of Sex Education & Therapy* 17 (1991): 32–41. In the online (and ongoing) CSLS, only 2 percent of respondents say they don't want to get married. Nine percent say they aren't sure.

3. Jeffrey Jensen Arnett, *Emerging Adulthood: The Winding Road from the Late Teens through the Twenties* (New York: Oxford University Press, 2004), 73.

4. Conducted in January and February 2004 by the Opinion Research Corporation of Princeton, New Jersey, for the National Marriage Project, the survey was based on a statistically representative national sample of 1,010 English speaking, heterosexual young men, aged 25 to 34, both married and single (36% had never been married).

5. Edward O. Laumann, John H. Gagnon, Robert T. Michael, and Stuart Michaels, *The Social Organization of Sexuality: Sexual Practices in the United States* (Chicago: University of Chicago Press, 1994).

6. Sessions Stepp, *Unhooked*.

7. Linda Waite and Maggie Gallagher, *The Case for Marriage: Why Married People Are Happier, Healthier, and Better Off Financially* (New York: Broadway, 2001).

8. Laumann et al., *Social Organization of Sexuality*.

9. Just under 50 percent of unmarried men aged 25–29 in the National Marriage Project's survey believe that "single men have better sex lives than married men."

10. Indeed, economists Adam Isen and Betsey Stevenson note that college-educated women have become slightly more likely over the past 15 years to believe that those who are married are happier than those who aren't. However, women who don't have a college degree have become notably less likely to think that married people are happier. See Adam Isen and Betsey Stevenson, "Women's Education and Family Behavior: Trends in Marriage, Divorce, and Fertility" (online), November 24, 2008. Available at http://bpp.wharton.upenn.edu/betseys/papers/Marriage_divorce_education.pdf (accessed July 21, 2009).

11. Stacy J. Rogers and Paul R. Amato, "Have Changes in Gender Relations Affected Marital Quality?" *Social Forces* 79 (2000): 731–53. An analysis of cumulative data in the 1972–2006 General Social Surveys reveals that the difference, however, is small: with respect to their marriages, 65 percent of men and 61 percent of women report being "very happy." Nevertheless, a slow pattern reveals itself: slightly fewer men and women report "very happy" marriages in each subsequent decade, beginning with the 1970s.

12. Waite and Gallagher, *The Case for Marriage*. See also W. Bradford Wilcox, "Religion and the Domestication of Men," *Contexts: Understanding People in Their Social Worlds* 5 (2006): 42–46.

13. Barbara Dafoe Whitehead and David Popenoe, *Why Men Won't Commit: Exploring Young Men's Attitudes about Sex, Dating, and Marriage* (New Brunswick, NJ: The National Marriage Project, 2002).

14. Evelyn L. Lehrer, "The Role of Religion in Union Formation: An Economic Perspective," *Population Research and Policy Review* 23 (2004):161–85; Xiaohe Xu, Clark D. Hudspeth, and John P. Bartkowski, "The Timing of First Marriage: Are There Religious Variations?" *Journal of Family Issues* 26 (2005): 584–618.

15. William G. Axinn and Arland Thornton, "The Influence of Parental Resources on the Timing of the Transition to Marriage," *Social Science Research* 21 (1992): 261–85; Scott J. South, "The Variable Effects of Family Background on the Timing of First Marriage: United States, 1969–1993," *Social Science Research* 30 (2001): 606–26.

16. Arland Thornton, "Influence of the Marital History of Parents on the Marital and Cohabitational Experiences of Children," *American Journal of Sociology* 96 (1991): 868–94.

17. Whitehead and Popenoe, *Why Men Won't Commit*.

18. Paula Kamen, *Her Way: Young Women Remake the Sexual Revolution* (New York: New York University Press, 2000), 134.

19. Matthew D. Bramlett and William D. Mosher, "Cohabitation, Marriage, Divorce, and Remarriage in the United States," National Center for Health Statistics, *Vital and Health Statistics*, Series 23, no. 22 (2002).

20. Bramlett and Mosher, "Cohabitation, Marriage, Divorce, and Remarriage." See also Norval Glenn, Jeremy E. Uecker, and Robert Love, "Later First Marriage and Marital Success," *Social Science Research*, forthcoming.

21. Page 406 from Tim B. Heaton, "Factors Contributing to Increasing Marital Stability in the United States," *Journal of Family Issues* 23 (2002): 392–409.

22. Norval Glenn, *With This Ring . . . : A National Survey on Marriage in America*, National Fatherhood Initiative (online), 2005. Available at http://www.fatherhood.org/downloadable_files/NationalMarriageSurvey.pdf (accessed October 20, 2008).

23. Glenn, Uecker, and Love, "Later First Marriage and Marital Success."

24. Barbara Dafoe Whitehead and David Popenoe, *Who Wants to Marry a Soul Mate? New Survey Findings on Young Adults' Attitudes about Love and Marriage* (New Brunswick, NJ: The National Marriage Project, 2001).

25. Whitehead and Popenoe, *Who Wants to Marry a Soul Mate?*

26. Barbara Dafoe Whitehead and David Popenoe, *Sex without Strings, Relationships without Rings: Today's Young Singles Talk about Mating and Dating* (New Brunswick, NJ: The National Marriage Project, 2000).

27. Page 33 from Ron Lesthaeghe and Karel Neels, "From the First to the Second Demographic Transition—An Interpretation of the Spatial Continuity of Demographic

Innovation in France, Belgium, and Switzerland," *European Journal of Population* 18 (2002): 325–60.

28. In the National Marriage Project survey of men, 56 percent of unmarried 25- to 29-year-old men said they "wouldn't want to marry until they could afford to own a home."

29. Kristin Rowe-Finkbeiner, "Oops, I Forgot to Have Kids," *Bust* (Summer 2002): 44–49.

30. Jane Lawler Dye, *Fertility of American Women: 2006*, Current Population Reports, P20–558, U.S. Census Bureau, 2008. According to the CDC, the chance of a 42-year-old woman completing a pregnancy using her own eggs is less than 10 percent, even with the help of technology.

31. Monica Gaughan, "The Substitution Hypothesis: The Impact of Premarital Liaisons and Human Capital on Marital Timing," *Journal of Marriage and Family* 64 (2002): 407–19.

32. It's ironic that talk of sexual chemistry and talk of the changing self tend to be mutually exclusive conversations. Not only does the human sex drive display robust gender differences, on average, it also changes with age.

33. Psychologist Michael Wiederman notes on page 497 of "The Gendered Nature of Sexual Scripts," *The Family Journal* 13 (2005): 496–502, that "as a couple builds a history together, each member learns how his or her sexual scripts overlap and how they differ, and gradually each constructs his or her own mutually held scripts for sexual activity. However, between the start of their first sexual interaction together and the period during which an established couple enjoys the comfort of a mutually constructed set of scripts for sexual activity, the likelihood of some degree of disharmony is high."

34. See Valerie K. Oppenheimer, "A Theory of Marriage Timing," *American Journal of Sociology* 94 (1988): 563–91; Valerie K. Oppenheimer, "Women's Rising Employment and the Future of the Family in Industrial Societies," *Population and Development Review* 20 (1994): 293–342.

35. Gaughan, "The Substitution Hypothesis," 417.

36. Tracy Clark-Flory, "Why Do Women Have Sex?" *Salon* (online), October 5, 2009. Available at http://www.salon.com/mwt/feature/2009/10/05/why_women_have_sex (accessed October 16, 2009).

37. Naomi Schaefer Riley, "The Young and the Restless: Why Infidelity Is Rising among 20-Somethings," *The Wall Street Journal* (online), November 27, 2008. Available at http://online.wsj.com/article/SB122782458360062499.html (accessed December 3, 2008).

38. Daniel T. Lichter and Zhenchao Qian, "Serial Cohabitation and the Marital Life Course," *Journal of Marriage and Family* 70 (1994): 861–78.

39. Larry L. Bumpass, "What's Happening to the Family? Interactions between Demographic and Institutional Change," *Demography* 27 (1990): 483–98; David John Frank and Elizabeth H. McEneaney, "The Individualization of Society and the Liberalization of State Policies on Same-Sex Sexual Relations, 1984–1995," *Social Forces* 77 (1999): 911–43; Ron Lesthaeghe and Johan Surkyn, "Cultural Dynamics and Economic Theories of Fertility Change," *Population and Development Review* 14 (1988): 1–45; Scott J. South, "The Variable Effects of Family Background on the Timing of First Marriage: United States, 1969–1993," *Social Science Research* 30 (2001): 606–26.

40. Whitehead and Popenoe, *Who Wants to Marry a Soul Mate?*

41. Page 735 from Jennifer Lundquist, "When Race Makes No Difference: Marriage and the Military," *Social Forces* 83 (2004): 731–57. Even in combat zones, spouses can remain together: the army dropped its spousal segregation policy for forward operations housing in 2006.

42. Ibid.

43. Jennifer Hickes Lundquist and Herbert L. Smith, "Family Formation among Women in the U.S. Military: Evidence from the NLSY," *Journal of Marriage and Family* 67 (2005): 1–13.

44. Jay Teachman, "Race, Military Service, and Marital Timing: Evidence from the NLSY-79," *Demography* 44 (2007): 389–404.

45. David P. Schmitt and David M. Buss, "Human Mate Poaching: Tactics and Temptations for Infiltrating Existing Mateships," *Journal of Personality and Social Psychology* 80 (2001): 894–917.

46. Galena K. Rhoades, Scott M. Stanley, and Howard J. Markman, "Couples' Reasons for Cohabitation: Associations with Individual Well-Being and Relationship Quality," *Journal of Family Issues* 30 (2009): 233–58; Sheela Kennedy and Larry Bumpass, "Cohabitation and Children's Living Arrangements: New Estimates from the United States," *Demographic Research* 19 (2008): 1663–92.

47. Robert Schoen, Nancy S. Landale, and Kimberly Daniels, "Family Transitions in Young Adulthood," *Demography* 44 (2007): 807–20.

48. Wendy D. Manning and Pamela J. Smock, "Measuring and Modeling Cohabitation: New Perspectives from Qualitative Data," *Journal of Marriage and Family* 67 (2005): 989–1002; Scott M. Stanley, Galena K. Rhoades, and Howard J. Markman, "Sliding versus Deciding: Inertia and the Premarital Cohabitation Effect," *Family Relations* 55 (2006): 499–509.

49. R. Kelly Raley, "Recent Trends in Marriage and Cohabitation: The United States," in *The Ties That Bind: Perspectives on Marriage and Cohabitation*, ed. Linda J. Waite, Christine Bachrach, Michelle Hindin, Elizabeth Thomson, and Arland Thornton (Hawthorne, NY: Aldine de Gruyter, 2000), 19–39.

50. Pamela J. Smock, Wendy D. Manning, and Meredith Porter, "'Everything's There Except Money': How Money Shapes Decisions to Marry among Cohabitors," *Journal of Marriage and Family* 6 (2005): 680–96.

51. Schoen, Lansdale, and Daniels, "Family Transitions in Young Adulthood."

52. Gaughan, "The Substitution Hypothesis," 409.

53. Rhoades, Stanley, and Markman, "Couples' Reasons for Cohabitation."

54. Karen Benjamin Guzzo, "Marital Intentions and the Stability of First Cohabitations," *Journal of Family Issues* 30 (2009): 179–205.

55. Paula Y. Goodwin, William D. Mosher, and Anjani Chandra, "Marriage and Cohabitation in the United States: A Statistical Portrait Based on Cycle 6 (2002) of the National Survey of Family Growth," *Vital Health Statistics* 23 (2010).

56. Lichter and Qian, "Serial Cohabitation and the Marital Life Course"; Jay Teachman, "Premarital Sex, Premarital Cohabitation, and the Risk of Subsequent Marital Dissolution among Women," *Journal of Marriage and Family* 65 (2003): 444–55.

57. Christian Smith and Patricia Snell, "The Darker Side of Sexual Liberation," Unpublished manuscript, 2009.

58. Cable News Network, "Live from the Headlines: Interview with Claire Kamp Dush, Andrea Miller, Sanjay Bhatnagar" (online), aired August 8, 2003. Available at http://transcripts.cnn.com/transcripts/0308/08/se.16.html (accessed August 20, 2008).

59. Page 848 of Andrew J. Cherlin, "The Deinstitutionalization of American Marriage," *Journal of Marriage and Family* 66 (2004): 848–61.

Chapter 7

1. Barbara Dafoe Whitehead and David Popenoe, *The Marrying Kind: Which Men Marry and Why* (New Brunswick, NJ: The National Marriage Project, 2004).

2. David Eggebeen and Jeffrey Dew, "The Role of Religion in Adolescence for Family Formation in Young Adulthood," *Journal of Marriage and Family* 71 (2009): 108–21.

3. Mark Regnerus, *Forbidden Fruit: Sex and Religion in the Lives of American Teenagers* (New York: Oxford University Press, 2007).

4. Benjamin Edelman, "Red Light States: Who Buys Online Adult Entertainment?" *Journal of Economic Perspectives* 23 (2009): 209–20.

5. The respondents we include here are either in college, already graduated from college, or not in college at all, which (intentionally) leaves a segment of the sample population out of

this analysis—those who dropped out of college and those who are pursuing an associate's degree. The conservative/liberal label comes from answers to the question, "In terms of politics, do you consider yourself conservative, liberal, or middle-of-the-road?" We grouped together those who said they were "conservative" or "very conservative," as well as those who claimed to be "liberal" or "very liberal." For these tables, those who identified as middle-of-the-road are not included.

6. Nevertheless, waiting to bear children will typically issue in modest fertility differences, as we certainly see in red and blue states. While such differences may seem minor, they compound over several decades and across generations, leading in part—together with relocation trends—to the political realignments we've begun to see as bluer states continue to grow at much slower rates than red ones. Texas, Arizona, and Nevada—which boast total fertility rates (TFR) above 2.2—have each added Congressional representatives since the 2000 census, while New York, Pennsylvania, Connecticut, Michigan, and Wisconsin—each of whose TFR is 1.9—lost seats in Congress. Vermont, whose TFR is below 1.7, cannot lose any seats, since it only has one. See Joyce A. Martin, Brady E. Hamilton, Paul D. Sutton, Stephanie J. Ventura, Fay Menacker, and Martha L. Munson, *Births: Final Data for 2003*, National Vital Statistics Reports Vol. 54 (2) (Hyattsville, MD: National Center for Health Statistics, 2005).

7. For similar arguments applied to family breakups, see Paul J. Boyle, Hill Kulu, Thomas Cooke, Vernon Gayle, and Clara H. Mulder, "Moving and Union Dissolution," *Demography* 45 (2008), 209–22; Andrew J. Cherlin, *The Marriage Go-Round: The State of Marriage and the Family in America Today* (New York: Knopf, 2009).

8. The correlation between living in a two-parent, intact family of origin and having moved within state is –0.11 and significant. There is no comparable association, however, with having moved between states.

9. Jonathan Haidt, *The Happiness Hypothesis: Finding Modern Truth in Ancient Wisdom* (New York: Basic Books, 2005).

10. Jeremy Uecker, Mark D. Regnerus, and Margaret Vaaler, "Losing My Religion: The Social Sources of Religious Decline in Early Adulthood," *Social Forces* 85 (2007): 1667–92.

11. While Danielle gets along better with her mother than her father—a very typical story among young women—her parents have been married for 25 years and set a good example for her, including how to fight: "There's always hard times, but it doesn't really feel like that with them. Even if they bicker, it's so funny, 'cause like they get over it, 'cause like my dad jokes about it and then, I don't know, my mom laughs, and then we're all laughing."

12. Paula Kamen, *Her Way: Young Women Remake the Sexual Revolution* (New York: New York University Press, 2000), 193.

13. For an excellent review of the issues and figures surrounding fertility decline, see S. Philip Morgan and Miles G. Taylor, "Low Fertility at the Turn of the Twenty-First Century," *Annual Review of Sociology* 32 (2006): 375–99.

14. Tom Smith, *GSS Trends in American Sexual Behavior* (Chicago: National Opinion Research Center, 2003); Lawrence Wu, "Cohort Estimates of Nonmarital Fertility for U.S. Women," *Demography* 45 (2008), 193–207.

15. Patrick Heuveline, Jeffrey M. Timberlake, and Frank F. Furstenberg Jr., "Shifting Childrearing to Single Mothers: Results from 17 Western Countries," *Population and Development Review* 29 (2003): 47–71.

16. Just under 80 percent of 25- to 29-year-old men in the National Marriage Project survey agreed that "the divorce laws favor women over men."

17. Andrew J. Cherlin, "The Deinstitutionalization of American Marriage," *Journal of Marriage and Family* 66 (2004): 848–61.

18. Ron J. Lesthaeghe and Lisa Neidert, "The Second Demographic Transition in the United States: Exception of Textbook Example?" *Population and Development Review* 32 (2006): 669–98; Dirk J. van de Kaa, "Europe's Second Demographic Transition," *Population Bulletin* 42 (Washington, DC: Population Reference Bureau, 1987).

19. Francesco C. Billari and Hans-Peter Kohler, "Patterns of Low and Lowest-Low Fertility in Europe," *Population Studies* 58 (2004): 161–76.

20. A country's total fertility rate (TFR) is the average number of children that would be born to a woman over her lifetime if she were to experience the exact current age-specific fertility rates throughout her lifetime, and if she were to survive from birth through the end of her reproductive career.

21. Lesthaeghe and Neidert, "The Second Demographic Transition." Interestingly, however, the authors note that early fertility is no guarantee of resisting subreplacement levels: Arkansas, Kentucky, West Virginia, Mississippi, and Wyoming all exhibit early "fertility schedules" that are nevertheless below 2.05 children, on average.

22. Bill Bishop, *The Big Sort: Why the Clustering of Like-Minded America Is Tearing Us Apart* (Boston: Mariner, 2008).

23. Ruy Teixeira, *The Coming End of the Culture Wars* (The Glaser Foundation: Center for American Progress, 2009).

24. Cherlin, *The Marriage Go-Round.*

25. Pippa Norris and Ronald Inglehart, *Sacred and Secular: Religion and Politics Worldwide* (Cambridge, UK: Cambridge University Press, 2004).

Chapter 8

1. Page 65 of Christian Smith, *Moral Believing Animals* (New York: Oxford University Press, 2003).

2. Page 43 of Jane D. Brown, "Mass Media Influences on Sexuality," *The Journal of Sex Research* 39 (2002): 42–45.

3. L. Monique Ward, "Does Television Exposure Affect Emerging Adults' Attitudes and Assumptions about Sexual Relationships? Correlational and Experimental Confirmation," *Journal of Youth and Adolescence* 31 (2002): 1–15.

4. Moreover, Americans have become more conservative about the morality of extramarital sex. Whereas in the 1970s until the mid-1980s around 70 to 75 percent of adults (in the GSS) said that "sex with a person other than your spouse" is "always wrong," the same figure since then has hovered at or above 80 percent.

5. As we did in chapter 3, we wish to remind readers that sexual economics theory is not our invention. Many of its ideas are helpfully summarized and elaborated upon in Roy Baumeister and Kathleen Vohs, "Sexual Economics: Sex as Female Resource for Social Exchange in Heterosexual Interactions," *Personality and Social Psychology Review* 8 (2004): 339–63.

6. Ashley Samelson, "Lipstick Jungle," paragraph 7, *Wall Street Journal* (online), September 26, 2008. Available at http://online.wsj.com/article/SB122238618931577035.html (accessed October 2, 2008).

7. Paula Kamen, *Her Way: Young Women Remake the Sexual Revolution.* (New York: New York University Press, 2000), 98.

8. Hephzibah Anderson, *Chastened: The Unexpected Story of My Year without Sex* (New York: Viking, 2010); Jessica Grose, "The Shame Cycle: The New Backlash against Casual Sex," *Slate* (online), March 3, 2010. Available at http://www.slate.com/id/2246553/ (accessed March 5, 2010); Ariel Levy, *Female Chauvinist Pigs: Women and the Rise of Raunch Culture* (New York: Free Press, 2006).

9. Page 307 from Stephen Ellingson, "Constructing Causal Stories and Moral Boundaries: Institutional Approaches to Sexual Problems," in *The Sexual Organization of the City*, ed. Edward O. Laumann, Stephen Ellingson, Jenna Mahay, Anthony Paik, and Yoosik Youm (Chicago: University of Chicago Press, 2004), 283–308.

10. Psychologist Michael Wiederman, who writes eloquently on sexual scripts in his article "The Gendered Nature of Sexual Scripts," *The Family Journal* 13 (2005): 496–502, includes references (on pages 498–499) to economic terms like "incentive," "investment," and "cost/benefit ratio."

Index

hooking up, 55, 75, 102–14, 118, 132, 135,
    151, 214, 217
    ambivalence about, 107–10, 217
    culture of, in college, 2, 106–7, 124, 129
    definitions of, 103
    perceived benefits to, 110–11
    prevalence of, 105–6
human papillomavirus (HPV), 41–43
    See also sexually transmitted infections

I am Charlotte Simmons, 114
institutionalization, of sexual scripts, 240–41,
    245, 248

Judaism, 176
Juno, 48

Kamen, Paula, 70, 139, 151, 179, 227
Kinsey, Alfred, 28

Laumann, Edward, 32
lesbians, 209
    See also homosexuality
"looking glass self," 90, 131
love, 35, 53, 62, 76, 90, 94, 107, 109–10, 121,
    124, 134, 151, 153, 156–60, 171, 212, 249

mainline Protestantism, 26, 176
marriage, 59, 65, 78, 149, 169–71, 192–93,
    215, 218, 229, 248
    age at, 2, 111, 169, 175–77, 179–96, 200,
        219, 232–33
    attitudes toward, 4, 94, 111, 229, 248–49
    benefits of, 170, 174–75, 181
    deinstitutionalization of, 170, 192–93, 204
    early, 179–81, 194–95, 197
    experience with, 176
    in the minds of men, 171–75
    scripts about postponing, 182–92
masturbation, 17, 94, 98–99, 157, 161, 244, 246
    gender differences in, 17, 53, 161
    mutual, 31
maturity, of men, 77–78, 122, 136, 249
Maxim, 86
media, mass
    influence of, on sex, 86, 239
    messages about sex, 18, 86, 129, 173, 239

military, influence of, on marriage, 179,
    194–96, 227–28
mobility, geographic, 219–22
Monitoring the Future, 203
moral hazard, 231–32
"morals," 228–29
Mormons, 176
mother, relationship with, 19, 109

narrative, 57–58, 116, 127, 137, 182–83, 187,
    204, 211, 219, 222, 236, 238, 250
National Health and Social Life Survey
    (NHSLS), 25, 32, 36, 85, 172
National Longitudinal Study of Adolescent
    Health. *See* Add Health Study
National Marriage Project, 192
National Study of Youth and Religion
    (NSYR), 11, 61
National Survey of Family Growth (NSFG),
    6, 8, 10, 19–20, 33, 36, 46, 180, 202,
    271n2
Natural Family Planning (NFP). *See* rhythm
    method of contraception
New York Times, 5–6, 27, 66, 124, 126
New Yorker, 205
nonmonogamy, 24, 81

oral sex, 27, 32–36, 43, 85, 87–88, 117
orgasm, 33, 53, 87, 106–7, 110–11, 152–53,
    157, 244
    faking, among women, 111
oxytocin, 152

Palin, Sarah, 205
parents, influence of, 3, 178, 188–89, 239
parties, 62, 108–9, 112, 172, 245
partners, number of sexual, 23–29, 41, 60–61,
    81–82, 118–19, 139–40, 143–49,
    152–53, 159, 161, 167, 212–13,
    221–22, 225
    different methods of estimating, 27–28
    perspectives about, 28–30
peer influence, 239
pill, 14, 46, 186
    side effects of, 47
    See also contraception
plausibility structure, 20, 29, 155–56, 217
pleasure, sexual, 227
    See also orgasm

prevalence of, 40
stigma associated with, 44
Smith, Christian, 203, 236
STDs. *See* sexually transmitted infections
social class, 3, 116
    differences in ideas about marriage or
        marital timing, 18, 111, 178,
        195, 248
    distinctions in sexual behavior, 31
social desirability bias, 27–29
social learning theory, 190, 222, 236,
    287n33
social networking, 130–33, 247
    See also Facebook
"soul mate," 192
South, the, 179–80, 197–98, 207, 220,
    248
Stepp, Laura Sessions, 23, 104, 173
syphilis, 43
    See also sexually transmitted infections

technical virginity, 21, 31, 58, 228
Texas, University of, 11, 53, 162, 194, 206
texting, 132–33
tolerance, 2, 112–14, 118, 129, 214
transactional sex. *See* casual sex; hooking up
True Love Waits, 227
    See also abstinence pledge

Twitter, 131–33, 192
    See also Facebook

unintended consequences, 64, 231–32,
    282n42
unwanted sex, 85–93
virginity, 14, 17–23, 65, 108, 123
    gift metaphor for, 55
    loss of, 22, 39, 115, 128, 139,
        217
    predictors of, 18–19
    prevalence of, among emerging adults,
        17–18, 117, 123, 225
    religiosity, as a primary reason for, 20–21,
        225
    social support for, 20
virginity pledges. *See* abstinence
Vohs, Kathleen, 52–53, 55–56, 59, 67

Washington Post, 28
withdrawal, as a method of contraception,
    45–46
Wolf, Naomi, 75, 80, 99, 282n51
women
    persistent marketability of, 25,
    plasticity of sexuality among, 53, 57, 166
    policing of each other by, 29, 248